Integrating African American Literature in the Library and Classroom

Integrating African American Literature in the Library and Classroom

Dorothy Littlejohn Guthrie

AN IMPRINT OF ABC-CLIO, LLC
Santa Barbara, California • Denver, Colorado • Oxford, England

Library of Congress Cataloging-in-Publication Data

Guthrie, Dorothy Littlejohn.
Integrating African American literature in the library and classroom / Dorothy Littlejohn Guthrie.
p. cm.
Includes bibliographical references and index.
ISBN 978-1-59884-751-2 (pbk. : acid-free paper) — ISBN 978-1-59884-752-9 (ebook)
1. African Americans—Study and teaching (Elementary)—Activity programs. 2. African Americans—Study and teaching (Secondary)—Activity programs. 3. African Americans—Juvenile literature--Bibliography. 4. American literature—African American authors—Bibliography. I. Title.
E184.7.G88 2011
973'.049607300712—dc23 2011017227

ISBN: 978-1-59884-751-2
EISBN: 978-1-59884-752-9

15 14 13 12 11 1 2 3 4 5

This book is also available on the World Wide Web as an eBook.
Visit www.abc-clio.com for details.

Libraries Unlimited
An Imprint of ABC-CLIO, LLC

ABC-CLIO, LLC
130 Cremona Drive, P.O. Box 1911
Santa Barbara, California 93116-1911

This book is printed on acid-free paper ∞
Manufactured in the United States of America

I am honored to have three special people in my life who have encouraged me to use my God-given talents, prayed for me, and encouraged me each day in some way. So, this is very special to me and my way of saying thank you from the deepest part of my heart. To my mother, Alma Robinson Littlejohn; my husband, Bobby Guthrie; and my son, Bobby Guthrie, II, this book I dedicate to you, and to the memory of my Grandmother, Massie Sims Robinson. And, a very special thanks to my aunt, Dr. Pauline Robinson Fulton.

—Love, Dorothy

Contents

Introduction: Why I Wrote This Book

As a child growing up in the rural South, I didn't have the opportunity to learn much about my history. Why? Because these books simply did not exist. When I stumbled across Russell Adams' book *Great Negroes Past and Present* in high school, I wanted to keep it. For the first time in my life, words seemed to jump off the pages—right into my heart and soul. That is when I realized that in addition to Harriet Tubman, Sojourner Truth, and Dr. Martin Luther King Jr., there were many others advocating for equal rights for all people.

My children's literature professor at South Carolina State College (now SC State University), in Orangeburg, South Carolina, shared the history and facts about African Americans who helped make this country, and she challenged her students to share these facts with others. I believed there were others who wanted to know this history but didn't have the resources, and I believed there were those who wanted to share what they knew but didn't know how. So, I wrote this book to meet the needs of those who want to learn about this history but whose resources are limited, and for those who want to teach and integrate more of these books into the curriculum but don't have the time for lesson planning. My goal in writing this book is to see that no more children are raised without knowing the rich cultural contributions that African Americans have made to American life.

Despite recent gains in acknowledging African American books, there is still much work to be done in promoting these authors and illustrators. A major accomplishment is the Coretta Scott King Award, which recognizes the work of these professionals.

Our role as leaders, educators, and parents is to tell all children about the great volumes of literature written and illustrated by and about African Americans. Please note that faith-based books and activities are also included, and many of the activities call for the use of the Bible for reading scriptures. Review the lesson plans and determine which activities are appropriate for your students. As you use this resource, it is my hope that you will find many enjoyable books and practical ideas for teaching your students about great African Americans and their roles in history.

Finally, it is my deepest desire that children will be motivated and encouraged by these books and activities and will be inspired by the examples to pursue their own places in history.

Chapter 1

ARTS

Introduce your students to books and activities that teach about the rich artistic heritage of African Americans, including literature and storytelling, graphic arts, music, dance, and other performing arts.

Belton, Sandra. *Beauty, Her Basket.* New York: Greenwillow/HarperCollins, 2004.

About the Author

Sandra Belton: Official Site. n.d. http://www.sandrabelton.com (accessed October 9, 2010).

Literary Element	Lexile Range	Teacher Resources and Supplies
Metaphor	—	Book A variety of baskets Craft supplies to make baskets Worksheet
Reading Level	**Accelerated Reader**	
K–Grade 3	0.5 Points	

Additional Title

Raven, Margot Theis. ***Circle Unbroken.***

Websites

http://www.knowitall.org/gullahnet/gullah/baskets/index.cfm
http://www.epa.gov/recyclecity
http://www.5min.com/Video/Sweet-Grass-Basket-Weaving-in-Charleston-SC-259884492
http://www.simplybaskets.com/SweetgrassBasketryInformation.html
http://www.lessonplanet.com/search?keywords=gullah&media=lesson
http://www.youtube.com/watch?v=D4WI1KvBH7s&feature=related
http://nativeamericans.mrdonn.org/baskets.html
http://beemp3.com/download.php?file=4025115&song=What+A+Wonderful+World

Brief Summary

This is a story of a little girl who sees beauty through the perspective of her Nana's stories. She learns that her ancestors brought more than their hard work and labor to America. Their gifts and contributions help cure the ills of slavery by spotlighting the talents that accompanied them.

Focus

- Culture
- Gifts
- Basket Weaving
- Jealousy

Teacher Input

- Ask the students to think of the things in life that they enjoy doing.
- Introduce the book and the Gullah people. Explain that basket making is a Gullah tradition and show the video found at http://www.knowitall.org/gullahnet/gullah/baskets/index.cfm.
- Have students tell what they know about basket making.
- Discuss recycling with students. Take them to http://www.epa.gov/recyclecity.
- Distribute index cards to students and write the phrase, "Beauty is only Skin Deep" on the board. Ask students to write their interpretations of the phrase and then discuss them in class.

Guided Practice

- Use the following online resource to show students how baskets are made: http://www.5min.com/Video/Sweet-Grass-Basket-Weaving-in-Charleston-SC-259884492.
- Plan a classroom event centered around the theme "***Know beauty? What is it? Design the picture—Help Me See.***" Discuss beautiful things, people, and places with students. Have them draw, write, or tell about one thing, person, or place that they find beautiful.
- Have students choose a classmate and list all of the beautiful things they like about that person.
- Discuss students' answers to these questions: Do you think Beauty was surprised to learn that Henry knew how to make baskets? Why? Do you think people are often judged by the way they look instead of their personality?
- List the gifts that the slaves brought with them to America, as described by Nana.
- Ask students to bring different types and designs of baskets to class. Have them share what they know about the baskets and how they are used in the home.
- Using the following online resource, have students view Native American basket making and discuss the differences and similarities with Gullah baskets: http://nativeamericans.mrdonn.org/baskets.html.

Independent Practice

- Using the song "***What a Wonderful World***" by Louis Armstrong or Sam Cooke as background, ask students to create a Photo Story or PowerPoint story titled "***Beauty Today.***"

Closure

- Give students time to share "***beauty***" compliments about classmates.
- Sponsor a "***Basket Day***" at your school. Students will design a basket using paper, straws, or pipe cleaners.
- Share "Beauty Today" projects.

Assessment

- Student interest, project development, and sharing their "beauty" comments with classmates.

Me and My Basket Worksheet

A Three-Day Assignment Give students the opportunity to get help from their parents or caregivers. This may provide great ideas for sharing! Draw your favorite basket.	My Basket (List the room where it is used.)	How Do I Use It? Let Me List the Ways (Tell how basket is used.)

List and define at least five basket compound words.	1. 2. 3. 4. 5.
Using the following website, name one ingredient the Indians used to make their baskets: http://nativeamericans.mrdonn.org/baskets.html.	
List ingredients Gullah people use for basket making (see http://www.knowitall.org/gullahnet/gullah/baskets/index.cfm).	

Name one item that you could use to make a basket.

What Slaves Brought to America The Gift and the Purpose	1. 2. 3. 4.

Name the Basket Needed Based on the Names Given	
Example: Paper plates, sandwiches, napkins, and cookies	Picnic Basket/Answers
Michael Jordan in the arena. Dori Sanders and her peach orchard. Mom and the clothes she picked up from my room. Grandma just made hot biscuits!	Basketball

***Cameron, Dan, et al., editors. Dancing at the Louvre: Faith Ringgold's French Collection and Other Story Quilts.* New York: New Museum of Contemporary Art, 1998.**

About the Author

Faith Ringgold. n.d. http://www.faithringgold.com (accessed October 9, 2010).

Literary Elements	Lexile Range	Teacher Resources and Supplies
Art Culture Personal Narratives	—	Books Worksheet Sample quilt Digital camera Color printer Miracle Fabric Sheets A seamstress
Reading Level Grades 9–12	**Accelerated Reader** —	
Additional Titles Lyons, Mary. ***Talking with Tebé: Clementine Hunter, Memory Artist.*** Ringgold, Faith. ***Tar Beach.*** Ringgold, Faith. ***We Flew over the Bridge: The Memoirs of Faith Ringgold.*** **Website** http://www.faithringgold.com		

Brief Summary

This is a brilliant volume featuring work artist Faith Ringgold has produced. She uses her eyes, heart, and hands to tell the stories of her people, revealing their joys, pains, and sorrows. Ringgold's work is her voice, and through this book, she teaches readers how to enjoy the simple pleasures of life in an inexpensive way, using paper, a creative mind, and a strong memory.

Focus

- Quilts
- Design and Balance
- Family Heirlooms
- Photography
- Storytelling

Teacher Input

- Discuss what kinds of items are considered heirlooms.
- Discuss the art of quilt making.
- Survey the class to see whether they have family quilts in their homes.
- Share Faith Ringgold's book *Tar Beach* with the class.

Guided Practice

- Distribute blank paper squares (7 x 7 inches) to each student. Instruct students to create a geometric design for a quilt block honoring African Americans. On the other side of the square, have students explain the reason for their geometric design.
- Read the quote on page 53 of *Tar Beach.* Ask students to draw a picture of what first comes to mind after hearing the quote.
- Divide the class into three groups. Distribute the worksheet and instruct each group to complete the following by using this website: http://www.faithringgold.com.
    - Group 1: Life of Faith Ringgold
    - Group 2: Quilt Stories
    - Group 3: Chronology of Faith Ringgold's Work
- Distribute index cards to students for the virtual field trip, "**Here's What I Saw.**" Using Ringgold's website (see http://www.faithringgold.com/ringgold/collect.htm#exhibitions), have students visit her public collections and record what they saw by viewing Ringgold's works. Describe the locations where some of Ringgold's paintings can be found.

Independent Practice

- Using the following quilt-making website, have students design their own stories and quilts for classroom presentations: http://www.youtube.com/watch?v=0tobn9KHyHo&feature=related

Closure

- Hold a "***We're Just a Bunch of Squares***" art show in the school library or classroom. Invite other classes to view your work.
- Introduce the parent volunteer or seamstress who will stitch the story squares together to create a quilt, which will appropriately be called the ***Faith Story Quilt.***

Assessment

- Classroom discussions, student artwork, project presentations.

"Voices of Faith" Worksheet

We See, But Not the Same Thing—Designed to Make a Difference

On page 14 in the chapter "The French Collection," Michele Wallace writes about a trip to Europe that her mother Faith took at age nine with her grandmother Mommy Fay and her great-great-grandmother Momma Jones.

- For Momma Jones, Europe offered opportunities to see such greats as Josephine Baker, Bricktop, and Sidney Bechet.
- In Europe, Faith saw legends such as James Brown and Chester Himes. This was the trip that inspired her to create story quilts.

Identify the following people and describe how each made an impact on others' lives.

Josephine Baker	
Bricktop	
James Brown	
Chester Himes	
Group 1: Report on Faith Ringgold's early life and the impact the following artists had on her career.	
Life of Faith Ringgold	
Pablo Picasso	
Henri Matisse	
Vincent van Gogh	
Group 2: Visit http://www.faithringgold.com and watch Faith Ringgold at http://www.youtube.com/watch?v=EzEWJJUnTlk&feature=related. List the various types of story quilts Ringgold has designed.	
Group 3: Develop a timeline of Ringgold's art creations titled "Chronology of Faith Ringgold's Work."	
The French Collection: Divided into three categories as seen through the eyes of Momma Jones, Mommy Fay, and Michele Wallace.	1. Dancing at the Louvre: Describe the stories behind each of the quilts. 2. Wedding on the Seine 3. Matisse's Chapel
Describe Clementine Hunter's artwork.	

Duggleby, John. *Story Painter: The Life of Jacob Lawrence.* San Francisco: Chronicle Books, 1998.

About the Author

Gwendolyn Knight Lawrence. Jacob Lawrence. 2003. Available at http://www.cs.washington.edu/building/art/JacobLawrence (accessed October 9, 2010).

Literary Elements	Lexile Range	Teacher Resources and Supplies
Arts Art and Photography Biography Harlem Renaissance	950L	Book Worksheet Newsprint
Reading Level YA	**Accelerated Reader** 1.0 point	

Additional Title
Spires, Elizabeth. ***I Heard God Talking to Me: William Edmondson and His Stone Carvings.***

Websites
http://www.phillipscollection.org/research/over_the_line/teacher_main.html
http://mercury.educ.kent.edu/database/eureka/detail_book.cfm?BooksID=1422
http://www.columbia.edu/itc/history/odonnell/w1010/edit/migration/migration.
html http://xroads.virginia.edu/~MA02/easton/vaudeville/vaudevillemain.html

Brief Summary

This is a biography depicting the life of a painter who lived during the Harlem Renaissance. His book is inviting to art lovers and those in search of a story told through the eyes and hands of an artist. These powerful images evoke emotions about an artist who dedicated his life to developing expressive art and educating his people through his paintings.

Focus

- Harlem
- Amateur Night
- Charles Alston
- Tempera Paints

Teacher Input

- Introduce students to Jacob Lawrence by using this website: http://www.phillipscollection.org/research/over_the_line/index.html
- Discuss the importance of the Harlem Renaissance.
- Discuss who Professor Seyfert was.

- Discuss Lawrence's painting process.
- Have students define the term amateur. Read (page 47).

Guided Practice

- Students examine Jacob Lawrence's life, his painting style, and the mediums he used through this website: http://www.pbs.org/wnet/aaworld/arts/lawrence.html
- Students design and create their own works of art using Lawrence's work as a model (see http://www.jacoblawrence.org; http://www.whitney.org/www/jacoblawrence/meet/index.html).
- Students complete the sentence "The Harlem Renaissance was ______________."
- Students work together to plan "soapbox lectures" related to today's issues.
- Divide the class into four groups. Each group will create a collage of the following:
    1. Group One: Collage of the Home
    2. Group Two: Collage of the Family
    3. Group Three: Collage of the School
    4. Group Four: Collage of the Community
- Students will make a coloring book of Harlem and use tempera paints to color pages using Lawrence's method of painting.
- Students will describe vaudeville by listing various acts and performers.

Independent Practice

- Have students write a TV commercial and design a recipe sheet with instructions showing how to make scrapple.
- Using PowerPoint or Photo Story software, create and design a project spotlighting the Harlem Renaissance.
- Display students' artwork, talk about mediums used, and allow students to share what motivated them to create the work.

Closure

- Hold a "From the Eyes of a Young Artist Day," allowing students to display their collage creations.

Assessment

- Student reporting, presentations, interactions, and brainstorming.

From the Eyes of Jacob Lawrence Worksheet

Write what you know about Jacob Lawrence: ______________________________

____

____

____

____

List What You Know About the Following People and Places	
Professor Seyfert	
Toussaint L'Ouverture	
President Jimmy Carter	
Metropolitan Museum of Art	
Cotton Club	
Adam Clayton Powell	
Duke Ellington	
Cab Calloway	

Which works earned Lawrence his popularity (see http://www.jacoblawrence.org)?

____

____

____

Lawrence was the first African American to have his work in which famous museum.

____

____

____

Find three books written by or about Jacob Lawrence.

1. ______________________________

2. ______________________________

3. ______________________________

Hudson, Cheryl Willis. *My Friend Maya Loves to Dance.* New York: Abrams, 2010.

About the Author

Cheryl W. Hudson. n.d. http://www.cherylwhudson.com (accessed October 9, 2010).

Literary Elements	Lexile Range	Teacher Resources and Supplies
Ballet Dance Rhyming	—	Books Worksheet
Reading Level K–Grade 3	**Accelerated Reader** Points: 0.5 Book Level: 2.3	
Additional Titles Michelson, Richard. ***Happy Feet: The Savoy Ballroom Lindy Hoppers and Me.*** Shahan, Sherry. ***Willie Covan Loved to Dance.*** **Websites** http://freeology.com/graphicorgs/pdf/venn1.pdf http://www.nytimes.com/2007/05/06/arts/dance/06kour.html http://www.pbs.org/wnet/freetodance/biographies/index.html		

Brief Summary

In this book, Hudson has captured the aspiration of the many young girls who dream of becoming great dancers. Maya is determined to dance and to do it well. She knows that to craft her skill to her own satisfaction, she must practice daily. Thus, readers will find her dancing everywhere she goes and to different genres of music. As the author takes her readers on this artistic journey, students will also see the integration of culture woven into the text.

Focus

- Ballet
- Dancers
- Hobbies

Teacher Input

- Offer a brief history of black dance. Use the Internet (http://www.pbs.org/wnet/freetodance/biographies/index.html) to introduce students to some of the many famous African American dancers.
- Divide the class into teams by gender. Introduce Michelson's and Shahan's books to students. Explain how students will use the books. In the first exercise, the girls will be assigned to read Michelson's book and the boys Shahan's book.

Guided Practice

- Describe the attitude of the main character in each book.
- Have the gender teams list what they like best about each book. Next, the teams exchange books and follow the same procedure.
- Use the worksheet to list and compare the similarities and differences found between Michelson's and Shahan's books and list the commonalities of these books to Hudson's books.
- Discuss whether there is a surprise ending in either book.
- Ask the students to explain what is meant by "dancing with grace."
- Use online resources to learn more about black male and female ballet dancers.

Independent Practice

- Ask students to write their own poems titled "(Student's Name) Loves to (whatever the student loves to do)." Students may develop flip charts or PowerPoint slides for sharing their work.

Closure

- Students share the results of their teamwork by sending a representative from each group to transfer information from graphic organizer to the board.
- Students share their individual poems.

Assessment

- Student participation, discussions, and projects.

The Feet Worksheet

List the unique features you discovered in *Happy Feet*.

List the unique features you discovered in *Willie Covan Loved to Dance*.

How were the books similar? How were they different?

Which book did you like best? Would you recommend it or both to other readers? Why or Why not?

Bibliography

Belton, Sandra. *Beauty, Her Basket.* New York: Greenwillow/HarperCollins, 2004.

Cameron, Dan. *Dancing at the Louvre: Faith Ringgold's French Collection and Other Story Quilts.* New York: New Museum of Contemporary Art, 1998.

Duggleby, John. *Story Painter: The Life of Jacob Lawrence.* San Francisco: Chronicle Books, 1998.

Hacker, Carlotta. *Great African-Americans in the Arts.* New York: Crabtree, 1997.

Hudson, Cheryl Willis. *My Friend Maya Loves to Dance.* New York: Abrams, 2010.

Webliography

62 Gullah Lesson Plans Reviewed by Teachers. Lesson Planet. 1999–2010. http://www.lessonplanet.com/search?keywords=gullah&media=lesson (accessed June 28, 2011).

AR BookFinder US—Welcome. Renaissance Learning. 2010. http://www.arbookfind.com/UserType.aspx (accessed November 2, 2010).

Cheryl W. Hudson. n.d. http://www.cherylwhudson.com (accessed October 9, 2010).

Eureka! AGORA. Ohio Literacy Resource Center. n.d. http://mercury.educ.kent.edu/database/eureka/detail_book.cfm?BooksID=1422 (accessed December 5, 2010).

Faith Ringgold. January 1, 2002. http://www.faithringgold.com (accessed October 9, 2010).

Faith Ringgold—Art Collections. Art in Context Center for Communications. 1997–2002. http://www.faithringgold.com/ringgold/collect.htm#exhibitions (accessed December 5, 2010).

Graphic Organizers (free printable graphic organizers). Freeology. n.d. http://freeology.com/graphicorgs/pdf/venn1.pdf (accessed November 28, 2010).

The Great Migration: A Story in Paintings by Jacob Lawrence. n.d. http://www.columbia.edu/itc/history/odonnell/w1010/edit/migration/migration.html (accessed October 9, 2010).

Making Baskets. Gullah Net website. ETV Commission. 2001–2008. http://www.knowitall.org/gullahnet/gullah/baskets/index.cfm (accessed November 25, 2010).

Henry Louis "Skip" Gates, Jr. (African American Lives 2: Profiles). PBS website. Educational Broadcasting Corporation. 2008. http://www.pbs.org/wnet/aalives/profiles/index.html (accessed October 29, 2010).

Information and History About Sweetgrass Basket and Basketry Information. 1993–2010. http://www.simplybaskets.com/SweetgrassBasketryInformation.html (accessed October 9, 2010).

Interview—Barbara Smith Conrad: Opera Singer. PBS website. 2009. http://video.pbs.org/video/1435210705 (accessed October 9, 2010).

Jacob Lawrence. 2001–2010. http://www.jacoblawrence.org (accessed December 5, 2010).

Jacob Lawrence: Exploring Stories. Whitney Museum of American Art. 2002. http://www.whitney.org/www/jacoblawrence/meet/index.html (accessed November 28, 2010).

Carlotta Hacker. Kids Can Press website. 2003. http://www.kidscanpress.com/Canada/CreatorDetails.aspx?cid=83 (accessed October 9, 2010).

Lawrence, Gwendolyn Knight. *Jacob Lawrence.* 2003. http://www.cs.washington.edu/building/art/JacobLawrence (accessed October 9, 2010).

The Lexile Framework for Reading. Lexile.com. MetaMetrics. 2010. http://lexile.com (accessed November 2, 2010).

Louis Armstrong—What a Wonderful World (Free MP3 Download). Beemp3.com. n.d. http://beemp3.com/download.php?file=4025115&song=What+A+Wonderful+World (accessed December 5, 2010).

Native American Baskets. Native Americans in Olden Times for Kids. n.d. http://nativeamericans.mrdonn.org/baskets.html (accessed November 26, 2010).

Recycle City. November 24, 2010. http://www.epa.gov/recyclecity (accessed November 25, 2010).

Sweet Grass Basket Weaving in Charleston SC (video). n.d. http://www.5min.com/Video/Sweet-Grass-Basket-Weaving-in-Charleston-SC-259884492 (accessed October 9, 2010).

Vaudeville: A Dazzling Display of Heterogeneous Spendor (a history). n.d. http://xroads.virginia.edu/~MA02/easton/vaudeville/vaudevillemain.html (accessed October 9, 2010).

"Where Are All the Black Swans?" (black ballet dancers). *New York Times.* 2007. http://www.nytimes.com/2007/05/06/arts/dance/06kour.html?_r=1 (accessed October 9, 2010).

Additional Reading Materials

Allen, Debbie. *Dancing in the Wings.* New York: Scholastic, 2000.

A young girl named Sassy dances her way right through her critics and those telling her that she will never make it. Inspired by her uncle never to lose hope, she is determined to reach her goal. While she is auditioning at the summer dance festival, the judge remarks negatively on her performance, but that makes her work even harder. When the final decision is made, Sassy is fighting to hold back the tears.

Barnwell, Ysaye M. *There Are No Mirrors in My Nana's House.* New York: Harcourt Children's Books, 1998.

If you want to know how much you're loved, spend some time with your nana (grandmother). In this lovely book, a child's barrier from the world's problems is her loving grandmother.

Belton, Sandra. *Pictures for Miss Josie.* New York: Greenwillow Books/An Imprint of HarperCollins, 2003.

A father takes his young son to learn from a lady who was his mentor, only to discover that the world has changed drastically since he was a boy and living under the wings of this now elderly woman.

Bolden, Tonya. *Wake Up Our Souls: A Celebration of Black American Artists.* New York: Harry N. Abrams, 2004.

Bolden has compiled information about the work of thirty-two artists, including their styles, mediums, and history.

Campbell, Mary Schmidt, et al. *Harlem Renaissance: Art of Black America.* New York: Abradale Press/Harry N. Abrams, 1987.

Recapture the beauty of the gifts contributed by the men and women artists who lived and worked during the Harlem Renaissance and learn how they helped to rejuvenate the lives of those who lived during that period in history.

Chambers, Veronica. *The Harlem Renaissance.* Langhorne, PA: Chelsea House, 1998.

This is a book full of rich paintings and vivid pictures from the various styles of artists that contributed to the Harlem Renaissance.

Dawes, Kwame Senu Neville. *I Saw Your Face.* New York: Dial, 2005.

Looking at people from all over the world, this book captures the stories their faces tell.

Dillon, Leo, and Diane Dillon. *Jazz on a Saturday Night.* New York: Scholastic, 2007.

The authors describe how the musicians look forward to the weekend after entertaining folks with their music all week long (Coretta Scott King Book Award).

Dillon, Leo, and Diane Dillon. *Rap A Tap Tap: Here's Bojangles—Think of That!* New York: Scholastic, 2002.

Children will have fun acting out the moves as they share this fascinating story about one of the greatest dancers to ever dance: Bill Bojangles Robinson (Coretta Scott King Illustrator Honor Book).

Haskins, James. *Black Dance in America: A History Through Its People.* New York: HarperTrophy/A Division of HarperCollins, 1990.

This is a book that provides readers with historic information on the origin and perfection of black dance and dancers in America, which is a vital part of African American culture (Coretta Scott King Book Award).

Hest, Amy. *Jamaica Louise James.* Cambridge, MA: Candlewick Press, 1996.

A young girl uses her eyes and crayons to share her thoughts about what she's seeing by sketching or coloring the things around her. When she gets a beautiful paint set for her eighth birthday, she describes how she brightened up the subway where her grandmother worked and changed the mood of the passengers waiting to ride the rails.

Johnson, Angela. *Lily Brown's Paintings.* New York: Orchard Books/An Imprint of Scholastic, 2007.

Lily Brown paints a world where everyone and everything is beautiful. She begins by flying through space and painting the stars and planets before she returns to make the world smile through a mirage of colors.

McKissack, Patricia C. *Mirandy and Brother Wind.* New York: Dragonfly Books/Alfred A. Knopf, 1988.

With a strong desire to win the Cake Walk Dance Contest, Mirandy devises a way to capture Brother Wind to have as her partner (Coretta Scott King Book Award).

Medearis, Angela Shelf. *Treemonisha.* New York: Henry Holt and Company, 1995.

This beautiful story tells of how a young girl uses her intelligence to fight a giant of ignorance and evil. The opera on which the book is based was composed by Scott Joplin, a prominent ragtime musician. This is a wonderful book to introduce with *Aida*, a book written by Leontyne Price.

Myers, Walter Dean. *Jazz.* New York: Holiday House, 2006.

Myers creates an array of moods and feelings through his stories about jazz. Using rhyme as the format, his vivid descriptions enable readers to be in whatever location his stories are set. A glossary of jazz terms is included to help readers better understand this genre of music

Nikola-Lisa. *Can You Top That?* New York: Lee & Low Books, 2000.

I CAN beat that! As young children compete in a sidewalk drawing challenge, the author makes the colors blend, showing how children can unite to use their remarkable imaginations to share tales through art.

Price, Leontyne. *Aida.* New York: Harcourt Brace & Company, 1990.

Based on Verdi's opera *Aida*, Price vividly captures the hearts of readers through her telling of the enslaved Aida, a princess from Ethiopia, and Radames, a young captain of the Egyptian army. Although many attempts are made to keep them apart, they find a way to finally be together (Coretta Scott King Book Award).

Raven, Margot Theis. *Circle Unbroken.* New York: Farrar, Straus & Giroux, 2007.

A grandmother shares the secret of basket making with her granddaughter, telling her how the artistry came to be and the many ways of using such a craft. From an enslaved group to a freed people, this art was passed on from generation to generation by the Gullah, who have proudly maintained their heritage and culture.

Ringgold, Faith. *Tar Beach.* New York: Crown, 1991.

Fly with Cassie as she takes readers on an aerial view of her world through descriptive storytelling (Caldecott Honor Book).

Ringgold, Faith. *We Flew Over the Bridge: The Memoirs of Faith Ringgold.* New York: A Bulfinch Press Book/Little, Brown and Company, 1995.

Faith continues her story in this book, emphasizing the importance of sharing art and developing an appreciation for the works of artists.

Roberts, Brenda C. *Jazzy Miz Mozetta.* New York: Farrar, Straus & Giroux, 2004.

In her red dress and red shoes, Miz Mozetta leaves her home with a desire to dance. Her friends tell her that they are too old and tired to dance, and the young group tells her that she's too old, causing her dream of dancing that evening to vanish. But once she returns home and turns on her music and starts to tap, the sounds and rhythm become contagious. Soon her friends join her in a frolicking good time by dancing their beloved jitterbug (Coretta Scott King Book Award).

Smalls, Irene. *My Nana and Me.* New York: Little, Brown and Company, 2005.

A young girl recalls the wonderful activities she participates in with her nana, who shows her, through play and conversation, just how much she is loved.

Tate, Eleanora E. *African American Musicians.* New York: John Wiley & Sons, 2000.

This is a collective biography about twenty-seven artists who share their dreams, desires, and accomplishments. Each made a major contribution that helped many to develop an artistic appreciation for both the visual and performing arts.

Taylor, Debbie A. *Sweet Music in Harlem.* New York: Lee & Low Books, 2004.

A young boy goes in search of his uncle's hat, only to discover some of Harlem's finest jazz musicians and lovers of the music. This delightful cumulative tale lends itself to information recall that gives readers the opportunity to strengthen their memories.

Williams, Karen Lynn. *Painted Dreams.* New York: Lothrop, Lee & Shepard Books, 1998.

A young Haitian girl must paint! She sees the pictures in her head and must let them out for the world to see. In this poignant story, a young girl's ability to create beautiful pictures using goat hair and moss and by adding water to empty paint tubes helps her family sell their vegetables at the market.

Chapter 2

AUTOBIOGRAPHY, BIOGRAPHY, AND MEMOIRS

If I like myself well enough to share my life with you, then what I write is my autobiography. If I write about the things I have done, accomplished, or experienced in my life, then that is my memoir. If people like me well enough to write about me, then that is my biography. In this section, you will find a wonderful selection of some of the best titles to read or share with students who have been challenged to overcome obstacles in their lives.

Bolden, Tonya. *Portraits of African American Heroes.* New York: Dutton Children's Books, 2003.

About the Author

Tonya Bolden . . . An Author for the Ages. Tonya Bolden Books. 2007–2010. http://www.tonyaboldenbooks.com (accessed October 10, 2010).

Literary Elements	Lexile Range	Teacher Resources and Supplies
Collected Biography Nonfiction Activists Arts Biography History	1140L	Book Paper Paints Potato Worksheet
Reading Level Grades 4 and up		**Accelerated Reader** Points: 3.0 Book Level: 8.3

Brief Summary

The stories in this book are from turbulent times, yet the heroes portrayed excelled in their lives, setting an example for young people to persevere and believe in themselves.

Focus

- Careers and Occupations
- Education and Skills
- Community Leaders and Humanitarians
- Religion

Teacher Input

- Show examples of both biographies and collected biographies, explaining the difference between the two, and introduce students to this website: http://raahistory.com.
- Lead a discussion on what makes a good leader.
- List on the board names of local community advocates, well-known abolitionists, and past and present educators who have made an impact on people's lives.
- Play the song "***Wind Beneath My Wings,***" available at http://beemp3.com/download.php?file=1058603&song=Wind+Beneath+My+Wings.

Guided Practice

- Ask students to define "gender jobs."
- Have students locate additional information about one of the heroes listed in this book and design their own drawing, collage, or poster to share with the class.
- Using online resources, have students explain why the NAACP was formed and then list its founders (see http://www.naacp.org/pages/naacp-history).
- Ask students to cite examples that indicate the need for such an organization today.
- Instruct students to design a collage telling the stories of "Women on the Go" as the author describes in the book.
- Ask students to compare and contrast the differences and similarities between Malcolm X and Dr. Martin Luther King, Jr.

Independent Practice

- Construct a collage of the NAACP founders.
- Choose a hero from this volume and write a poem about that person, or create a PowerPoint presentation with music relevant to the subject matter.

Closure

- Students share their projects with the class.
- Show "Gifted-Hands: The Ben Carson Story": http://www.megavideo.com/?v=2DY97SZD.

Assessment

- Student reports, brainstorming, questions, and projects.

The Heroes I Need to Know Worksheet

1. What does the acronym NAACP mean? See http://www.naacp.org/content/main.

 ____

2. Why do we still need an organization like the NAACP today? Provide some examples.

 ____

 ____

 ____

3. Which jobs are traditionally done more often by men? Which are traditionally done by women? Should both sexes be able to do any job that interests them? See the following website to learn more: http://www.thedigeratilife.com/blog/index.php/2007/05/29/traditional-jobs-for-men-and-women-the-gender-divide.

 ____

 ____

 ____

4. Now that you've read *Portraits of African American Heroes*, fill in the blanks below with the names of the heroes you learned about.

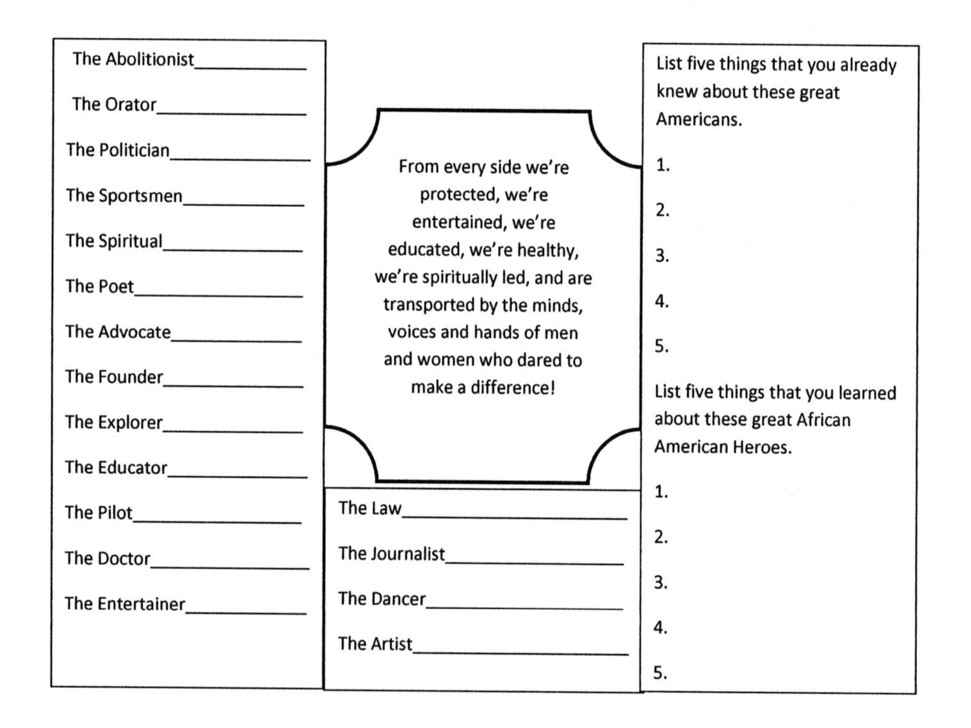

The Abolitionist__________

The Orator__________

The Politician__________

The Sportsmen__________

The Spiritual__________

The Poet__________

The Advocate__________

The Founder__________

The Explorer__________

The Educator__________

The Pilot__________

The Doctor__________

The Entertainer__________

From every side we're protected, we're entertained, we're educated, we're healthy, we're spiritually led, and are transported by the minds, voices and hands of men and women who dared to make a difference!

The Law__________

The Journalist__________

The Dancer__________

The Artist__________

List five things that you already knew about these great Americans.

1.

2.

3.

4.

5.

List five things that you learned about these great African American Heroes.

1.

2.

3.

4.

5.

Answers: Abolitionist – Frederick Douglass; The Orator – Paul Robeson; The Politician – Shirley Chisholm; Sportsmen – Satchel Paige, Joe Louis; The Spiritual – Pauli Murray; The Explorer – Matthew Henson; The Educator – Mary McLeod Bethune; The Pilot – Bessie Coleman; The Doctor – Ben Carson; The Entertainer – Dizzy Gillespie; The Law – Thurgood Marshall; The Journalist – Charlayne Hunter-Gault; The Dancer – Judith Jamison; The Artist – Jacob Lawrence

Now that you've read about Martin Luther King, Jr. and Malcolm X, describe how they were similar. What were some of their specific differences?

 ____

 ____

Greenfield, Eloise, and Lessie Jones Little. *Childtimes: A Three-Generation Memoir.* New York: HarperCollins, 1979.

About the Author

"Meet the Author: Eloise Greenfield." Houghton Mifflin Reading. Houghton Mifflin. n.d. http://www.eduplace.com/kids/hmr/mtai/greenfield.html (accessed October 10, 2010).

Literary Elements	Lexile Range	Teacher Resources and Supplies
Boston Globe–Horn Book Award Honor Carter G. Woodson Outstanding Merit Book Coretta Scott King Book Award Library of Congress Children's Book Notable Children's Trade Book in Social Studies Memoir	1000L	Book Worksheet
Reading Level Grades 5–12	**Accelerated Reader** Points: 4.0 Book Level: 5.0	
Additional Titles Davis, Tanita. ***Mare's War.*** Johnson, Angela. ***Toning the Sweep.*** **Website** http://teacher.scholastic.com/writeit/memoir/teacher		

Brief Summary

The lives of three women provide readers with ideas for recording and preserving their family history. These recorded memories can then be shared at family gatherings and passed down to future generations. This book will inspire readers to document and share their family histories.

Focus

- Women
- Preservation of Family Memories
- Genealogy

Teacher Input

- Introduce this book by asking students to share what they would write about themselves for others to know.
- Ask students to define "memoir."
- Ask students what title they would use for their memoirs.

Guided Practice

- Have students identify the three women in the book and compare them to members in their families who have similar habits. Students then create a chart and tell why they choose to match the pair.
- Students describe and explain the demographics of Parmele, North Carolina.
- The author notes that farming was the main source of income for residents living in Parmele at the time. Using online resources, have students examine farming today. Students choose five types of farms and explain how they are important. As a special feature, use the step-by-step instructions provided at http://42explore.com/farming.htm to create a shoebox or hat box farm diorama with a written description about your special farm.
- Greenfield identified John Mercer Langston as a lawyer in her book. Using online resources to locate additional information about Langston, have students explain why he was well known.
- Students locate and listen to music by Billie Holiday, Ella Fitzgerald, and Billy Eckstine. Using a rating scale of 1 to 3, with 1 being highest, have students rate the performers.
- Have students interview members of their families to gather information to write their memoirs. They should be prepared to use at least three family resources to construct their memoirs.
- Have students explain why they think this book received so many awards, including the Coretta Scott King Author Honor Book Award.

Independent Practice

- Suggest that students write their own memoir based on data collected from family members or create a multimedia memoir. Use the following online resource for ideas: http://www.brighthub.com/education/k-12/articles/19463.aspx.

Closure

- Students share their memoirs.

Assessment

- Student dedication to project, interviews, and project presentation.

Childtimes—Family Worksheet

What is a memoir?
1. Describe the geographic region of Parmele, North Carolina, today.

2. These characters from the book remind me of members in my family.	Name of family member
Character 1:	
Character 2:	
Character 3:	

Web and Print Resources for Research

John Mercer Langston:

http://www.oberlin.edu/external/EOG/OYTT-images/JMLangston.html

Billie Holiday:

http://www.last.fm/listen/artist/Billie%2BHoliday/similarartists

Books by and about Billie Holiday: *God Bless the Child* (Coretta Scott King Book Award);

Don't Explain: A Song of Billie Holiday (Coretta Scott King Book Award);

Becoming Billie Holiday (Fictional Memoir; Coretta Scott King Book Award)

Ella Fitzgerald: http://www.ellafitzgerald.com/		
Billy Eckstine: http://www.google.com/search?sourceid=navclient&aq=0&oq=Billy+ec&ie=UTF-8&rlz=1T4TSNA_en___US387&q=billy+eckstine		

What did you like best about this book?

Grimes, Nikki. *Barack Obama: Son of Promise, Child of Hope.* New York: Simon & Schuster Books for Young Readers, 2008.

About the Author

Nikki Grimes. n.d. http://www.nikkigrimes.com.

Literary Elements	Lexile Range	Teacher Resources and Supplies
Biography CBC/NCSS Notable Social Studies Trade Book Volunteer State Book Award Master List National *New York Times* Best Seller	AD630L	Book
Reading Level K–Grade 5	**Accelerated Reader** AR Points: 0.5	
Additional Title Edwards, Roberta. ***Barack Obama: United States President.*** **Websites** http://www.dailymotion.com/video/x7tupr_sam-cooke-a-change-is-gonna-come_webcam http://www.youtube.com/watch?v=8ZZ6GrzWkw0 http://www.whitehouse.gov/administration/president-obama http://www.buzzle.com/articles/importance-of-education-to-youths.html		

Brief Summary

The author takes the reader on a historical journey through the life events of Barack Obama, the first African American president of the United States. At an early age, he welcomed "hope" into his life and decided to team up with it to bring joy and happiness into the lives of others. Realizing that he would be hated, despised, and misunderstood for his actions, he allowed God to direct his decision making.

Focus

- First African American President of the United States
- Perseverance
- Education, Goal Setting
- Empathy for Others

Teacher Input

- Introduce the biography of the first African American president of the United States with this video clip: http://www.dailymotion.com/video/x7tupr_sam-cooke-a-change-is-gonna-come_webcam

- Survey students to determine what they know about the forty-fourth president of the United States (see President Obama's Message for America's Students: http://www.youtube.com/watch?v=8ZZ6GrzWkw0).
- Ask students to record times when they felt different or were treated differently because of their skin color or another difference.

Guided Practice

- Allow students to discuss certain areas in their lives that challenge them today.
- Have students draw a picture of President Barack Obama and write a short essay about concerns they would like him to address to provide hope in their lives.
- Ask students to analyze the author's description of the Golden Rule: "***Be honest. Be Kind. Be fair.***"
- Have students compare the percentage of male African American students attending Harvard University with that of other ethnic groups.
- Using online resources, ask students to locate and record specific information about Pali Mountain.

Independent Practice

- Plan a gallery or art show reflecting "***A Photo Wall of History Makers,***" after viewing this online site: http://www.biography.com/video.do?name=blackhistory.
- Have students write a "***Yes, We Can Succeed!***" speech after selecting and listening to at least one of the speeches made by an African American located at this website: http://www.blackpast.org/?q=african-american-history-major-speeches.

Closure

- Students deliver their speeches.
- Students explain how they feel about Barack Obama, an African American, being elected the forty-fourth president of the United States.

Assessment

- Student discussions, reports, and project design.

Johnson, Delores. *Onward: A Photobiography of African-American Polar Explorer Matthew Henson.* Washington, DC: National Geographic, 2006.

About the Author

Who Wrote That? Featuring Dolores Johnson. California Kids. December 2001. Available at http://www.patriciamnewman.com/johnson.html (accessed October 10, 2010).

Literary Elements	Lexile Range	Teacher Resources and Supplies
Biography Photography Science	—	Book Map Globe Worksheet
Reading Level Grades 5–8	**Accelerated Reader** Points: 2.0 Book Level: 7.6	
Additional Title Hoena, B.A. ***Matthew Henson.*** **Websites** http://www.matthewhenson.com/photos.htm		

Brief Summary

This is a beautiful book packed with information and photos tracking the life of Matthew Henson and his expeditions to the North Pole.

Focus

- Expeditions, North Pole
- Education, Race Relations
- Photography

Teacher Input

- Use the following website to take students on a virtual trip to the North Pole: http://www.matthewhenson.org/North_Pole_Trip2.htm.
- Present the book and lead a discussion on how the way we present ourselves to others has an impact on the way people treat us.
- List the people responsible for Henson's early education and what he was taught.
- Ask students the question "Have you ever had a great idea only to have someone else take it from you and use it as their own? If so, how did that make you feel?"

Guided Practice

- Have students participate in a "Weather Poll" by answering the question "Do you prefer hot or cold weather?"
- Ask students to draw a picture of a magnetic compass and provide some historical background for this tool, using the following website: http://inventors.about.com/od/cstartinventions/a/Compass.htm.
- Have students locate and list the names of three ships Henson and Peary used for their expeditions.
- Read a passage from page 14 and ask students to explain what they think Peary meant when he made the statement about Henson's heritage before sailing.
- Invite students to tell why they believe the Inuit (Eskimos) grew fond of Henson.
- Allow students to explain what type of education the Inuit boys and girls received.
- Have students research other explorers who claimed to have reached the North Pole before Henson and Peary and the evidence (or lack of) on which their claims are based.
- Invite students to debate who reached the North Pole first. Was it Henson or Peary? Have them support their answers.
- Ask students to explain why they believe Booker T. Washington and Adam Clayton Powell, Sr., celebrated Henson.

Independent Practice

- Suggest that students create their own virtual photo story of Matthew Henson's life by using Photo Story or PowerPoint. Use Google to download free images.

Closure

- Sponsor a "Day at the North Pole with Matthew Henson and Peary." Take both men on a tour of the North Pole to show them how it looks today. Use this online site to plan the event: http://iguide.travel/North_Pole.

Assessment

- Classroom discussions, report sheets, and project design.

The Exploration Worksheet

Describe Captain Childs. Why was his role in Matt Henson's life so important?	
What subjects did Henson master under Childs's guidance?	
Define "compass." Explain how one is used.	What does the word "Inuit" mean?
What is bartering?	Name the three ships used in the explorations.
Who was Robert Edwin Peary?	Why do you think Booker T. Washington and Adam Clayton Powell, two notable African Americans, celebrated Henson?

Both Peary and Henson were vying to be the first to arrive at the North Pole. Based on information in this book, who do you think placed the American flag? Tell why.

____

____

____

____

____

____

____

____

____

Miller, William. *Zora Hurston and the Chinaberry Tree.* New York: Lee & Low Books, 1994.

About the Author

Alabama Bound Author William Miller. May 11, 2001. http://www.alabamabound.org/AuthorPages/Miller William.htm (accessed October 10, 2010).

Literary Elements	Lexile Range	Teacher Resources and Supplies
Biography Fiction Nonfiction Literature	640L	Book
Reading Level All grades	**Accelerated Reader** Points: 0.5 Book Level: 3.0	
Additional Title Taylor, Mildred. ***Song of the Trees.*** **Websites** http://www.youtube.com/watch?v=Z81SViX2VIg http://www.arborday.org/kids/teachingYouth.cfm		

Brief Summary

The author unravels this story in a stereotypical way by naming those general mundane tasks that girls should do, while leaving the adventurous activities to the boys. Receiving little help from her father about changing these views, Zora refuses to be limited by her surroundings. Her strength, encouragement, and wisdom come from her dying mother, who teaches Zora never to give up climbing—not just to the top of the highest branches on her favorite tree but to the top of the world that holds her dreams.

Focus

- Stereotypes, Tomboy
- Dreams, Trees, Death

Teacher Input

- Present this book by reciting "Trees" by Joyce Kilmer (see http://www.poetry-archive.com/k/trees.html).
- Discuss how we benefit from trees. Read the poem, "What Do We Plant?" by Henry Abby (see http://www.dltk-kids.com/crafts/arborday/what_do_we_plant_poem.htm).
- Use online resources to discuss trees and their usefulness with students.
- Ask students what a tomboy is. Ask whether any of them have ever been called a tomboy and why.
- Tell students that the author mentioned Bream and Catfish in the beginning of the story. Ask what they know about fish and fishing.

Guided Practice

- Ask students whether their parents influence the way they dress.
- Using the author's description of Zora sitting in the tree, high above and away from the real conditions that existed below, have students describe what they believe was happening on the ground below to make her want to stay in the tree forever.
- Have students list Zora's progress as she ventures out to learn more about her world.
- Ask students to write an essay titled "**Why I Want to Stay in the Tree.**"
- Instruct students to draw a picture of Zora sitting in the tree. Play Louie Armstrong's "**What a Wonderful World.**"
- Zora's father warned what would happen to girls who refused to be obedient to their fathers. Invite students to debate whether he was trying to intimidate her or was offering her sound advice.
- Ask students whether they have ever experienced a death in their family or known someone who died. What did the older adults in Zora's house do after her mother's death?
- Have students read "**Mother to Son,**" a poem by Langston Hughes.
- Locate and read to students the story of John Henry or listen to this online resource: http://www.npr.org/programs/morning/features/patc/johnhenry/index.html.

Independent Practice

- Have each student write a mother-to-daughter or mother-to-son poem.

Closure

- Students present their assignments and projects.

Assessment

- Student brainstorming, reading and discussions, and project presentations.

Myers, Walter Dean. *Bad Boy: A Memoir.* New York: HarperCollins, 2001.

About the Author

Walter Dean Myers Author. n.d. http://www.walterdeanmyers.net/ (accessed October 10, 2010).

Literary Elements	Lexile Range	Teacher Resources and Supplies
Autobiography Character Education Classics Memoir	970L	Book
Reading Level Grades 9–12	**Accelerated Reader** Points: 8.0 Book Level: 6.5	
Additional Title Greenfield, Eloise, and Lessie Jones Little. ***Childtimes: A Three-Generation Memoir*** (Coretta Scott King Book Award). **Website** http://www.asha.org/public/speech/disorders		

Brief Summary

A teacher can see more of you than just your physical appearance. She can see and determine many of your needs by observing your behavior in the classroom and how well you get along with others.

Focus

- Student Behavior in Classroom
- Speech Impediments

Teacher Input

- Ask students: "Do you expect to see the same excitement and enthusiasm from your teachers in middle and high schools that you saw when you first began school? If so, why? If not, why?"
- How do you feel about reading comics in the classroom? See http://www.comicsintheclassroom.net.
- Poll students to see who has read a graphic novel.
- Ask students if they know what a memoir is and what a classic is. Explain the genres.

Guided Practice

- Have students visit Walter Dean Myers's website (www.walterdeanmyers.net) to learn about this award-winning author.
- Divide students into groups and have them address the topic, "***Have you ever been called bad?***" Have each group cite the reason for such negative labeling and describe their feelings about being labeled "bad."

- Have students compare and contrast the memoir of Walter Dean Myers to that of Maritcha Remond Lyons, two memoirs listed as additional reading. What role does education play in each story?
- Have students write a paper titled "***The Causes of Speech Disorders***" after viewing this online resource: http://kidshealth.org/parent/system/ill/speech_therapy.html.
- Assign students the following classics to read:
  - ***Ivanhoe*** http://www.publicbookshelf.com/regency/ivanhoe
  - ***The Prince and the Pauper*** http://www.online-literature.com/twain/princepauper/1
  - ***Tom Sawyer and Huck Finn*** http://www.pagebypagebooks.com/Mark_Twain/Tom_Sawyer
- Have students read poetry written by Kipling and Tennyson.

Independent Practice

- Suggest that students design and write their own memoirs, giving them creative titles.

Closure

- Students write their interpretation of the following passage found in Myers's book: "***Books are often touted by librarians as vehicles to carry you far away. I most often saw them as a way of hiding one self inside the other.***"

Assessment

- Class participation, motivation to read additional classics, oral and written reports.

Bibliography

Bolden, Tonya. *Portraits of African-American Heroes.* New York: Dutton Children's Books, 2003.

Dolores Johnson. California Kids. December 2001. http://www.patriciamnewman.com/johnson.html (accessed October 10, 2010).

Grimes, Nikki. *Barack Obama: Son of Promise, Child of Hope.* New York: Simon & Schuster Books for Young Readers, 2008.

Johnson, Delores. *Onward: A Photobiography of African-American Polar Explorer Matthew Henson.* Washington, DC: National Geographic, 2006.

Miller, William. *Zora Hurston and the Chinaberry Tree.* New York: Lee & Low Books Inc., 1994.

Myers, Walter Dean. *Bad Boy: A Memoir.* New York: HarperCollins, 2001.

Nikki Grimes. n.d. http://www.nikkigrimes.com/ (accessed October 9, 2010).

Tonya Bolden . . . An Author for the Ages. Tonya Bolden Books. 2007–2010. http://www.tonyaboldenbooks.com/ (accessed October 10, 2010).

Walter Dean Myers Author. n.d. http://www.walterdeanmyers.net/ (accessed October 10, 2010).

William Miller. Alabama Bound. May 11, 2001. http://www.alabamabound.org/AuthorPages/MillerWilliam.htm (accessed October 10, 2010).

Webliography

Bette Midler—Wind Beneath My Wings (free MP3 download). beemp3.com. n.d. http://beemp3.com/download.php?file=1058603&song=Wind+Beneath+My+Wings (accessed December 9, 2010). http://www.ovguide.com/movies_tv/gifted_hands_the_ben_carson_story.htm

COMICS IN THE CLASSROOM: A Comic Site for Teachers, Parents and Librarians. Scott Tingley. 2005–2010. http://www.comicsintheclassroom.net/ (accessed December 9, 2010).

History of the Compass. About.com. 2010. http://inventors.about.com/od/cstartinventions/a/Compass.htm (accessed December 27, 2011).

Importance of Education to Youths. 2010 Buzzle.com. 2000–2009. http://www.buzzle.com/articles/importance-of-education-to-youths.html (accessed October 10, 2010).

John Henry, Present at the Creation. National Public Radio. n.d. http://www.npr.org/programs/morning/features/patc/johnhenry/index.html (accessed December 28, 2010).

The King Center. The King Center. 2010. http://www.thekingcenter.org/MrsCSKing/ (accessed October 31, 2010).

MalcolmX.com. Estate of Malcolm X. n.d. http://www.malcolmx.com (accessed December 9, 2010).

Matthew A. Henson, "Photo Gallery." 2009. http://www.matthewhenson.com/photos.htm (accessed October 10, 2010).

NAACP (National Association for the Advancement of Colored People). 2009–2010. http://www.naacp.org/content/main (accessed December 27, 2010).

"1909 Expedition to the North Pole." Matthew Henson—Legend of the Arctic. 2003. http://www.matthewhenson.org/North_Pole_Trip2.htm (accessed December 27, 2010).

President Barack Obama. The White House. n.d. http://www.whitehouse.gov/administration/president-obama (accessed October 10, 2010).

President Obama's Message for America's Students. n.d. http://www.youtube.com/watch?v=8ZZ6GrzWkw0 (accessed December 27, 2010).

The Prince and the Pauper by Mark Twain: Chapter 1. Jalic. 2000–2010. http://www.online-literature.com/twain/princepauper/1/ (accessed December 28, 2010).

Read Ivanhoe Online-Free. PublicBookshelf. 2011. http://www.publicbookshelf.com/regency/ivanhoe/ (accessed December 28, 2010).

Real African American Heroes. Dr. Von L. Burton. 2010. http://raahistory.com (accessed October 10, 2010).

Sam Cooke—A Change Is Gonna Come. Dailymotion.com. n.d. http://www.dailymotion.com/video/x7tupr_sam-cooke-a-change-is-gonna-come_webcam (accessed December 27, 2010).

Speech and Language Disorders and Diseases. American Speech Language-Hearing Association. 1997–2010. http://www.asha.org/public/speech/disorders (accessed October 10, 2010).

Speech-Language Therapy. The Nemours Foundation. 1995-2010. http://kidshealth.org/parent/system/ill/speech_therapy.html (accessed December 28, 2010).

Teaching Youths About Trees with Resources from arborday.org. n.d. http://www.arborday.org/kids/teachingYouth.cfm (accessed October 10, 2010).

Tom Sawyer, by Mark Twain, Read It Now for Free! Page by Page Books. n.d. http://www.pagebypagebooks.com/Mark_Twain/Tom_Sawyer/ (accessed December 28, 2010).

Trees, by Joyce Kilmer. Poetry-Archive.com. 2002. http://www.poetry-archive.com/k/trees.html (accessed December 11, 2010).

What Do We Plant? Poem. DLTK. 1998–2010. http://www.dltk-kids.com/crafts/arborday/what_do_we_plant_poem.htm (accessed December 28, 2010).

Zora Neale Hurston's "Their Eyes Were Watching God." n.d. http://www.youtube.com/watch?v=Z81SViX2VIg (accessed December 27, 2010).

Additional Reading Materials

Altman, Susan. *Extraordinary Black Americans: From Colonial to Contemporary Times.* Chicago: Children's Press, 1993.

Readers will find this historical collection of biographies motivating as the author shares the lives of patriots who fought to provide hope and freedom for all people.

Bridges, Ruby. *Through My Eyes.* New York: Scholastic Press, 1999.

Ruby Bridges shares her feelings and the experience of her first day in an integrated school. Readers will learn how her experience changed the process for educating students in the South. Her recollection of the compassion her teacher showed and the bond that developed between them helped Ruby face daily obstacles

Dominy, Jeannine. *Katherine Dunham.* New York: Chelsea House, 1992.

This book gives readers a clear understanding about the life and personal interests of a determined and dedicated woman who found personal triumphs through dance.

Edwards, Roberta. *Barack Obama: An American Story.* New York: Grosset & Dunlap, 2008.

This beginner reader tells the story and shares the life of Barack Obama, the forty-fourth president of the United States. This story is unique in that children just learning to read may read about the country's first African American president.

Freedman, Russell. *The Voice That Challenged a Nation: Marian Anderson and the Struggle for Equal Rights.* New York: Clarion Books, 2004.

Marian Anderson dreamed of performing at Constitution Hall, but knowing that it was not within her reach at the time, she was content supporting her family while waiting for the opportunity. When the time arrived for her to perform at Constitution Hall where the world could hear and appreciate her gift, there were groups that did not accept her because of her skin color.

Hearth, Amy Hill. *Reach High.* Nashville, TN: Abingdon Press, 2002.

Sharing the lives of two sisters, this award-winning book profiles Bessie and Sadie who kept hope alive while fighting racism through faith, their love for each other, and family encouragement. The sisters persevered in pursuit of their dreams.

Hoena, B. A. *Matthew Henson.* Mankato, MN: Pebble Books, 2006.

For young readers interested in explorations, this is another good story of how Matthew Henson arrived at the North Pole with Robert Peary.

King, Martin Luther, Jr. *Why We Can't Wait.* New York: Signet Classic, 2000.

Dr. King worked tirelessly during his lifetime to ensure civil rights for all people. His words still ring true today. We can't wait for others to do what we should do. This book is required reading on the Common Core Standards list for high school students.

Manheimer, Ann S. *James Beckwourth: Legendary Mountain Man.* Minneapolis, MN: Twenty-First Century Books, 2006.

Running away from the degradation of slavery, James Beckwourth surrounded himself with nature and felt that he could adapt to anything—if he were free. Finding it easy to become a member of the Native American Crow Tribe where he learned survival skills, he helped others fight for fairness by working with the U.S. Army.

Myers, Walter Dean. ***Malcolm X: By Any Means Necessary.*** **New York: Scholastic Inc., 1993.**

Myers gives his readers the opportunity to discover how and what leads to the greatness of Malcolm X and then to his demise. In this novel is a valuable lesson for young readers: it is necessary to understand concepts before trying to apply them. Although Malcolm's influence is still prevalent today, many continue to misunderstand his philosophy because of the concept of violence he attached to it in the early years of his crusade.

Myers, Walter Dean. ***Now Is Your Time!: The African-American Struggle for Freedom.*** **New York: HarperCollins, 1991.**

This is a collection of stories about the men and issues that affected the struggle of African Americans to acquire and maintain freedom. Myers has carefully adapted important documents to help readers understand them.

Myers, Walter Dean. ***Slam!*** **New York: Scholastic, 1996.**

Although Greg may be "bad" on the basketball court, his manners leave a lot to be desired. He learns the hard way—through academics, his dysfunctional family, and a shortage of manners—that developing positive relationships with family and friends can strengthen his ability to earn the nickname "Slam!"

Nobisso, Josephine. ***John Blair and the Great Hinckley Fire.*** **Boston: Houghton Mifflin, 2000.**

Readers will be impressed by the leadership skills displayed by John Blair, a man who was fully committed to his job. A porter on a train bound for Hinckley, Blair shows the characteristics of a hero when during a raging fire he controls his passengers and carries out his responsibilities.

Poitier, Sidney. ***The Measure of a Man: A Spiritual Autobiography.*** **New York: Harper San Francisco/A Division of HarperCollins, 2000.**

In his book Poitier gives honor and praise where it is due—to God—for the blessings he received. He details the principles that helped him to achieve his high level of success as an actor and performer.

President Obama: A Day in the Life of America's Leader. **Des Moines, IA: Time, 2009.**

Time has created this beautifully illustrated book for young people to learn about the historical election of the first African American president of the United States. Information about the president's family, cabinet, and staff are included.

Richardson, Ben Albert. ***Great Black Americans.*** **New York: Crowell, 1976.**

A revised edition of an important resource originally compiled by Russell Adams, this book shares the achievements and accomplishments of men and women whose lives were dedicated to serving others. Many, like Duke Ellington, Paul Robeson, and Jesse Owens, not only entertained but also advocated to help others survive in a world where freedom was available to only a few.

Sterling, Kristin. ***Mary McLeod Bethune: A Life of Resourcefulness.*** **Minneapolis, MN: Lerner, 2008.**

Mary McLeod Bethune was an educational and political activist who worked tirelessly to a create better way of life for her people by advocating for women's rights, educating children, and collaborating effectively with government officials about the needs and issues affecting the African American family.

Swanson, Gloria Borseth, and Margaret V. Ott. ***I've Got an Idea!: The Story of Frederick McKinley Jones.*** **Minneapolis, MN: Runestone Press, 1994.**

Called a "black Thomas Edison," Frederick Jones showed at any early age that he was a genius with gadgets. In this book, he and a friend build a car and use it to win a race with an airplane. Later he makes history when he invents a way to keep food fresh by transporting it by truck. Afterward he spends his time working for a company known as Thermo King.

Turner, Glennette Tilley. ***Take a Walk in Their Shoes: Biographies of Fourteen Outstanding African Americans with Skits About Each to Act Out.*** **New York: Puffin Books/Penguin Group, 1992.**

Young readers can learn much about history by acting out the events and occurrences that were a part of the black experience. Using many prominent names such prominent names, from Leontyne Price and her amazing performance of *Aida* to Garret Morgan and his invention of the traffic light, readers will be amazed by the steps made and the imprint left by these great heroes and heroines.

Wiebe, Ruth Lent. ***African Americans.*** **Broomall, PA: Mason Crest, 2009.**

This is a great resource book that profiles prominent African Americans and the hardships many of them experienced while helping to change how blacks in America are viewed today in every profession.

Chapter 3

BE A GOOD SPORT

Introduce your students to books and activities about legendary athletes who dreamed big and worked hard to accomplish their goals, and who succeeded despite racism and sexism. From the books in this chapter, students will learn about professional boxer Muhammad Ali, champion cyclist Major Taylor, tennis pro Althea Gibson, and many other stand-out athletes.

Bolden, Tonya. *The Champ*. New York: Random House, 2004.

About the Author

Tonya Bolden Books—Tonya Bolden . . . An Author for the Ages. 2007–2010. http://www.tonyaboldenbooks.com/ (accessed October 10, 2010).

Literary Elements	Lexile Range	Teacher Resources and Supplies
Biography Boxing Culture History Repetition Metaphor	AD820L	Book Boxing gloves Worksheet U.S. flag
Reading Level Grades 5–7	**Accelerated Reader** Points: 0.5 Book Level: 5.0	
Additional Titles Antle, Nancy. ***Staying Cool.*** Miller, William. ***Joe Louis, My Champion.*** Shange, Ntozake. ***Float Like a Butterfly.*** **Websites** http://www.ali.com http://www.time.com/time/covers/20060116/puzzles		

Brief Summary

This is a great and powerful book about a man whose quest for greatness is achieved through perseverance and hard work.

Focus

- Sports
- Boxing
- Physical and Mental Training

Teacher Input

- Define "calisthenics" for the class.
- Ask the class to explain what they think the phrase "Throwing a rock and hiding behind it" means.
- Ask the students to tell what Ali meant when he said he was prepared and committed to his goal. Have students explain in their own words what they think this means.
- Define the word "metaphor" and provide examples for the class.

Guided Practice

- Direct students to participate in the online Brain Calisthenics Workout at http://www.time.com/time/covers/20060116/puzzles.
- Encourage students to use this online site to learn more about the draft or Selective Service. http://www.sss.gov.
- Discuss or debate whether Muhammad Ali's punishment for saying "No," to the draft was justifiable. Ask students whether they think that by making such a decision, he loved his country less. Have them explain why.
- Instruct students to search for and list metaphors found in Bolden's book.

Independent Practice

- Suggest that students develop a PowerPoint or Photo Story timeline of Ali's career showing examples of his success before and after the Supreme Court decision not to send him to jail.

Closure

- Invite a boxer or boxing coach to discuss the sport with the class.

Assessment

- Student participation, reports, interactions, and project designs.

A Page for the Champ Worksheet

1. What was Muhammad Ali's name before he joined the Nation of Islam?

2. Define the term "metaphor."

3. List at least three metaphors found in Bolden's book.

Cline-Ransome, Lesa. *Major Taylor: Champion Cyclist.* New York: Atheneum Books for Young Readers, 2004.

About the Author

Lesa Cline-Ransome, Writer & Editor Rhinebeck, New York. n.d. http://www.lesaclineransome.com (accessed October 10, 2010).

Literary Elements	Lexile Range	Teacher Resources and Supplies
Biography Cyclist Making Inferences and Analyzing	AD1020L	Book Worksheet
Reading Level Grades 2 and up	**Accelerated Reader** Points: 0.5	
Additional Title Crews, Donald. ***Bicycle Race.*** **Websites** http://www.majortaylorassociation.org/who.htm http://www.fi.edu/pieces/silverman/taylor.htm http://www.lancearmstrong.com		

Brief Summary

Major Taylor, an African American cyclist, used his skills and ingenuity to peddle his way into history. Taylor's success is due in part to his tremendous love for the sport and his ability to communicate with people even when some didn't have his best interest at heart. It is important to introduce children to great African Americans who excelled in fields other than baseball, basketball, football, tennis, and golf. This is an excellent resource to provide young readers the name of a champion cyclist.

Focus

- Sports Other Than Basketball
- Cycling
- Transportation

Teacher Input

- Survey students to find out who among them are bike riders.
- Discuss using a bicycle to get the job done or to have some fun. Have students view the following website: http://bicycling.about.com/od/organizedbikeevents/a/bikerodeo_event.htm. There are various ways for bike lovers to use their bicycles. At this website, students will discover that some people use bicycles while trying to earn a living and others use them merely for recreation. Ask students how they use their bicycles.
- Ask students to comment on what kinds of jobs require a bicycle.

Guided Practice

- Define the term "***Penny-Farthing***" and discuss how it differs from the tricycle.
- Have students draw picture of a bicycle and label its parts. Explain why each part is important.
- Instruct students to write an essay titled "***You've Got Talent, but You've Got to Keeping Working.***"
- Have students view websites about both Major Taylor and Lance Armstrong to compare the similarities and differences between the two great bikers. Students may record their findings on the worksheet provided.
- Poll students to determine which brakes they use most often on their bicycles—the handbrakes or the pedal brakes.

Independent Practice

- Suggest that students develop a bicycle safety video.
- Divide students into two groups. Have them debate the topic "***Every Trial Is an Opportunity.***"

Closure

- Invite a police officer to talk to the class about bicycle safety.

Assessment

- Student reports and project design.

I've Got Wheels! Worksheet

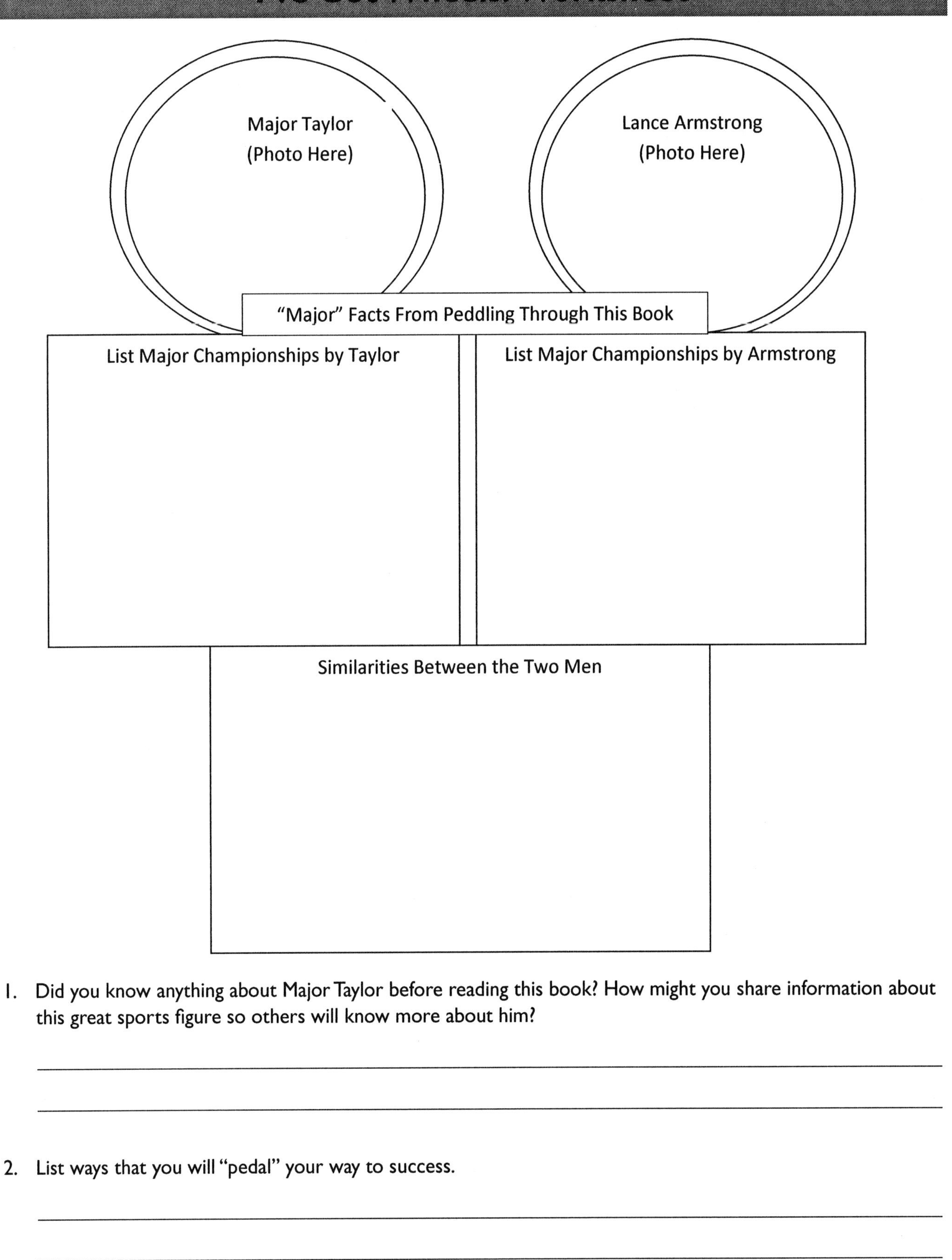

1. Did you know anything about Major Taylor before reading this book? How might you share information about this great sports figure so others will know more about him?

____

____

2. List ways that you will "pedal" your way to success.

____

____

Peddling Through History on a Bike Timeline

Part A: Draw a Bicycle

Create a Timeline

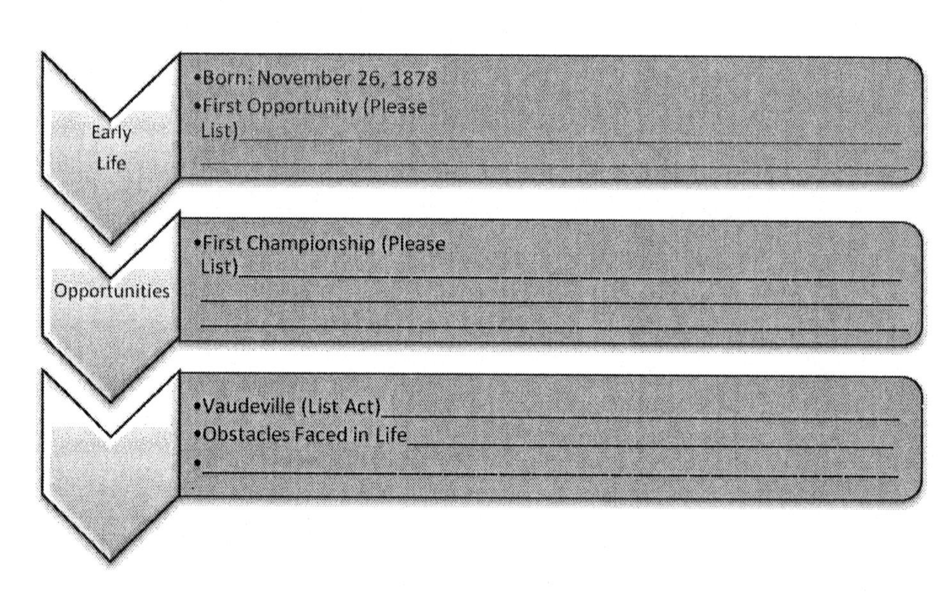

Part B: Match the Bicycle with the Job It Performs Best

1. Kids	a. Off-road cycling
2. Bike path	b. Used on the beach
3. Mountain	c. Powered by a battery
4. Cruiser	d. Mountain and racing bike combination
5. Hybrid	e. City bike
6. Urban	f. Young riders
7. Road	g. Long-distance bike
8. Electric	h. Neighborhood bike

Part C: Research the following cyclists, record one fact about them, and cite your reference.

Arthur Zimmerman

____

Willie Windle

____

Louis "Birdie" Munget

____

Edmond Jacquelin

____

Deans, Karen. *Playing to Win: The Story of Althea Gibson.* New York: Holiday House, 2007.

About the Author

Karen Deans. n.d. http://karendeans.com (accessed October 10, 2010).

Literary Elements	**Lexile Range**	**Teacher Resources and Supplies**
Biography Female Athletes Dropouts	890L	Book Worksheet Tennis ball and racket
Reading Level Grades 2–6	**Accelerated Reader** Points: 0.5 Book Level: 5.6	
Additional Titles Stauffacher, Sue. ***Nothing but Trouble: The Story of Althea Gibson.*** Mantel, Paul. ***Arthur Ashe: Young Tennis Champion.*** **Websites** http://www.tuskegee.edu/global/Story.asp?s=1372200 http://www.williamssisters.org		

Brief Summary

Although life is a gift, we do not always have the opportunity to enjoy it to the fullest because of barriers that may be impossible to eradicate. We don't always get what we deserve, and life can be disappointing at times. Althea Gibson faced many such barriers, but she was determined to persevere because she felt she had something inside that needed to come out. Tempted to drop out of school, faced with racial disadvantages, and lacking faith in herself, she overcame these obstacles to become the number one African American woman to compete on the world tennis tour.

Focus

- Tennis
- Women Athletes
- Education; Motivation to Stay in School
- School Dropouts

Teacher Input

- Discuss family life and how family members can encourage each another.
- Ask students to talk about their favorite sport(s). Survey the class to determine whether any are tennis players.
- Ask students to state their favorite school subject and why it is the one thing they like best.
- Ask students to name role models in the community, and then discuss the importance of community role models.

Guided Practice

- Ask students to brainstorm and discuss why they believe students skip or drop out of school.
- Define the meaning of "physical skills." Have students list and explain five physical skills.
- Enlist the help of students who understand and play tennis in the "***Serving on My Terms***" game. The purpose is to teach interested students how to play the game. This activity may consist of a variety of mediums, such as charts, posters, brochures, PowerPoint presentations, and the like.
- Invite students to view the following online resource to learn more about the Peters sisters, who played tennis before Venus and Serena Williams: http://www.tuskegee.edu/global/Story.asp?s=1372200. Ask them to talk about Margaret "Pete" and Matilda Roumania "Repeat" Peters.
- Ask students to describe in writing the similarities and differences between the Peters and the Williams sisters.

Independent Practice

- Encourage students to develop a script for a news show, "***Life Is a Game—Play Hard and Never Give Up!***"

Closure

- Invite a professional or skilled tennis player to discuss tennis with the class. Contact a local athletic club for a potential speaker.

Assessment

- Student brainstorming, research, and project presentations.

Gibson's Life Serve

Althea Gibson was born in ____. List three things about this town and state.

1.	2.	3.

Briefly describe Gibson's family. ____

With which relatives was Gibson sent to live? Where were they? ____

Name the sports that Gibson was most interested in playing. ____

Who was Buddy Walker? ____

Where did Gibson attend college? ____

Write a statement about the African American Cosmopolitan Club and the impact it had on Gibson. ____

What does the acronym ATA mean? ____

Johnson, Angela. *Just Like Josh Gibson.* New York: Simon & Schuster Books for Young Readers, 2004.

About the Author

Angela Johnson. AALBC.com, LLC. 1997–2010. http://aalbc.com/authors/angela.htm (accessed October 10, 2010).

Literary Elements	Lexile Range	Teacher Resources and Supplies
Point of View Repetition Similie	AD920L	Book Worksheet Baseball and bat
Reading Level Grade 2	**Accelerated Reader** Points: 0.5 Book Level: 3.2	
Additional Title Green, Michelle Y. ***A Strong Right Arm: The Story of Mamie "Peanut" Johnson.*** **Websites** http://www.joshgibson.org http://www.america.gov/st/pubs-english/2003/June/20050606084701pssnikwad0.4582025.html http://www.npr.org/templates/story/story.php?storyId=1164167		

Brief Summary

A young girl tells the story of how her grandmother loved baseball player Josh Gibson because of her father's love for the player. She later masters the sport, even though she knows that girls can never play the game. However, after an accident, the game plans change and she is allowed to play and use her skills to help the team win and enjoy the championship.

Focus

- Girls, Sports, and Baseball
- Girls and Skills
- Grandmothers

Teacher Input

- Instruct students to imagine they're putting together a task force to advocate for females to play professional baseball or football. What would their argument be? List on paper.
- Using online resources, introduce students to NCAA women's basketball teams.

Guided Practice

- Survey students to discover the number of girls who play on softball teams, the positions they play, and whether they feel they're treated differently from the boys on the team. Allow students to discuss why they think this is.

- Guide students to identify conditions and attitudes that may prevent women from playing the game professionally.
- Instruct students to create a book titled ***The ABCs of Why There Should Still Be a Professional Baseball League for Women.*** To support their positions, have students search for African American women who have been successful in other sports.
- Encourage students to debate the question "Should Women Play Professional Baseball? Why? Why not?"
- ***"Stop Joshing Around!" Here Are the Facts.*** Group students by gender. Assign one group the task of examining the number of African Americans playing professional baseball in the American League, and assign the other group to follow the same procedure for those players playing in the National League. Ask each group to draw an illustration of each team's logo.

Independent Practice

- Have the two groups create a slideshow of African American players and team logos.

Closure

- Group students by gender and sponsor an American League versus National League Tournament designed to see which group can identify or name the most teams in their league based on team logos. Winners receive Babe Ruth and Oh Henry! candy bars (although the latter was not named after Henry "Hank" Aaron).
- Have each student present and talk about the construction of their book.

Assessment

- Students interests, group participation, and project sharing.

Stop Joshing Around Worksheet: Women at Home Plate

Toni Stone (Player One)

With what team did Stone sign in 1953? ______________________________

What was her batting average? ______________________________

What was considered to be Stone's greatest success? ______________________________

List the teams Stone played with during her career. ______________________________

What position did Stone play? ______________________________

In what year did she retire? ______________________________

Toni Stone became a pioneer member of which organization? ______________________________

Connie Morgan (Player Two)	**Mamie "Peanut" Johnson (Player Three)**
How old was Morgan when she signed to play with Indianapolis?	How many years did Johnson play?
What position did she play?	What positions did she play?
How long did she play for Indy?	What is the average number of innings Johnson could pitch?
What was the name of the Indianapolis team?	What are two other skills that Johnson possessed? 1. 2.
Who did Morgan replace when she went to Indianapolis?	Where did Johnson get her higher education?
Using the Internet, find another interesting fact about Morgan. List it here.	What did Johnson do after she stopped playing baseball?

Draw a picture of your favorite African American sports hero.

Nelson, Kadir. *We Are the Ship: The Story of Negro Baseball.* New York: Jump at the Sun/Hyperion Books, 2008.

About the Author

About the Artist: Artist's Biography—The Art of Kadir Nelson. Little Blue Room Web Design. n.d. http://www.kadirnelson.com/Artist-Biography.html (accessed October 10, 2010).

<table>
<tr><td>Literary Elements
Point of View
Repetition
Similie</td><td>Lexile Range
AD920L</td><td>Teacher Resources and Supplies</td></tr>
<tr><td>Reading Level
Grade 2</td><td>Accelerated Reader
Points: 0.5
Book Level: 3.2</td><td>Book
Worksheet
Baseball and bat</td></tr>
<tr><td colspan="3">Additional Title
McKissack, Patricia C., and Fredrick McKissack, Jr. Black Diamond: The Story of the Negro Baseball League.
Websites
http://www.joshgibson.org
http://www.america.gov/st/pubs-english/2003/June/20050606084701pssnikwad0.4582025.html
http://www.satchelpaige.com
http://mlb.mlb.com/mlb/history/mlb_negro_leagues.jsp</td></tr>
</table>

Brief Summary

This incredible informational book about America's favorite pastime provides a comprehensive history of the role the Negro League that played in the 1920s. Nelson's poignant story of the league's origin combined with his bold and strong illustrations is captivating. For the many young men who dream about making their fortunes in baseball, this book is highly motivational because it shows how one can achieve such a dream through hard work and perseverance.

Focus

- Negro Baseball Leagues
- Baseball
- Perseverance

Teacher Input

- Survey the class to determine which students participate in softball or baseball teams.
- Share baseball language with the class.

Guided Practice

- Direct students to develop classroom monologue or skit presentations using the theme "***Life Is Like a Baseball Game.***"

- Group students and assign a compare-and-contrast activity about the lives of President Barack Obama, Jackie Robinson, Ruby Bridges, and Rosa Parks. Have students assess what they believe to be the driving force behind their successful actions.

Independent Practice

- Suggest that students create projects that include photos, online sites, flipcharts, and PowerPoint presentations.

Closure

- Students identify their favorite baseball teams.

Assessment

- Student participation.
- Student reports and worksheets.

A "Historic Grand Slam" Worksheet

Search for information on these great heroes and heroines. Identify the role they played in history, tell what you know about their character, and describe in the ball-shaped circle how they were similar. List your resources or references in the second column.

Barack Obama	Reference
Jackie Robinson	Reference
Ruby Bridges	Reference
Rosa Parks	Reference

Did you learn something new about one of the heroes or heroines that you didn't already know? If so, explain.

List your three favorite baseball teams.

1. ____________________

2. ____________________

3. ____________________

Bibliography

Bolden, Tonya. *The Champ.* New York: Random House, 2004.

Cline-Ransome, Lesa. *Major Taylor: Champion Cyclist.* New York: Atheneum Books for Young Readers, 2004.

Deans, Karen. *Playing to Win: The Story of Althea Gibson.* New York: Holiday House, 2007.

Dungy, Tony. *You Can Do It!* New York: Little Simon Inspirations, 2008.

Johnson, Angela. *Just Like Josh Gibson.* New York: Simon & Schuster Books for Young Readers, 2004.

Krull, Kathleen. *Wilma Unlimited: How Wilma Rudolph Became the World's Fastest Woman.* New York: Voyager Books, 1996.

McKissack, Patricia C., and Fredrick McKissack, Jr. *Black Diamond: The Story of the Negro Baseball League.* New York: Scholastic , 1994.

Nelson, Kadir. *We Are the Ship: The Story of Negro Baseball.* New York: Jump at the Sun/Hyperion Books, 2008.

Pinkney, Andrea D. *Bill Pickett: Rodeo-Ridin' Cowboy.* San Diego, CA: Gulliver Books/Harcourt Brace & Company, 1996.

Robinson, Sharon. *Slam Dunk!* New York: Scholastic Press, 2007.

Weatherford, Carole Boston. *Jesse Owens.* New York: Walker, 2007.

Webliography

About the Artist: Artist's Biography—The Art of Kadir Nelson. Little Blue Room Web Design. n.d. http://www.kadirnelson.com/Artist-Biography.html (accessed October 10, 2010).

Althea Gibson. About.com. 2010. http://womenshistory.about.com/od/gibsonalthea/a/althea_gibson.htm (accessed December 27, 2010).

AR BookFinder US—Quick Search. Renaissance Learning Inc. 2010. http://www.arbookfind.com/Default.aspx (accessed December 7, 2010).

Black Female Baseball. Free Articles Directory. 2009–2010. http://sportarticles.net/2010/02/black-female-baseball (accessed December 8, 2010).

Carole Boston Weatherford. n.d. http://www.caroleweatherford.com (accessed October 10, 2010).

ESPN.com:Johnson doubled the difficulty. ESPN. 2007. http://espn.go.com/sportscentury/features/00016046.html (accessed December 8, 2010).

Florence Griffith Joyner. The Estate of Florence Joyner. n.d. http://www.florencegriffithjoyner.com (accessed December 8, 2010).

Gibson, Josh—Negro League Baseball Player. Negro League Baseball Players. 2000–2007. http://www.nlbpa.com/gibson_josh.html (accessed December 8, 2010).

JesseOwens.com. Jesse Owens Trust. 2009. http://www.jesseowens.com (accessed December 8, 2010).

The Lexile Framework for Reading. Lexile.com. MetaMetrics, Inc. 2010. http://lexile.com (accessed November 2, 2010).

Mamie "Peanut" Johnson, Pitching Pioneer: NPR. National Public Radio. February 18, 2003. http://www.npr.org/templates/story/story.php?storyId=1164167 (accessed December 8, 2010).

Wilma Rudolph—An Uphill Battle. n.d. http://www.youtube.com/watch?v=igl8DmcKRhQ (accessed December 26, 2010).

Wilma Rudolph.net—Biography, Picture, Videos, & Quotes. Mosaic. n.d. http://www.wilmarudolph.net (accessed December 8, 2010).

Additional Reading Materials

Antle, Nancy. *Staying Cool.* New York: Dial Books for Young Readers, A Division of Penguin Books USA, 1997.

A young boy's dream of winning the Golden Glove competition is put on hold until his grandfather—who is his personal trainer—gives his approval, signaling that he is ready for this event. Until that time, the boy knows that he must both study to show that he is mastering the skills in the classroom and practice to develop and improve his boxing skills, so that when his grandpa gives the signal, nothing is left undone.

Barber, Tiki. *By My Brother's Side.* New York: Simon & Schuster Books For Young Readers, 2004.

This interesting book details the story of the Barber twins, who made it big in football after spending most of their lives playing the sport. Performing on advice from their mother—to always believe in themselves—they dreamed of playing in the Super Bowl, and both went on to do so.

Burleigh, Robert. *Stealing Home. Jackie Robinson: Against the Odds.* New York: A Paula Wiseman Book/Simon & Schuster for Young Readers, 2007.

Burleigh has created a story that will excite young readers and motivate older ones to develop an appreciation for both baseball and the hero of this book. This is the story of a man whose life was dedicated to others. The general manager of the Dodger's organization dared Robinson to be different, knowing that Robinson needed to be challenged to strengthen him against the racial remarks and poor treatment he would receive because of his growing popularity in the sport.

Cline-Ransome, Lesa. *Satchel Paige.* New York: Aladdin Paperbacks/An Imprint of Simon & Schuster Children's Publishing Division, 2000.

Satchel Paige was no average man. He pitched his way through history by playing with the Negro major leagues and then the Cleveland Indians. He was finally elected to the Baseball Hall of Fame in Cooperstown, New York, becoming the first African American to receive this honor (see http://www.satchelpaige.com).

Crews, Donald. *Bicycle Race.* New York: Greenwillow Books, 1985.

This is a delightful counting book from one to twelve featuring cyclists and bicycles.

Dingle, Derek T. *First in the Field: Baseball Hero Jackie Robinson.* New York: Scholastic, 1998.

Jackie had his brother Mack to thank for asking his friends to allow younger brother Jackie to play on one of their afternoon school baseball teams. From that game until he died, Jackie Robinson loved baseball. He excelled in the game and never once lost his cool, even when he heard baseball fans' jeers and faced racism. His love of the game and his commitment to putting the interests of the team above his personal feelings contributed to breaking the racial barriers in baseball.

Green, Michelle Y. *A Strong Right Arm: The Story of Mamie "Peanut" Johnson.* New York: Dial Books for Young Readers/A Division of Penguin Young Readers Group, 2002.

Who said girls can't play professional baseball? It's not so! Mamie "Peanut" Johnson, a young girl living with her grandmother in Ridgeway, South Carolina, was one of three African American women to play the sport professionally. Readers will be intrigued by this young woman whose dreams were fulfilled on the baseball field, where she worked hard to prove to her critics that women can play the game—and play it well.

Hubbard, Crystal. *The Last Black King of the Kentucky Derby: The Story of Jimmy Winkfield.* New York: Lee & Low Books, 2008.

This is an incredible book that reveals the life of a young man who overcame many obstacles to become King of the Kentucky Derby. Jimmy "Wink" Winfield had a successful but brief career as a jockey cut short because of his ethnic background and social position. This book encourages readers to persevere and never give up.

Johnson, Dolores. *What Kind of Baby-Sitter Is This?* New York: Scholastic, 1991.

What kind of babysitter is this one going to be? The kind that has the skills and tools to win over the heart of a young boy who is reluctant to accept her into his home to care for him. Soon he is able to observe the sitter's interests and discovers that the two of them love the same thing—baseball. Mother leaves home concerned about her son, only to return to see him happily sitting beside his new friend.

Jordan, Deloris, and Roslyn M. Jordan. *Salt in His Shoes: Michael Jordan in Pursuit of a Dream.* New York: Scholastic, 2000.

Deloris Jordan tells the story of her son Michael, who prayed to grow taller so that he could improve his chances of playing basketball. Michael thought that salt would make him taller, so he tried "putting salt in his shoes."

Lester, Julius. *Black Cowboy, Wild Horses: A True Story.* New York: Dial Books/A Member of Penguin Putnam, 1998.

Based on the life story of Bob Lemmons, Lester has created a fictional account of a man determined to catch and control a group of wild stallions. When an unfortunate mishap happens to a colt, Lemmons decides to take advantage of the situation and gain control of the herd with the help of his horse.

Mantel, Paul. ***Arthur Ashe: Young Tennis Champion.*** **New York: Aladdin Paperbacks, 2006.**

This biography discusses the life and legacy of Arthur Ashe, who was the first black man to earn success in tennis. Readers will learn how he dealt with attitudes and behaviors in his struggle to become one of the greatest tennis players of all times.

Mathis, Sharon Bell. ***Red Dog Blue Fly: Football Poems.*** **New York: Puffin Books/Published by the Penguin Group, 1991.**

This book of poems will make a touchdown with readers who love football. Mathis carefully crafted a series of rhymes related to the joys and disappointments of the game.

Mathis, Sharon Bell. ***Running Girl: The Diary of Ebonee Rose.*** **New York: Browndeer Press/Harcourt Brace & Company, 1997.**

Mathis presents the reader with an array of prominent female stars in track and field. Realizing that star runners may have felt the jitters just as she did before the All-City Track Meet, Ebonee uses the coaching and encouragement provided by her predecessors to get motivated. Read more at http://findarticles.com/p/articles/mi_m1355/is_n17_v90/ai_18657498.

Miller, William. ***Joe Louis, My Champion.*** **New York: Lee & Low Books, 2004.**

A young boy wants to become a boxer like Joe Louis and learns that it is important to be yourself and strive to do your best at all times. He discovers that his idol had to overcome prejudice, work hard, and "keep getting up" to earn the title "Heavy Weight Champion of the World."

Myers, Walter Dean. ***The Journal of Joshua Loper: A Black Cowboy.*** **New York: Scholastic, 1999.**

Walter Dean Myers has woven a piece of diverse history into this fictional journal that is part of the Dear America series. A young African American boy of sixteen shares his account of how rugged and dangerous life was on the trail.

Raven, Margot Theis. ***Let Them Play.*** **Ann Arbor, MI: Sleeping Bear Press, 2005.**

In the 1950s, an all-black Little League Baseball team's dreams were shattered when no white team wanted to play them for a championship game. In fact, the white team pulled out of the league so that they wouldn't have to play the black team. But a father and a coach go behind closed doors to advocate for the boys. When they take the field and hear the cheers from the crowd, they are overwhelmed and feel just like Jackie Robinson.

Smith, Charles R., Jr. ***Hoop Kings: Poems by Charles R. Smith Jr.*** **Somerville, MA: Candlewick Press, 2004.**

Readers who love basketball will also love this collection of poems by Charles Smith. Smith uses famous basketball stars to drive home the point that hard work, determination, and endurance are just a few of the qualities needed to become successful at the game.

Stauffacher, Sue. ***Nothing but Trouble: The Story of Althea Gibson.*** **New York: Alfred A. Knopf, 2007.**

Everyone needs a mentor, and Althea Gibson found one in Buddy Walker, a Harlem musician. Facing many conflicts in her life, including hearing that she was a tomboy as well as a problem at home and in the community, Gibson was about to become a gifted dropout. However, once Walker watched her play paddle tennis, he knew that with careful guidance, Gibson would change the way the world thought about her.

Stewart, Mark. ***Florence Griffith-Joyner.*** **New York: Children's Press, 1996.**

Known as "Flo-Jo," this beautiful woman of track and field was at one time the fastest woman alive. In this book, readers will learn about her struggles, battles, and hardships as she raced her way to the top to become the world's fastest female runner.

Chapter 4

BOYS WILL BE BOYS—"BELIEVING BROTHERS"

A brother is someone who will reach down to your level and lift you up. A brother can be a mentor, a friend, a father, a grandfather, a neighbor, or an uncle. A brother does not see color as a barrier. A brother is someone who will recognize your potential even when you don't see it or can't believe it. These titles will help teachers and parents make recommendations to children looking to improve their situations or who are in search of hope for family improvement.

Davis, Sampson. *We Beat the Street: How a Friendship Pact Led to Success.* New York: Dutton Children's books/A Division of Penguin Young Readers Group, 2005.

About the Author

The Three Doctors, Inc. Media Relations. 2001–2007. http://www.threedoctors.com (accessed October 11, 2010).

Literary Elements	Lexile Range	Teacher Resources and Supplies
Autobiography Biography Bullying Character Education	860L	Book Worksheet
Reading Level Grades 9–12	**Accelerated Reader** AR points: 7.0 Book Level: 5.8	
Additional Titles Greenfield, Eloise. ***Night on Neighborhood Street*** (Coretta Scott King Book Award). **Websites** http://www.threedoctors.com/ourstory.php http://www.ojjdp.gov		

Brief Summary

You CAN change your life with courage, determination, and perseverance. In this book, three young doctors take charge of their lives and work hard to help others shape positive futures.

Focus

- Socioeconomic Background
- Setting Goals
- Dealing with Drug Abuse

Teacher Input

- Introduce the book with this video: http://www.threedoctors.com.
- Ask students to describe what makes a good neighborhood and who makes a good neighbor.
- Ask students to describe themselves as neighbors and what they expect from their neighborhood.
- Ask students to comment on the issue of bullying and whether they have been affected by bullying.
- Play the song "Taking It to the Street" to the class: http://beemp3.com/download.php?file=218949&song=Takin'+It+To+The+Streets.
- Read Chapter 11 aloud. Have students share their thoughts about Rameck's behavior and tell what they would have done if they had been in the biology teacher's position.

Guided Practice

- Invite students to describe the three profiles of the boys growing up and to tell which profile they feel best represents them personally.
- Ask students to give their definition of a good teacher.
- Instruct students to think about the event that took place between "The Bomb" and the addict and to then explain what their response might have been if they had witnessed such a cruel act.
- Use this resource to locate a poem written by poet Amiri Baraka and read it aloud: http://www.poemhunter.com/imamu-amiri-baraka/poems.
- Have students name another great and notable American who believed that changes could be made using nonviolence as the mechanism.
- Invite the class to discuss other peaceful measures that might be used to change a situation.
- Have the class analyze why it was important for the students in the book to boycott their school's diversity practices and policies. Allow them to comment on whether they think their school is doing enough to promote diversity.

Independent Practice

- Suggest that students write a letter to a person in the community explaining how and why it is important to encourage youth never to lose hope and to maintain their faith in themselves.

Closure

- Invite a juvenile court counselor, doctor, or judge to speak to your class.

Assessment

- Student discussions, interest in project design, and questions.

The Healing Worksheet

List some characteristics of a "good" neighborhood.

1.

2.

3.

4.

5.

Read Eloise Greenfield's book, ***Night on Neighborhood Street.*** Compare her poems with the vignettes described in ***We Beat the Streets.*** Identify the common threads between the two.

____

____

____

____

Use this online resource to locate the poem "Ka 'Ba" by poet Amiri Baraka. What is the message of this poem? http://www.english.illinois.edu/maps/poets/a_f/baraka/onlinepoems.htm

____

____

____

____

The Doctors Three—Tell What You Like Best and Least in the Lives of the Three Doctors

Profile: Dr. Sampson Davis	**Profile: Dr. Rameck Hunt**	**Profile: Dr. George Jenkins**
Best Part of His Life:	Best Part of His Life:	Best Part of His Life:
Least Favorite Part:	Least Favorite Part:	Least Favorite Part:

Harper, Hill. *Letters to a Young Brother.* New York: Penguin Group, 2006.

About the Author

Manifest Your Destiny. ForRealSolutions.com. n.d. http://www.manifestyourdestiny.org (accessed December 28, 2010).

Literary Elements Psychology Writing	**Lexile Range** —	**Teacher Resources and Supplies** Book Worksheet
Reading Level All grades	**Accelerated Reader** Points: 7.0 Book Level: 6.7	
Additional Title Harper, Hill. ***Letters to a Young Sister.*** **Website** http://www.manifestyourdestiny.org		

Brief Summary

Hill Harper used his fame and financial resources to establish a foundation for encouraging and motivating young boys. Harper used his friends who were enjoying successful careers to provide answers to some of the questions raised by the young men featured in this book. The answers provided by his friends include letters answered by Oprah Winfrey and President Barack Obama. Simply by reading the early childhood biographies of Hill Harper, Oprah Winfrey, and Barack Obama, readers learn that not even poor or single-parent conditions can stop someone who is focused on achieving a goal.

Focus

- Reading
- Writing
- Goal Setting

Teacher Input

- Discuss goals, careers, and future endeavors with the class and invite students to make personal comments.
- Discuss the concept of educational preparation with the class and invite students to tell what their educational plans are or what they would like to do for a living.
- Divide the students into two groups to discuss the differences between Harper's two books for brothers and sisters.

Guided Practice

- Have students refer to this online resource to learn how to enhance their test-taking skills: http://www.studygs.net/tsttak1.htm.
- Have students share their perspectives on some of the questions raised by the boys in their letters to Hill.

- Suggest that students view this online resource to learn about developing good work ethics: http://library.adoption.com/articles/instilling-a-good-work-ethic-in-your-teens.html.
- Help students establish and develop a "Mentors Bank" that allows them to shadow a career professional in the community, enabling them to cultivate social skills.

Independent Practice

- Suggest that students write to Hill at Hill@manifestyourdestiny.net to thank him for sacrificing his time to gather the human resources to provide guidance to young people.

Closure

- Invite a local reporter or television personality to speak to the class.

Assessment

- Student participation in discussions, questions asked, and interest level in project.

Helping to Reach My Goals Letter

Identify the leaders in your city, county, state, and federal governments. Write a letter to one official to inform him or her of your goals and ambitions in life.

Support Leaders	List Names Here
Name of Your Father or Mother	
Name of Your School Principal	
Name of Your School Superintendent	
Names of Your Board of Education	
Names of City or Town Council and Mayor	
Names of County Commissioners	
Name of Faith-based Leader	
Name of State Governor	
Name of member of House Representatives	
Name of State Senator	
Name of President of United States of America	

Compose your letter on the back of this sheet.

Langan, Paul. *The Bully.* New York: Scholastic, 2002.

About the Author

Biography of Paul Langan. IRA/NCTE. 2004. http://www.readwritethink.org/files/resources/lesson_images/lesson390/bio.pdf (accessed October 11, 2010).

Literary Elements Bluford High Books in Series 5 Character Education	**Lexile Range** 700L	**Teacher Resources and Supplies** Book Worksheet
Reading Level Grades 6 and up	**Accelerated Reader** Points: 5.0 Book Level: 4.7	
Additional Title Paulsen, Gary. ***Hatchet.*** **Websites** http://www.stopbullyingnow.hrsa.gov/kids http://pbskids.org/itsmylife/friends/bullies		

Brief Summary

After moving to another state, Darrell Mercer learns to stand up to a bully by reading a book his teacher gives him. He grows tired of living in fear of a school bully who demands his lunch money. He even confronts his own cousin whom he sees bullying another family member. Readers will learn the importance of standing up to a bully from this book.

Focus

- Moving; Making New Friends
- Bullying, Bibliotherapy
- Sports

Teacher Input

- Invite students to comment on the challenges of relocating to a new town, city, or school.
- Discuss bullying with the class, and invite students to comment on their own experiences.
- Ask students if they have ever had a problem with bullying.
- Ask students to comment on the negative effects of bullying.
- Ask students if they would report any type of bullying they saw or experienced. Why or why not?

Guided Practice

- Have students write their own definition of bullying.
- Invite students to describe how Gary Paulsen's book ***Hatchet*** might help to dispel fear and doubt in Darrell's life.
- Have students read and discuss the first paragraph on page 86, write down why it is important for students to report bullying to an adult when they see it occurring within their school or community, and explain their answer.

- Have students interpret Mr. Mitchell's remarks on page 94 and engage in a classroom discussion on the topic.
- Suggest that students create a "***Stop Bullying***" video and word game for the class and school.
- Suggest that students design "***We're Against Bullying***" posters and flyers to distribute around and throughout the school.

Independent Practice

- Invite students to write a news script for the school news program titled "***Bullying Is NOT for Me!***" Discuss the possible mental and physical effects of bullying.
- Help students organize a "***What My Parents Should Know About Bullying Conference***" which includes having them talk with parents, community leaders, law enforcement personnel, and clergy leaders.

Closure

- Invite your school counselor, law enforcement, community leaders, and parents to discuss bullying throughout the year.

Assessment

- Student discussions, brainstorming , and projects.

You Can't Bully Me Worksheet

Design a Poster on Bullying.

List five things that you would include as you develop your school news show on bullying.

1.

2.

3.

4.

5.

October is National Bullying Prevention Month. Use this website to gather ideas for observing the month: http://www.pacer.org/bullying/bpam.

Plans for Week One:
Plans for Week Two:
Plans for Week Three:
Plans for Week Four:

Wiles, Deborah. *Freedom Summer.* New York: Atheneum Books for Young Readers, 2001.

About the Author

Deborah Wiles, Novelist. September 2009. http://deborahwiles.com (accessed October 11, 2010).

Literary Elements Coretta Scott King Book Award Ezra Jack Keats Award Historical Fiction	**Lexile Range** AD460L	**Teacher Resources and Supplies** Book Worksheet
Reading Level Grades 2–5	**Accelerated Reader** AR points: 0.5 Book Level: 3.2	
Additional Title Woodson, Jacqueline. ***The Other Side.*** ***Website*** http://www.core-online.org/History/freedom_summer.htm		

Brief Summary

Two boys look beyond their different skin colors to become best friends despite the racism around them. Together they devise ways to have fun and deal with those who treat them badly. Even though they witness the worst of times in their hometown, their friendship remains strong.

Focus

- Friendships
- Racism and Segregation
- Swimming as a Sport
- Improvising

Teacher Input

- Using the song at the following website, introduce *Freedom Summer* to the class: http://www.youtube.com/watch?v=sssqBjaTzOU.
- Ask students to define the meaning of true friendship.
- Read aloud books by Wiles and Woodson to the class.
- Use Dr. Martin Luther King's quote on character found at this website: http://www.brainyquote.com/quotes/quotes/m/martinluth115056.html. Invite students to discuss choosing to have friends who are different.
- Divide the class into two groups. Direct the students to identify in writing how the books are different and what they have in common.

Guided Practice

- Have students explain how John Henry Waddell and Joe became best friends.

- Ask students to analyze whether their families approved of such a friendship and state evidence to support their remarks.
- Invite students to describe how they feel when someone is hateful toward them.
- Distribute handouts for students to read about *Freedom Summer* and the Civil Rights Act of 1964. See http://www.timeforkids.com/TFK/kids/news/story/0,28277,660464,00.html.
- Ask students to discuss how John Henry must have felt when he expressed his desire to be able to do things just like Joe.
- Have students draw a picture of Will, John Henry's brother, illustrating how he must have felt knowing that his brother wanted to swim in the pool that he had just filled with tar.

Independent Practice

- Using role playing, give students the opportunity to pair up and write their own scripts to share with the schooling, classroom, or community.
- Suggest that students interview an older adult to learn how they handled racism and used the experience to help others.

Closure

- Invite an older American to discuss his or her experience with "bridging the racial divide" with the class.

Assessment

- Completion of the Freedom Summer Worksheet, classroom discussions, and projects.

Freedom Summer Worksheet

1. What was Freedom Summer? ___

2. Explain the purpose of the Council of Federated Organizations (COFO). ___

3. What was CORE? What was its role in Freedom Summer? ___

4. Why did the NAACP and SNCC become involved? ___

Williams, Mary. *Brothers in Hope.* New York: Lee & Low, 2005.

About the Author

BookTalk—Mary Williams. n.d. http://www.leeandlow.com/p/williams.mhtml (accessed October 11, 2010).

Literary Elements Coretta Scott King Book Award Historical Fiction	**Lexile Range** 670L	**Teacher Resources and Supplies**
Reading Level Grades 3 and up	**Accelerated Reader** Points: 1.0 Book Level: 4.7	Book Parental Consent Form
Additional Title Myers, Walter Dean. ***Fallen Angels.*** **Websites** http://www.lostboysfilm.com		

Brief Summary

This is truly a heartfelt story about a group of boys whose faith, perseverance, and moral support of each other helped them make the rugged journey to America after their country was devastated by war.

Focus

- Sudan
- Ethiopia
- Orphans
- Caring
- Refugee Camps
- Education

Teacher Input

- Present the book to the class using the following online resource: http://travel.nationalgeographic.com/travel/countries/sudan-facts/http://beemp3.com/download.php?file=5760594&song=The+Impossible+Dream.
- Engage students in a discussion about whether they have been faced with doing something that seemed impossible yet were able to do it, just like the Lost Boys of Sudan.

Guided Practice

- Instruct students to use online resources to explore and develop background information about the boys. In their research, students should use Williams's book to explain how the boys became orphans: http://video.nationalgeographic.com/video/player/places/countries-places/sudan/sudan_thelostboy.html
- Have students define what "hope" means and name leaders that offered it to the boys long after they had been rescued.

- Ask the students to identify leaders who have made significant contributions to their community and to complete the sentence, "I hope that . . . ."
- Read and explain the scriptures at Matthew 12:48–50 from the Bible to the class.
- Invite students to list ways in which the boys showed love and provided hope for each other: http://www.npr.org/templates/story/story.php?storyId=3022317.
- Create a Refugee Camp in the classroom for one day. Obtain permission from the principal and students' parents first. The object is for the students to try doing without the everyday conveniences they are used to having to experience a small fraction of what life would be like without hope. This exercise requires students to sit on the floor for an entire day or at least part of the day and to eat their lunches without utensils. Do not use any audiovisuals for teaching. Explain what the author meant by the expression, "There are good people all around to help the unfortunate." Again, parental permission is needed to include children in this experience; see the example letter that follows.

Independent Practice

- Encourage students to design a video or speech using the theme "***Lost Without an Education.***"

Closure

- View the *Lost Boys of Sudan* documentary with the class: http://video.nationalgeographic.com/video/player/places/countries-places/sudan/sudan_thelostboy.html

Assessment

- Students' discussion of book, interpretations of scripture, and projects.

Parental Consent Letter to Participate in Classroom Refugee Camp

Date:

To:

From:

Dear Parents or Guardian:

Your child's class just completed reading a book titled *Brothers in Hope*. From reading this book, your child learned about the Lost Boys of Sudan and how these boys were able to survive difficult times. In an attempt to reenact on a small scale what life must have been like for these thousands of boys, the class would like to designate a day at school during which they volunteer to do without common conveniences. For example, the students will sit on the floor and will eat lunch without using utensils. The students will then discuss their experiences and the experiences of the boys in the book. The objective of this exercise is to get the students to think about what they would do and how they would persevere if they ever found themselves in a difficult situation that might appear hopeless.
I hope that you will consent for your child to participate in this activity. Please indicate your consent by signing this form and returning it to me. If you have any concerns or questions about this activity, please feel free to contact me at [telephone number] to discuss them.

Thank you.

I give consent for my child ____ (student's name) to participate in this activity.

Parent's signature____

Bibliography

Biography of Paul Langan. IRA/NCTE. 2004. http://www.readwritethink.org/files/resources/lesson_images/lesson390/bio.pdf (accessed October 11, 2010).

BookTalk—Mary Williams. n.d. http://www.leeandlow.com/p/williams.mhtml (accessed October 11, 2010).

Davis, Sampson. *We Beat the Street: How a Friendship Pact Led to Success.* New York: Dutton Children's Books/A Division of Penguin Young Readers Group, 2005.

Deborah Wiles, Novelist. September 2009. http://deborahwiles.com (accessed October 11, 2010).

Harper, Hill. *Letters to a Young Brother.* New York: Penguin Group, 2006

Langan, Paul. *The Bully.* New York: Scholastic, 2002.

Letters to a Young Brother. New York: Penguin Group, 2006.

The Three Doctors. Media Relations. 2001–2007. http://www.threedoctors.com (accessed October 11, 2010).

Wiles, Deborah. *Freedom Summer.* New York: Atheneum Books for Young Readers, 2001.

Williams, Mary. *Brothers in Hope.* New York: Lee & Low, 2005.

Webliography

Amiri Baraka Online Poems. Modern American Poetry. n.d. http://www.english.illinois.edu/maps/poets/a_f/baraka/onlinepoems.htm (accessed January 4, 2011).

Doobie Brothers. "Takin' It to the Streets." Free MP3 Download. Beemp3.com. n.d. http://beemp3.com/download.php?file=218949&song=Takin'+It+To+The+Streets (accessed January 4, 2010).

Ebony & Ivory (Music Video) by Paul McCarthy and Stevie Wonder. n.d. http://www.youtube.com/watch?v=sssqBjaTzOU (accessed December 28, 2010).

Echoes of the Lost Boys of Sudan. National Public Radio. 2010. http://www.npr.org/templates/story/story.php?storyId=3022317 (accessed December 28, 2010).

Freedom Summer. 2006. http://www.core-online.org/History/freedom_summer.htm (accessed October 11, 2010).

Instilling a Good Work Ethic in Your Teens. Adoption Media. 1995–2010. http://library.adoption.com/articles/instilling-a-good-work-ethic-in-your-teens.html (accessed December 28, 2010).

It's My Life, Family, Sibling Rivalry, *You vs. Them.* PBS Kids GO! CastleWorks. 2005. http://pbskids.org/itsmylife/family/sibrivalry (accessed November 3, 2010).

Ka 'Ba by Imamu Amiri Baraka. PoemHunter.com. 2010. http://www.poemhunter.com/imamu-amiri-baraka/poems (accessed December 28, 2010).

Landsberger, Joe. "Ten Tips for Test Taking." *Study Guides and Strategies.* 1996. http://www.studygs.net/tsttak1.htm (accessed December 28, 2010).

Lost Boys of Sudan. A Documentary Film by Megan Mylan and Jon Shenk. n.d. http://www.lostboysfilm.com (accessed October 11, 2010).

Manifest Your Destiny. ForRealSolutions.com. n.d. http://www.manifestyourdestiny.org (accessed December 28, 2010).

Martin Luther King, Jr. Quotes. BrainyQuote.com. 2001–2010. http://www.brainyquote.com/quotes/quotes/m/martinluth115056.html (accessed December 28, 2010).

Office of Juvenile Justice and Delinquency Prevention. July–August 2010. http://www.ojjdp.gov (accessed October 11, 2010).

Stop Bullying Now! n.d. http://stopbullyingnow.hrsa.gov/kids (accessed October 10, 2010).

Sudan Facts, Sudan Flag—National Geographic. National Geographic Society. 1996–2010. http://travel.nationalgeographic.com/travel/countries/sudan-facts (accessed December 28, 2010).

Sudan: The Lost Boy—National Geographic. National Geographic Society. 1996-2010. http://video.nationalgeographic.com/video/player/places/countries-places/sudan/sudan_thelostboy.html (accessed December 28, 2010).

The Three Doctors. Media Relations. 2001–2007. http://www.threedoctors.com (accessed October 11, 2010).

Time for Kids: Marking a Civil Rights Milestone. SI Kids.com. 2010. http://www.timeforkids.com/TFK/kids/news/story/0,28277,660464,00.html (accessed December 28, 2010).

Williams, Andy—The Impossible Dream. Free MP3 download. Beemp3.com. n.d. http://beemp3.com/download.php?file=5760594&song=The+Impossible+Dream (accessed December 28, 2010).

Additional Reading Materials

Adoff, Jamie. *Jimi & Me.* New York: Jump at the Sun/Hyperion Books for Children, 2005.

This story tells of a boy who must relocate after the death of his father. To comfort him through this grieving process, he listens to the music of Jimi Hendrix, a great musician. During this move, he discovers more than just what it's like to have a bully as a schoolmate. Suddenly, the love and grieving for his father are gone and replaced with anger. Readers will be eager to discover what caused this change and why his father kept a secret (CSK John Steptoe Award/New Talent, 2006).

Boyd, Candy Dawson. *Chevrolet Saturdays.* New York: Puffin Books/Penguin Group, 1993.

How do you deal with a stepfather, class bully, and failing grades all at the same time? This is what young Joey Davis asked himself when his mother remarries and his stepfather moves in. He wants to remain loyal to his father. His stepfather's business and a Chevrolet truck play a major role in uniting Joey and his stepfather and helping them develop a closer relationship.

Bunting, Eve. *Your Move.* Orlando, FL: Harcourt Brace, 1998.

An older brother makes the right decision to say no to a gang after his younger brother is nearly shot by an opposing gang. After that incident, the brothers decide to entertain themselves by playing checkers.

Curtis, Christopher Paul. *Elijah of Buxton.* New York: Scholastic, 2007.

Elijah, known for his skinny frame and hardly anything else, must take on the role of detective to find the thief who stole his friend's money which was going to be used to buy his family's freedom.

Curtis, Gavin. *The Bat Boy & His Violin.* New York: Aladdin Paperbacks/An Imprint of Simon & Schuster, 1998.

A father in need of a bat boy for his losing baseball team assigns his son to do the job. But the boy is more interested in learning how to play the violin, so he brings it along to practice. The effects of his music motivate the players and cause them to renew their commitment to the team.

Davis, Anthony, and Jeffrey Jackson. "*Yo, Little Brother . . .*": *Basic Rules of Survival for Young African American Males.* Sauk Village, IL: African American Images, 1998.

This is a straightforward and basic book that provides positive advice and suggestions to young African American males to help them develop character and integrity.

Draper, Sharon. *The Buried Bones Mystery.* New York: Aladdin Paperbacks, 2006.

The adventure in *Lost in the Tunnel of Time* (see below) continues in this book. The boys try to identify the box of bones found in the backyard. Later they learn that the bones belonged to slaves who couldn't be identified, so out of respect for the dead, the bones were gathered and given a decent burial.

Draper, Sharon. *Lost in the Tunnel of Time.* New York: Aladdin Paperbacks, 2006.

A group of boys learn that their school is built on an area once used by the Underground Railroad. They decide to explore the secret passages under their school to learn more about the tunnels used by those involved with the Underground Railroad. They go on a field trip and discover that they're lost in the Tunnel of Time. Study Guide and Discussion Questions are located also included.

Greenfield, Eloise. *Night on Neighborhood Street.* New York: Dial, 1991.

This book provides a poetic description of sights and sounds of the city.

Howard, Elizabeth Fitzgerald. *Virgie Goes to School With Us Boys.* New York: Simon & Schuster Books for Young Readers, 2000.

A little girl longs to go to school like her brothers. Because the school is so far away and her brothers must stay all day, at first her father will not allow her to go, but she is persistent. Her brothers promise they'll watch over her and give her the delight of attending school to learn. Virgie, determined not to grow tired on the way, amuses herself and her brothers by singing and playing games.

Mollel, Tololwa M. ***Kele's Secret.*** **New York: Lodestar Books/An Affiliate of Dutton Children's Books, 1997.**

A young boy living with his grandparents is curious about his pet hen who lays her eggs in some unusual places. He decides to follow her one day to see whether she will lead him to other unknown places where she might be leaving her eggs. He gets the surprise of his life.

Myers, Walter Dean. ***Fallen Angels.*** **New York: Scholastic, 1988.**

Walter Dean Myers' riveting fictional reflection on the Vietnam War describes seventeen- and eighteen-year-old young men who go into war without ever having experienced life itself. This award-winning novel is exceptional because the young men it features volunteered even though the draft was in place. When they looked at their future, they saw futility, hopelessness, and the possibility of an early death from unhealthy community circumstances. And so they enlisted and went to war.

Myers, Walter Dean. ***Handbook for Boys: A Novel.*** **New York: HarperCollins, 1988.**

This outstanding book is relevant to bridging the communication gap between generations. A barber and his friends and customers provide leadership and guidance to young boys in their community to help them make sound decisions.

Uhlberg, Myron. ***Dad, Jackie, and Me.*** **Atlanta, GA: Peachtree, 2005.**

This is a fictional account of a boy and his deaf father who follow Jackie Robinson's performance as he makes his debut with the Brooklyn Dodgers in 1947. This book shares how Robinson remained calm even when those around him shouted insults and even tried to cause him physical harm.

Woodson, Jacqueline. ***Locomotion.*** **New York: Penguin Group, 2003.**

Lonnie T. Motion—"Locomotion" for short—was orphaned at an early age and separated from his sister. He keeps a diary to record his thoughts. He considers himself a poet and is inspired by his teacher to write down his feelings. He is also fortunate to have a foster mother who encourages him never to lose hope and who makes every effort to see that he is able to visit his sister.

Woodson, Jacqueline. ***Miracle's Boys.*** **New York: G. P. Putnam's Sons/A Division of Penguin Putnam Books for Young Readers, 2000.**

A dying mother tries hard to keep her three boys out of trouble, although one boy is destined for jail. After her death, the brothers must find a way to trust, learn, forgive, and forget.

Chapter 5

CELEBRATIONS AND HOLIDAYS

No matter what the occasion, a holiday or celebration is a special event. Family, friends, and neighbors tend to forgive and to forget their problems at such times. Young and old alike will enjoy the titles in this section. Introduce your students to books and activities about celebrations and holidays that are significant to African American heritage.

Branch, Muriel Miller. *Juneteenth: Freedom Day.* New York: Cobblehill/Dutton, 1998.

About the Author

Muriel Miller Branch (1943–). n.d. http://biography.jrank.org/pages/671/Branch-Muriel-Miller-1943.html (accessed October 9, 2010).

Literary Elements Nonfiction Visual Literacy	**Lexile Range**	**Teacher Resources and Supplies**
Reading Level Grades 3 and Up	**Accelerated Reader** Points: 1.0	Book Plain paper Crayons and pencils Art teacher Worksheet
Additional Title Weatherford, Carole Boston. ***Juneteenth Jamboree.*** **Websites** http://www.juneteenth.com/index.html http://www.socialstudiesforkids.com/subjects/juneteenth.htm http://www.juneteenth.us		

Brief Summary

This book provides an overview of the historical account that led to Juneteenth and the importance of celebrating and sharing this day with others. The author takes the reader on a journey to the origins of this celebration, including recollections of how slaves reacted to hearing that they were free.

Focus

- Calendar
- Liberty Bell
- Slavery and Literacy
- Celebrations

Teacher Input

- Ask students to tell what they know about Juneteenth.
- Introduce and discuss factors that led to the origin of Juneteenth.
- Read ***Juneteenth Jamboree*** to the class.
- Ask students what they think are the advantages and disadvantages of being able to read.
- Use the following online resource that demonstrates how to make a paper cube: http://www.wikihow.com/Make-a-Paper-Cube.

Guided Practice

- Have students list the holidays that are significant to African Americans and why.
- Instruct students to compare and contrast the African American holidays of Juneteenth and Kwanzaa.
- Divide students into two working groups, each of which will develop a list of reactions and feelings from slaves as described by the author, and ask them to write a short skit to reenact.
- Ask students to describe in writing how the slaves reacted to the news of being free.

Independent Practice

- Have each student develop a Juneteenth Learning Cube explaining the day on one side, the reason for celebrating on another, where it's celebrated on another, and why it's important to celebrate on another.

Closure

- Invite students to share their editorials and projects.
- Have students present their skit about Juneteenth.

Assessment

- Student interest and participation, small-group discussions, worksheets, and projects.

Juneteenth

What is Juneteenth?

____

Name two special documents read during a Juneteenth celebration.

____

____

List other names considered for this celebration before Juneteenth was officially accepted.

____

____

Name the representative who introduced a bill in the Texas legislature to make Juneteenth a holiday. ____________

____

Draw a map of Galveston, Texas, where the first Juneteenth was held.

Juneteenth Only	July 4th Only
1.____________________	1.____________________
2.____________________	2.____________________
3.____________________	3.____________________
4.____________________	4.____________________
5.____________________	5.____________________
6.____________________	6.____________________
7.____________________	7.____________________
8.____________________	8.____________________

McKissack, Patricia. *The All-I'll-Ever-Want Christmas Doll.* New York: Schwarz & Wade Books/An Imprint of Random House Children's Books, 2007.

About the Author

Patricia McKissack. n.d. Kids@Random. http://www.randomhouse.com/kids/catalog/author.pperl?authorid=20049 (accessed October 9, 2010).

Literary Elements	Lexile Range	Teacher Resources and Supplies
ALA Notable Children's Book List Historical Fiction Read-Aloud Science	—	Books Dolls Worksheet Old socks
Reading Level Grades 2–5	**Accelerated Reader** Points: 0.5 Book Level: 3.3	
Additional Title Hamilton, Virginia. ***Brer Rabbit and the Tar Baby Girl.*** Nelson, Vaunda Micheauz. ***Almost to Freedom.*** Porter, Connie. ***Addy's Christmas.*** Stuve-Bodeen, Stephanie. ***Elizabeti's Doll.*** **Websites** http://www.pbs.org/wgbh/americanexperience/films/rails http://news.nationalgeographic.com/news/2005/12/1216_051216_jonkonnu.html http://www.solutions-site.org/artman/publish/article_47.shtml http://www.educationworld.com/a_curr/curr077.shtml http://www.birdsforever.com/chickdee.html		

Brief Summary

A young girl's dream comes true when she gets the doll she wants for Christmas. But she nearly ruins her holiday because of her selfishness when she refuses to let her sisters play with the doll. Her sisters admit that she did most of the work to get the doll, and they go off to find other activities to keep them busy, leaving her alone with it. She soon realizes that no doll can replace the great times the sisters have together.

Focus

- Gifts
- Sharing
- Siblings

Teacher Input

- Introduce the book by booktalking additional titles and asking students to view the following video online: http://www.youtube.com/watch?v=ybDa0gSuAcg. Brainstorm with students about the factors they believe led to the decision the children made.
- Briefly discuss the Great Depression to help students understand this period in history.

- Ask students if they know of anyone who didn't get gifts at Christmas because their family couldn't afford them. Ask students how they feel about such a situation.
- Share this chickadee website with students: http://www.birdsforever.com/chickdee.html.
- Explain that the author referred to the sisters as "chickadees" because of their chattering together. Ask students if they can think of anyone they would call chickadees and why.

Guided Practice

- Invite students to discuss whether they have ever had to share a Christmas gift with another family member.
- Ask students to discuss a time when they were disappointed with a gift or when they didn't get the gift they wanted.
- Have students identify three reasons why Nella made the decision to allow her sisters to play with the doll Baby Betty.
- Allow students to use books and online resources to find at least five interesting things to report about the chickadee.
- Ask students what Christmas symbol has replaced the "goody" sack and its contents, which the author references in the story.
- Listen to the song "You Are My Sunshine" and ask students to comment on how it makes them feel (http://bussongs.com/songs/your_are_my_sunshine.php).
- Have students list five songs they like to sing at Christmas.
- Ask students whether they think parenting is difficult or easy and to explain why. Middle and high school students may want to view these online sites to learn more about parenting and parenting skills: http://www.educationworld.com/a_curr/curr077.shtml and http://www.solutions-site.org/artman/publish/article_47.shtml.
- Summarize the Brer Rabbit and Tar Baby story for the class.
- Have students use Google Images Online to locate dolls for a doll fashion show. Explain that the show include five categories, such as sports, evening, and so forth.

Independent Practice

- Suggest that students use the following online resource to write about Jonkonnu: http://news.nationalgeographic.com/news/2005/12/1216_051216_jonkonnu.html.
- Invite students to write a paper titled "My Best Christmas Gift Ever" to share with the class.
- Have students make their own sock dolls.
- Instruct students to complete the Dolls Worksheet.
- Suggest that students design and present a doll fashion show.

Closure

- Have students share their written papers with the class.
- Invite an older American, possibly someone who lived through the Great Depression, to tell the class about the gifts he or she received at Christmas as a child.
- Have students conduct a doll fashion show.

Assessment

- Student sharing, discussions, and projects.

The Dolls Worksheet

Directions: Read the following books about dolls and then fill out the worksheet.

Book Title and Doll's Name	Historic Period	What Was the Doll Made From?	What Effect Does the Doll Have on the Girl's Life?
The All-I'll-Ever-Want Christmas Doll Betty Doll			
Almost to Freedom Sally			
Meet Addy: An American Girl Addy			
Elizabeti's Doll Eve			

After filling out the chart, read "'Baby' Helps Teens Think It Over!" (http://www.educationworld.com/a_curr/curr077.shtml). Share your thoughts and opinions about this special kind of doll.

Medearis, Angela Shelf. *Seven Spools of Thread: A Kwanzaa Story.* Park Ridge, IL: Albert Whitman & Company, 2000.

About the Author

The Kitchen Diva. Diva Productions. 2009. http://www.medearis.com (accessed October 9, 2010).

Literary Elements	**Lexile Range**	**Teacher Resources and Supplies**
Folktale Notable Book for Children Notable Books for a Global Society Honor Book Notable Social Studies Trade Book for Young People	430L	Book Seven spools of thread
Reading Level K–3	**Accelerated Reader** Points: 0.5 Book Level: 3.9	
Additional Titles McGee, Randel. ***Paper Crafts for Kwanzaa.*** Otto, Carolyn. ***Celebrate Kwanzaa.*** **Websites** http://www.holidays.net/kwanzaa http://thirdgrade.okaloosaschools.wikispaces.net/Reading+Unit+4#Seven Spools of Thread http://activities.macmillanmh.com/OralLanguageActivities/main1.php?selectionID=144 http://www.kentecloth.net/category/kente-cloth-designs-meaning		

Brief Summary

Seven quarreling and disagreeable brothers learn how to work together to create peace and harmony in hopes of gaining their late father's inheritance. What they discover is the power of their relationship when they learn how to treat each other with dignity and respect. The author uses the Kwanzaa principles to weave a tale that's relevant and applicable to both young and old.

Focus

- Unity
- Ghana
- Decreed
- African Proverbs
- Cloth

Teacher Input

- Show a map of Ghana to the class.
- Bring kente cloth to class and discuss its history.
- Collaborate with an art teacher to acquire threads and yarns for class designs and projects.

- Brainstorm with the students about what is involved in getting along with people. View the following website: http://treasures.macmillanmh.com/florida/students/grade3/book2/unit4/seven-spools-of-thread.
- Show students a copy of the Bible and discuss the Book of Proverbs and its value in life today.

Guided Practice

- Allow students to use online resources to select other Ghana stories to tell.
- Ask students to identify how the behavior of each brother affected the lives of the others.
- Have students list ways that they might try to get along with people who cause problems.
- Have students list the color of thread each brother received from the village chief.
- Ask students to identify the ways the brothers showed responsibility toward each other in order to gain their inheritance.
- Have students use online resources to locate meanings for various types of kente cloth (e.g., http://www.kentecloth.net/category/kente-cloth-designs-meaning).
- Ask students to choose and explain one proverb from the Bible.
- Suggest that students designate a day for the African American who has had the greatest impact in your community and to give their reason why this day should be celebrated.
- Invite students to share some of their holiday traditions with the class.
- Ask students to explain what Jonkonnu is.

Independent Practice

- Using the instructions provided at the back of the book, have students choose threads and make their own belts.
- Suggest that students create a presentation of African proverbs or the meaning of kente cloth patterns by using one of the formats listed in the examples provided (e.g., PowerPoint, posters, brochures, videos using flip cameras).
- Suggest that students create and design a PowerPoint presentation, "Celebrating Christmas or Kwanzaa Around My House."

Closure

- Have students conduct a parade of the belts made from threads.
- Allow students to present their multimedia presentations to the class.

Assessment

- Class presentations, discussions, and interest level.

Smalls, Irene. *A Strawbeater's Thanksgiving.* Toronto: Little, Brown & Company (Canada), 1998.

About the Author

Meet Irene Smalls. n.d. http://web.me.com/ismalls107/Information/Welcome.html (accessed October 9, 2010).

Literary Elements Historical Fiction Slave Narrative	**Lexile Range** 570L	**Teacher Resources and Supplies** Book Worksheet
Reading Level Grades 2–5	**Accelerated Reader** —	
Additional Title McKissack, Patricia C. ***Mirandy and Brother Wind.*** **Websites** http://ministry-to-children.com/book-of-ruth-video http://www.oldhatrecords.com/cd1005.html http://videos.howstuffworks.com/hsw/25486-african-culture-call-and-response-song-video.htm		

Brief Summary

This book tells the story of how slaves celebrated the end of the harvest and Thanksgiving. Interwoven throughout is the story of two young boys who are competing for the honor of serving as strawbeater for the fiddler during the big dance that takes place at the end of the corn-shucking event. The story demonstrates that endurance—not size—matters—if you just believe in yourself.

Focus

- Thanksgiving Celebration
- Slavery
- Competition
- Bullying
- Gleaning

Teacher Input

- Establish a background for understanding the genre of music that slaves used in their celebrations by using the following resource: http://www.oldhatrecords.com/cd1005.html.
- Ask students what they think the word "perseverance" means.
- Read aloud Langston Hughes Poem "***Mother to Son***" and ask students to comment on how a person can persevere.
- Write on the board "***Competition Is Good When . . .***" and "***Competition Is Bad When . . . .***"Ask students to cite examples from their own competitive experiences.
- Read aloud the book *Mirandy and Brother Wind,* which will become a part of the student worksheet activity.

Guided Practice

- Ask students whether the older boy in the story is a bully. Have them list two reasons to support their conclusions.
- Have students write down the steps involved in the corn-shucking activity.
- Ask students to create a poem titled "***See Freedom's Sun Shine.***"
- Divide the students into two groups and assign them online reading from the biblical Book of Ruth, second chapter: http://ministry-to-children.com/book-of-ruth-video. Instruct each group to compare how the "trash gang" in Small's book with the gleaning in the chapter of Ruth.

A Harvest of Confidence and Perseverance

Use the following website to find out the best times for harvesting strawberries: http://www.life123.com/home-garden/gardening-tips/harvesting/strawberry-harvest-season.shtml.

1. Harvest times for strawberries vary. Explain why based on your reading.

2. As a slave, Jess's mother, Sis Wisa, wanted to see her son do well in life. In your own words, why do you think she wanted more for her son than what he was currently doing?

3. What is a strawbeater? Use the link below to see a strawbeater at work.
   http://www.louisianafolklife.org/FOLKLIFEimagebase/FLImagesListing.asp?Page=358

4. What does the word "conflict" mean? Explain in the space below why there was conflict between Jess and Nathaniel.

5. List the activities described by the author that were a part of the slaves' celebration.
   a.
   b.
   c.

6. Explain why you think the author made a point to mention the size of Jess and Nathaniel in the story.

7. Compare the similarities and differences between *The Strawbeater's Thanksgiving* by Irene Smalls and *Mirandy and Brother Wind* by Patricia McKissack. Use the middle column to note similarities. Identify the main characters and explain why they were persistent.

Differences	Similarities	Characters/Persistence

Wright, Courtni C. *Jumping the Broom.* New York: Holiday House, 1994.

About the Author

Children's Literature—Meet Courtni C. Wright. n.d. http://www.childrenslit.com/childrenslit/mai_wright_courtni.html (accessed October 9, 2010).

Literary Elements	Lexile Range	Teacher Resources and Supplies
Historical Fiction Society of School Librarians International's List of Best Books Symbolism	—	Book Broom
Reading Level Grades: 3 Up	**Accelerated Reader** —	
Additional Titles Black, Sonia W. ***Just for You! Jumping the Broom.*** Woodson, Jacqueline. ***Show Way.*** **Websites** http://www.do-it-yourself-weddings.com/wedding-broom.html http://www.celebrateintimateweddings.com/ceremonybroom.html		

Brief Summary

A young girl can hardly wait to celebrate her sister's marriage, known and celebrated by slaves as "Jumping the Broom." She and other slaves living on the plantation know how to gather and make all they will need for this special celebration, from her mother choosing wild flowers for her sister's plaits to the star quilt needed for the bed in the new cabin. Readers will be inspired when they learn why this story is a part of African American culture.

Focus

- Culture and Customs
- Slave Life

Teacher Input

- Hold up the broom and ask students to explain the importance of a broom in an African American wedding. Use online resource to give students a greater understanding of the broom's relevance: http://www.helium.com/items/1255115-weddings.
- Bring a sewing kit to class and explain the different implements and their uses to the students.
- Invite parents to bring family quilts to display to the students and tell the story of their quilt.
- Discuss the history of the broom with the class.

Guided Practice

- Ask students to define the word "tradition" and list the traditions observed by their families.
- Invite students to tell each other their favorite holidays and describe how they celebrate it.
- Have students list the three events noted by the author when slaves were free to gather together.

- Ask students what method is used in their home to prevent food from spoiling and tell how slaves preserved their food or kept it fresh.
- Discuss with students whether they think the slave masters were kind to their slaves when a special event was about to happen on their plantation. Ask them to explain how the slave owner helped slaves to celebrate the Jumping the Broom celebration.
- Have students describe how slaves got the materials to make their dresses, quilts, and other items.
- Ask students to summarize the steps involved in making quilts as explained by the author.
- Allow students to use online resources to learn more about the history of the broom and the African American tradition.
- Guide the students in designing a quilt using newsprint paper. Reenact the quilt-making process by playing songs such as "Go Down, Moses" and "Swing Low, Sweet Chariot" while designing the quilt. Ask the students to describe their feelings during this process.

Independent Practice

- Suggest that students think about the event discussed in the book and explain what they might have done if they had lived during the time of slavery.
- Suggest that students create a story to describe the event or create a board story, flip chart, or PowerPoint presentation to share with class.

Closure

- Allow students to present their individual projects to the class.

Assessment

- Student observations, project presentations, and interests.

Bibliography

Branch, Muriel Miller. *Juneteenth: Freedom Day.* New York: Cobblehill/Dutton, 1998.

The Kitchen Diva. Diva Productions. 2009. http://www.medearis.com (accessed October 9, 2010).

Meet Authors & Illustrators: Courtni C. Wright. Children's Literature. n.d. http://www.childrenslit.com/childrenslit/mai_wright_courtni.html (accessed October 9, 2010).

McKissack, Patricia. *The All-I'll-Ever-Want Christmas Doll.* New York: Schwarz & Wade Books/An Imprint of Random House Children's Books, 2007.

Medearis, Angela Shelf. *Seven Spools of Thread: A Kwanzaa Story.* Park Ridge, IL: Albert Whitman & Company, 2000.

Meet Irene Smalls. n.d. http://web.me.com/ismalls107/Information/Welcome.html (accessed October 9, 2010).

Muriel Miller Branch (1943–). n.d. http://biography.jrank.org/pages/671/Branch-Muriel-Miller-1943.html (accessed October 9, 2010).

Patricia McKissack. Kids@Random. n.d. http://www.randomhouse.com/kids/catalog/author.pperl?authorid=20049 (accessed October 9, 2010).

Smalls, Irene. *A Strawbeater's Thanksgiving.* Toronto: Little, Brown & Company (Canada), 1998.

Wright, Courtni C. *Jumping the Broom.* New York: Holiday House, 1994.

Webliography

Activities: Seven Spools of Thread. The McGraw-Hill Companies. n.d. http://treasures.macmillanmh.com/florida/students/grade3/book2/unit4/seven-spools-of-thread (accessed December 18, 2010).

African Culture: Call and Response Song. HowStuffWorksVideos. 1996–2010. http://videos.howstuffworks.com/hsw/25486-african-culture-call-and-response-song-video.htm (accessed October 9, 2010).

Attracting Chickadees. Wild Birds Forever. n.d. http://www.birdsforever.com/chickdee.html (accessed December 18, 2010).

Benjamin Banneker. Africans in America. Part 2. PBS. n.d. http://www.pbs.org/wgbh/aia/part2/2p84.html (accessed November 6, 2010).

Black Doll White Doll. n.d. http://www.youtube.com/watch?v=ybDa0gSuAcg (accessed December 17, 2010).

Book of Ruth Video Clip for Children. Ministry-to-Children. 2010. http://ministry-to-children.com/book-of-ruth-video (accessed December 18, 2010).

Dusick, Amber. *The Wedding Broom Jumping Ceremony: History, Ideas, and Modern Meanings.* 2004–2005. http://www.do-it-yourself-weddings.com/wedding-broom.html (accessed October 9, 2010).

Education World Curriculum: "Baby" Helps Teens Think It Over! Education World. 1996–2010. http://www.educationworld.com/a_curr/curr077.shtml (accessed December 18, 2010).

How to Make a Paper Cube (with pictures). wikiHow. n.d. http://www.wikihow.com/Make-a-Paper-Cube (accessed January 5, 2011).

James, Larry. *Jumping the Broom History.* 2010. http://www.celebrateintimateweddings.com/ceremonybroom.html (accessed October 9, 2010).

Kente Cloth Weave Patterns and Meaning. Kente Cloth. 2010. http://www.kentecloth.net/category/kente-cloth-designs-meaning (accessed December 18, 2010).

Myers, Rev. Ronald. *Juneteenth.* Myers Foundation. September 22, 2010. http://www.juneteenth.us (accessed October 8, 2010).

National Registry Juneteenth Organizations and Supporters. *Juneteenth.* National Registry Juneteenth Organizations and Supporters. June 17, 2010. http://www.juneteenth.com/index.html (accessed October 8, 2010).

Nelson, Vaunda Micheaux, and Drew Nelson. *Juneteenth* (On My Own Holidays). Minneapolis, MN: Millbrook Press, 2006.

Old Hat Records—Quality Reissues of Vintage American Music. Old Hat Enterprises. 2000–2008. http://www.oldhatrecords.com/index.html (accessed December 18, 2010).

Realityworks Infant Simulator and RealCare Parenting Program. Yale University Department of Biology HORIZON International. June 30, 2010. http://www.solutions-site.org/artman/publish/article_47.shtml (accessed December 18, 2010).

Revelers Revive the African American Holiday of Jonkonnu. National Geographic Society. December 16, 2005. http://news.nationalgeographic.com/news/2005/12/1216_051216_jonkonnu.html (accessed December 18, 2010).

Welcome to a Celebration of Kwanzaa, Festival of Lights. Holidays on the Net. 1995–2010. http://www.holidays.net/kwanzaa (accessed October 9, 2010).

White, David. *Social Studies for Kids.* 2002–2010. http://www.socialstudiesforkids.com/subjects/juneteenth.htm (accessed October 8, 2010).

Additional Reading Materials

Adams, Janus. *Freedom Days: 365 Inspired Moments in Civil Rights History.* New York: John Wiley & Sons, 1998.

This is an important resource for all ages. Adams gives the reader a reason to celebrate freedom all year long. She gives dreamers the opportunity to dream and the hopeless a reason to hope through the description provided about those who learned how to persevere during difficult times.

Chocolate, Deborah M. Newton. *My First Kwanzaa Book.* New York: Scholastic, 1992.

A child excited about Kwanzaa describes what the family does to prepare for the festivity and tells what is done to celebrate each Kwanzaa principle.

***Christmas Gif': An Anthology of Christmas Poems, Songs, and Stories.* Compiled by Charlemae Hill Rollins. New York: Morrow, 1993.**

Readers will be enthralled with the collection of resources found in this volume. This is a wonderful book to use when planning for the holidays.

Doering, Amanda. *Martin Luther King, Jr. Day: Honoring a Civil Rights Hero.* Mankato, MN: Capstone Press, 2006.

This book gives a brief but factual account of the life and achievements of Dr. Martin Luther King Jr., what and why he advocated for human rights, and why there is a federal holiday to commemorate his life.

Ford, Juwanda G. *K Is for Kwanzaa: A Kwanzaa Alphabet Book.* New York: Scholastic, 1997.

Young children will have fun repeating the alphabet and remembering the word each letter represents in this historic volume. The book lends itself to extending the vocabulary of readers by affording them the opportunity to design their own alphabet book related to a specific subject.

Gayle, Sharon Shavers. *A Kwanzaa Miracle.* Scholastic, 1996.

Two children are throwing snowballs, and one accidently hits a neighbor's window, changing an entire community. The children are summoned to the neighbor's home, thinking that they are in trouble for their actions. Once inside, they soon discover something more important. They learn that she is lonely and hardly has any family at all. So they decide to use Umoja, one of the principles of Kwanzaa, to change her life forever.

Grier, Ella. *Seven Days of Kwanzaa.* New York: A Holiday Step Book, 2004.

This is a beautiful book explaining the seven principles of Kwanzaa and providing examples for readers to understand each one.

Grimes, Nikki. *At Jerusalem's Gate: Poems of Easter.* Grand Rapids, MI: Eerdmans, 2005.

This is a spiritual account of the story of Easter told in poetic form. It describes how jealousy can influence others to destroy the lives of those whose intentions are to do good. This recollection of poems can also be used to empower readers of all ages to seek spiritual guidance through the Bible.

Hamilton, Virginia. *The Bells of Christmas.* New York: Harcourt Brace & Company, 1989.

Children today and those of long ago still share one thing in common related to Christmas: excitement. In this holiday story, a family prepares to celebrate by sharing and giving. The author's description of Christmas bells and beautiful white snow allows readers to create their own beautiful scenery for such a celebration.

Hamilton, Virginia. *Brer Rabbit and the Tar Baby Girl.* New York: Blue Sky Press, 2003.

A Gullah version from Joel Chandler Harris's *Uncle Remus Tales, Brer Rabbit and the Tar Baby Girl* is as entertaining today as Chandler's tale of yesteryear. While Chandler's listeners may grow older each year, it seems that Brer Rabbit is never too old to trick his way out of any situation. Young readers will delight in this tale.

Hoffman, Mary. ***An Angel Just Like Me.*** **New York: Dial Books for Young Readers, 1997.**

While helping to decorate the family Christmas tree, a young boy is troubled when he discovers that there is no angel that looks like him. Describing the boy's determination to find an angel that he can identify with, this book keeps the reader intrigued to the very end.

Hold Christmas in Your Heart: African-American Songs, Poems, and Stories for the Holidays. **Compiled by Cheryl Willis Hudson. New York: Scholastic, 1995.**

The stories, poems, and Christmas songs in this book get readers excited about the Christmas season. Hudson has combined a collection of resources from various authors and illustrators aimed at getting the whole family involved in one of the largest celebrations of the year.

Kroll, Virginia L. ***Wood-Hoopoe Willie.*** **Watertown, MA: Charlesbridge, 1995.**

Willie excites his readers by demonstrating his musical skills. This book encourages readers to look for the best in what they have and set goals to strive for excellence in using their innate gifts.

McKissack, Patricia C. ***Mirandy and Brother Wind.*** **New York: Dragonfly Books/Alfred A. Knopf, 1988.**

Mirandy is determined to win the Cakewalk Dance Contest, so she tries to figure out a way to catch Brother Wind to dance with her. During the times that she's trying her best to capture him, Ezel, her clumsy friend, is looking for a dance partner. Once Mirandy captures Brother Wind, readers will be amazed to learn the climax.

McKissack, Patricia C., and Fredrick McKissack. ***Christmas in the Big House, Christmas in the Quarters.*** **New York: Scholastic, 1994.**

This story compares and contrasts how the slave master and his slaves celebrate Christmas. While those who have and those who do not may differ, the excitement of celebrating Christmas is the same.

MacMillan, Dianne M. ***Martin Luther King, Jr. Day.*** **Berkeley Heights, NJ: Enslow, 2008.**

Young readers will learn why there is a Dr. Martin Luther King Day celebration and what they can do to keep Dr. King's legacy alive in their communities by performing good deeds.

Marzollo, Jean. ***Happy Birthday, Martin Luther King.*** **New York: Scholastic, 1993.**

We celebrate the birthday of Dr. King, who made the choice to speak, serve, and sacrifice his life for what he believed was the right thing to do for a people enslaved in both mind and spirit. Dr. King was a man who loved all people and who worked hard to show the importance and impact of love.

Nelson, Vaunda Micheauz. ***Almost to Freedom.*** **Mankato, MN: Carolrhoda Books, 2003.**

This is a sock doll tells how she provides comfort to a young slave girl as she and her family travel underground to freedom. When the young girl is suddenly forced to leave her safe haven, the doll is left behind and longs for her playmate—until one night when another little traveler discovers the doll.

Nelson, Vaunda Micheaux, and Drew Nelson. ***Juneteenth.*** **Minneapolis, MN: Millbrook Press, 2006.**

There are many meaningful special days, dates, and years for special people. This book provides readers with a greater opportunity to understand why, when, and how Juneteenth is celebrated.

O Holy Night: Christmas with the Boys Choir of Harlem. **Pictures by Faith Ringgold. New York: Amistad/HarperCollins, 2004.**

A beautiful book illustrating the Christmas story found in the King James Version of the Bible in the Chapter of Luke 2:1–20. The Harlem Boys Choir sings the songs featured on the CD that comes with the book.

Otto, Carolyn. ***Celebrate Kwanzaa.*** **Washington, DC: National Geographic Society, 2008.**

Readers will learn about the popular African American holiday that was created to celebrate and extend cultural pride.

Porter, A. P. ***Kwanzaa.*** **Mankato, MN: Carolrhoda Books, 1991.**

Candles are used for many celebrations. Here Porter shows how candles, fruits, and vegetables are used to create an environment for a special celebration that many families observe in keeping with their African heritage. This easy-to-read book contains information for any curious reader or for the family to celebrate by following its step-by-step instructions.

Porter, Connie. *Addy's Surprise: A Christmas Story* (American Girl). Middleton, WI: Pleasant Company, 1993.

Addy gets the surprise of her life as she and her mother prepare to celebrate Christmas without other members of her family. First, she receives a beautiful dress made from cloth that she has so admired. And just as the lights go down at church for the start of the Christmas play, in walks her dad. What a way to begin a Christmas celebration! Readers will once again marvel at this little heroine's character.

Raabe, Emily. *A Kwanzaa Holiday Cookbook.* New York: Rosen, 2002.

The author takes the reader through the seven principles of Kwanzaa with food and recipes for preparing various dishes. As a special feature, the book contains a glossary of terms, an index, and links to additional information related to the celebration.

Rau, Dana Meachen. *Kwanzaa.* New York: Scholastic Library, 2000.

Students learn how Kwanzaa is celebrated and the symbols that are used each day. They also learn how to make gifts that are just as meaningful as purchased gifts.

Stuve-Bodeen, Stephanie. *Elizabeti's Doll.* New York: Lee & Low Books, 2002.

Parents *can* make a difference by what they say and do in front of their children. Here in this delightful book, a young girl admires the tender love and care her mother gives to the baby in the family by adopting a rock as her baby and caring for it.

***'Twas the Night Before Christmas: An African-American Version.* Retold and illustrated by Melodye Rosales. New York: Scholastic, 1996.**

This is the African American version of Clement Moore's popular poem, ***The Night Before Christmas***. Readers will find this book interesting as well as entertaining.

Wangerin, Walter. *Probity Jones and the Fear Not Angel.* Minneapolis, MN: Augsburg Fortress, 1996.

Having to stay home because of an illness she suffered after bullies made her give up her coat on a snowy day, a young girl is disappointed because she is missing the Christmas Pageant. Left at home while her family attends the celebration, Probity is visited by the Fear Not Angel. Probity's angel wipes away disappointment by sweeping her up into her arms and soaring through the sky to allow her to enjoy the event.

Weatherford, Carole Boston. *Juneteenth Jamboree.* New York: Lee & Low Books, 2007.

There's a celebration in Texas, and it's not Fourth of July. In fact, a young girl is amazed by the way Juneteenth is celebrated by the people in the big state. As the day draws near, she joins in the excitement with many other families.

Winchester, Faith. *African-American Holidays.* Mankato, MN: Capstone Press, 1999.

Every teacher will find this book to be helpful toward instructional planning. The events covered can teach students about cultural differences and appreciation for different cultures.

Woodson, Jacqueline. *Show Way.* New York: Putnam, 2005.

There's a secret, and it's visible to the naked eye. However, if you don't know what the symbols mean, you don't know the secret. Many slaves were able to escape the degradation of slavery by learning and understanding the meanings of secrets embedded in quilts. This is a fantastic book for all readers that shares the ingenuity of the slaves who found a way out of slavery.

Chapter 6

CIVIL RIGHTS

Introduce students to the men and women who worked tirelessly—some sacrificing their lives—to bring civil rights to African Americans. Encourage your class to research topics such as the Civil Rights movement, Jim Crow laws, Martin Luther King, Jr., Rosa Parks, the Freedom Riders, and the U.S. Postal System to determine the role each played in this movement.

Dudley, Karen. *Great African Americans in Government.* New York: Crabtree, 1997.

About the Author

Welcome to Karen Dudley Profile. n.d. http://www.mbwriter.mb.ca/mapindex/d_profiles/dudley_k.html (accessed October 12, 2010).

Literary Elements	Lexile Range	Teacher Resources and Supplies
Biography Government History	930	Book Worksheet
Reading Level Grades 6 and up	**Accelerated Reader** Points: 2.0 Book Level: 6.8	
Additional Titles Meltzer, Milton. ***Mary McLeod Bethune: Voice of Black Hope.*** Sanders, Nancy I. ***America's Black Founders: Revolutionary Heroes & Early Leaders with 21 Activities*** (For Kids series). **Websites** http://www.un.org/en/index.shtml http://www.dar.org/library http://www1.umn.edu/humanrts/edumat/activities.shtm http://www.infoplease.com/spot/bhmbios1.html		

Brief Summary

This useful resource for young people is about African Americans who dedicated their lives to the service of mankind. These men and women were strong, faithful, and determined workers who overcame the many obstacles they encountered on the way to achieving their goals.

Focus

- African Americans in Government
- African Americans Firsts

Teacher Input

- Identify for the class examples of peacemakers in the United States.
- Use the following online resource to access the human rights links and give students the opportunity to choose from the list of topics or services that they would be interested in learning more about and sharing with classmates in a written report: http://www1.umn.edu/humanrts/edumat/activities.shtm.

Guided Practice

- Invite students to share and describe ways they have tried to bring about peace in their home, school, or community.
- Instruct students to research the United Nations to gain a greater understanding of its purpose.
- Have students locate online resources that cover a variety of human rights issues.
- Ask students to explain how Shirley Chisholm and Adam Clayton Powell developed strategies to empower blacks living in New York.
- Ask students to explain why a dispute arose between President Truman and Adam Clayton Powell.
- Have the class discuss reasons why the DAR may have been offensive to Powell.
- Instruct students to write a speech titled "What I Can Do to Support Local Government."

Independent Practice

- Suggest that students create a chart of African American firsts by using the online resource at http://www.infoplease.com/spot/bhmbios1.html.

Closure

- Students give speeches and present projects.

Assessment

- Group discussions, worksheet, and projects.

"Let's Govern Accordingly" Worksheet

Write a brief description of each of the following people.

Government Official	Most Notable Accomplishment
Ralph Bunche	
Yvonne Braithwaite Burke	
Shirley Chisholm	
Carol Moseley-Braun	
Adam Clayton Powell, Jr.	
Colin Powell	
L. Douglas Wilder	
Julian Bond	
David Dinkins	
W. Wilson Goode	
Sharon Pratt Kelly	
Constance Baker Motley	

Who is Eric Holder? ____

____

What does the acronym DAR mean (http://www.dar.org)?

____

What can you do to support your local government?

____

____

____

____

____

Haskins, Jim, and Kathleen Benson. *John Lewis in the Lead: A Story of the Civil Rights Movement.* New York: Lee & Low Books Inc., 2006.

About the Author

James Haskins—Department of English. October 16, 2007. http://www.english.ufl.edu/faculty/jhaskins (accessed October 12, 2010).

Literary Elements	Lexile Range	Teacher Resources and Supplies
Biography Character Civil Rights History	950L	Book
Reading Level Grades 3–8	**Accelerated Reader** Points: 0.5 Book Level: 5.9	
Additional Title Sirimarco, Elizabeth. ***The Civil Rights Movement.*** **Websites** http://johnlewis.house.gov http://www.blackpast.org/?q=aah/bloody-sunday-selma-alabama-march-7-1965 http://beemp3.com/download.php?file=1645856&song=Blowin'+In+the+Wind http://www.nps.gov/nr/travel/civilrights/players.htm http://www.infoplease.com/spot/civilrightstimeline1.html http://www.time.com/time/specials/packages/article/0,28804,1871648_1871684_1871650,00.html http://www.studyguide.org/cm101_persuasive_speech.htm http://www.pbs.org/wgbh/amex/eyesontheprize/tguide/elem.html		

Brief Summary

Readers will marvel at the bravery and desire to succeed that John Lewis modeled as he fought to avoid Jim Crow laws, segregation, and hatred in the South.

Focus

- Courage, Responsibility
- Sharecroppers, Bus Boycott, Protest
- Justice, Injustice, Nonviolence

Teacher Input

- Use the following online resource as a "hook" to introduce this great leader: http://beemp3.com/download.php?file=1645856&song=Blowin'+In+the+Wind.
- Introduce students to Congressman John Lewis.
- Describe his responsibility and passion to the class.
- Explain the conditions that led to the Civil Rights movement.

- Play Stevie Wonder's version of "***Blowin' in the Wind***" to the class (http://www.youtube.com/watch?v=AlsRWxC55I4).
- Write on the board, "***Why should you be allowed to cross the bridge to freedom?***" and ask students to comment on this question.

Guided Practice

- Assign students to write an opinion paper describing the significant impact of "walking hand-in-hand."
- Divide the class into two groups. Have students debate whether the "***Civil Rights Storm Is Over.***"
- Ask students to describe the treatment African Americans received by the election clerk when they came to vote. Have them research and describe Sheriff Jim Clark by visiting http://www.nps.gov/nr/travel/civilrights/players.htm.
- Have students use the following resource to learn about Bloody Sunday: http://www.infoplease.com/spot/civilrightstimeline1.html. Based on the author's description of how Lewis and his protesters responded to Sheriff Clark and law enforcement on the bridge, ask them to write their opinions of whether Bloody Sunday could have been avoided. They should support their answers with a ***why*** or ***why not.***
- Allow students to use online resources to learn more about Congressman John Lewis.
- After discussing and reviewing information in the book and from online resources, have students respond to the question on the board by writing and delivering a persuasive speech. Students may also use this online resource to help them: http://www.studyguide.org/cm101_persuasive_speech.htm.

Independent Practice

- Suggest that students develop a five-page booklet comparing how John Lewis advocated for Civil Rights in the 1960s and the impact he is making today to support President Barack Obama, the first African American president of the United States: http://www.time.com/time/specials/packages/article/0,28804,1871648_1871684_1871650,00.html.

Closure

- Each student expresses why he or she has the right to cross the "***Bridge of Freedom.***"
- Students read report results of their group discussions.

Assessment

- Student recall of information, reports, interests in project design, and discussions.

Shelton, Paula Young. *Child of the Civil Rights Movement.* New York: Schwartz & Wade Books, 2010.

About the Author

Interview with Paula Young Shelton and Raul Colon. 2009. http://bwibooks.com/articles/shelton-colon.php (accessed October 12, 2010).

Literary Element Civil Rights	**Lexile Range** AD960	**Teacher Resources and Supplies** Book Worksheet
Reading Level K–Grade 3	**Accelerated Reader** Points: 0.5 Book Level: 4.8	
Additional Title Meltzer, Milton. ***There Comes a Time: The Struggle for Civil Rights.*** **Websites** http://www.pbs.org/teachers/thismonth/civilrights/index1.html http://www.justice.gov/crt/voting/intro/intro_b.php		

Brief Summary

Andrew Young's daughter takes us back to the Civil Rights Era. This stirring book that recalls the issues that plagued African American men and women and motivated them to unite, plan, and sacrifice their lives to obtain opportunities and equality for all.

Focus

- Jim Crow, Segregation
- Protest, Sit-ins, Selma to Montgomery
- Right to Vote, Voting Rights Acts of 1965

Teacher Input

- Introduce this book by using resources from this website: http://www.pbs.org/teachers/thismonth/civilrights/index1.html.
- Ask the class if they know who Jim Crow was and what his name means to people. Tell the class what segregation means, and, if applicable, relate examples that took place in your community.
- Ask the students if they know of any ways that segregation takes place today.
- Lead a discussion about how conditions in a community can directly affect family relationships.

Guided Practice

- Have students summarize the main points in the book, including having them discuss and list the specific Jim Crow laws, identify the ***Freedom Riders*** and describe how they changed the pages in history. Also have them describe the author's first sit-in.

- Instruct students to write an essay titled "***Riding the Bus Together: What I See, What I Hear, and What I Believe.***"
- Ask students to define what significant role President Lyndon B. Johnson played in the Civil Rights movement. View http://www.justice.gov/crt/voting/intro/intro_b.php.
- Allow students to debate whether they feel that President Johnson was pressured into signing the Voting Rights Act of 1965.
- Ask students to identify families that advocate for Civil Rights today, and whether they believe these families play a major role in speaking out for the rights of others.

Independent Practice

- Suggest that students conduct and record interviews with adults who experienced the era of segregation, telling what they experienced, how they lived through it, and how they feel about their freedom today.
- Have students create a PowerPoint presentation using photos of the people who Shelton mentioned in the book who were a part of the Civil Rights Family. Shelton described these men and women as "instruments preparing for a performance" when they were all together talking in the same room. Create a slide show describing the individual and the instrument used to identify that person using the topic "The Vocal Band of Civil Rights."

Closure

- Invite an older American to your class to talk about Civil Rights.

Assessment

- Student interests, brainstorming, interactions and respect for individual differences and opinions, and individual reports.

My Right to Give You This Worksheet—Your Right to Complete It!

Using the online sites listed in the lesson plans, distribute this worksheet for students to complete within a week of assignment.

Question	Answer	Cite Source
Name the African American congressman from South Carolina.		
Name the first African American President of the United States of America.		
Who was the founder of Tuskegee Institute?		
Name the founders of the NAACP.		
Name the leader of the Freedom Rides.		
Who was the founder of the Universal Negro Improvement Association?		
Name the "Mother of the Civil Rights Movement."		
Name the first African American woman who refused to give up her bus seat in the South.		
Who did Dr. King use as a model to lead "peaceful" marches?		
State when and where Dr. King delivered his famous "I Have a Dream" speech.		
Who was Ruby Bridges?		
Who was Thurgood Marshall?		
What did Mary McLeod Bethune do to support the cause?		
Name the woman who led more than 300 slaves to freedom.		
Explain what the March on Washington was.		
Who were the Little Rock Nine?		
Summarize *Brown v. Board of Education of Topeka*: Challenging School Segregation in the Supreme Court.		
What was Greensboro, North Carolina, known for in the Civil Rights movement?		
What are the criteria for the Coretta Scott King Book Award?		
Who was Barbara Jordan?		
Name one important role Shirley Chisholm played in politics.		
Explain who Jim Crow was and what he is known for.		

Bibliography

About Phillip. 2009. http://www.philliphoose.com (accessed October 12, 2010).

Dudley, Karen. *Great African Americans in Government.* New York: Crabtree, 1997.

Haskins, Jim. *Delivering Justice: W. W. Law and the Fight for Civil Rights.* Somerville, MA: Candlewick Press, 2005.

Haskins, Jim, and Kathleen Benson. *John Lewis in the Lead: A Story of the Civil Rights Movement.* New York: Lee & Low Books Inc., 2006.

Hoose, Phillip. *Claudette Colvin: Twice Toward Justice.* New York: Melanie Kroupa Books/Farrar, Straus & Giroux, 2009.

Interview with Paula Young Shelton and Raul Colon. 2009. http://bwibooks.com/articles/shelton-colon.php (accessed October 12, 2010).

James Haskins—Department of English. October 16, 2007. http://www.english.ufl.edu/faculty/jhaskins (accessed October 12, 2010).

Shelton, Paula Young. *Child of the Civil Rights Movement.* New York: Schwartz & Wade Books, 2010.

Welcome to Karen Dudley Profile. n.d. http://www.mbwriter.mb.ca/mapindex/d_profiles/dudley_k.html (accessed October 12, 2010).

Webliography

500 Famous African American Biographies (A–Z). Infoplease.com. Pearson Education. 2000–2010. http://www.infoplease.com/spot/bhmbios1.html (accessed January 3, 2011).

AR BookFinder US—Quick Search. Renaissance Learning Inc. 2010. http://www.arbookfind.com/Default.aspx (accessed December 7, 2010).

Before Rosa Parks, There Was Claudette Colvin: NPR. NPR. 2010. http://www.npr.org/templates/story/story.php?storyId=101719889 (accessed December 11, 2010).

Bloody Sunday, Selma, Alabama (March 7, 1965). The Black Past: Remembered and Reclaimed. 2007–2009. http://www.blackpast.org/?q=aah/bloody-sunday-selma-alabama-march-7-1965 (accessed October 13, 2010).

Carlton Pearson (Mp3 downloads). skull.com. n.d. http://mp3skull.com/mp3/carlton_pearson.html (accessed December 11, 2010).

Civil Rights Division Home Page. July 25, 2008. http://www.justice.gov/crt/voting/intro/intro_b.php (accessed October 13, 2010).

Civil Rights Movement Timeline (14th Amendment, 1964 Act, Human Rights Law) Infoplease.com. Pearson Education. 2000–2010. http://www.infoplease.com/spot/civilrightstimeline1.html (accessed December 11, 2010).

DAR Library. National Society Daughters of the American Revolution. 2005. http://www.dar.org/library (accessed December 11, 2010).

Discovery Theater Presents—How Old Is Old? n.d. http://discoverytheater.org/education/guides/2007/How%20Old%20is%20a%20Hero.pdf (accessed December 11, 2010).

http://beemp3.com/download.php?file=1645856&song=Blowin'+In+the+Wind. n.d. http://beemp3.com/download.php?file=1645856&song=Blowin'+In+the+Wind (accessed December 11, 2010).

Human Rights Education—Activities. Human Rights USA. 1997, 1998, 1999, 2000. http://www1.umn.edu/humanrts/edumat/activities.shtm (accessed January 3, 2011).

John Lewis—Civil Rights and the Obama Presidency. Time. 2010. http://www.time.com/time/specials/packages/article/0,28804,1871648_1871684_1871650,00.html (accessed December 11, 2010).

The Lexile Framework for Reading. Lexile.com. MetaMetrics. 2010. http://lexile.com/ (accessed November2 2010).

New Georgia Encyclopedia: W. W. Law (1923–2002). 2004–2010. http://www.georgiaencyclopedia.org/nge/Article.jsp?id=h-2553 (accessed October 13, 2010).

The Online Office of Congressman John Lewis—Home. 2007. http://johnlewis.house.gov/ (accessed October 13, 2010).

PBS Teachers. Thematic Teaching. The Civil Rights Movement in American Literature. Public Broadcasting Service. February 2005. http://www.pbs.org/teachers/thismonth/civilrights/index1.html (accessed December 11, 2010).

Persuasive Speech—StudyGuide.org. StudyGuide.org. 2009. http://www.studyguide.org/cm101_persuasive_speech .htm (accessed December 11, 2010).

Rosa Parks: How I Fought for Civil Rights. Scholastic.com. Scholastic. 1996–2010. http://teacher.scholastic.com/rosa/ (accessed December 11, 2010).

Saying Goodbye to Rosa Parks. TVGuide.com. n.d. http://video.tvguide.com/The+Early+Show/Saying+Goodbye+ To+Rosa+Parks/2468067?autoplay=true&partnerid=OVG (accessed January 3, 2011).

This Far by Faith by W. W. Law. The Faith Project. PBS. 2003. http://www.pbs.org/thisfarbyfaith/witnesses/w_w_law.html (accessed December 11, 2010).

We Shall Overcome—The Players. nps.gov. n.d. http://www.nps.gov/nr/travel/civilrights/players.htm (accessed December 11, 2010).

Welcome to the United Nations. n.d. http://www.un.org/en/index.shtml (accessed December 9, 2010).

Additional Reading Materials

Anderson, Michael. *The Civil Rights Movement.* Chicago: Heinemann Library, 2004.

This book uses black-and-white photos as its focal point to lead readers through the journey of the Civil Rights movement and the many trials and triumphs that African Americans endured in their pursuit of equality. Topics include the Brown Ruling, the Montgomery Bus Boycott, Voting Rights, the Greensboro Sit-ins, the Little Rock Nine, and many others. A glossary helps readers to understand the terminology, along with a timeline chronicling the events. While young readers will enjoy the picture-book format, older readers will also find plenty of descriptive information.

Meltzer, Milton. *There Comes a Time: The Struggle for Civil Rights.* New York: Landmark Books/Random House, 2001.

This is a great history book for young adults who are interested in learning about the struggle for freedom and why we should respect those who paid the price to attain it.

Miller, Jake. *The Montgomery Bus Boycott: Integrating Public Buses.* New York: Rosen, 2004.

This is one of several books in a series that explains the Civil Rights movement, as well as the issues that led up to it, those involved in it, and how students today benefit from the movement.

Parks, Rosa, and Jim Haskins. *Rosa Parks: My Story.* New York: Scholastic, 1992.

Rosa Parks speaks about her personal trials and triumphs in this autobiography. She shares a little childhood humor and the joy she experienced going fishing with her grandparents before she threw herself into the Civil Rights movement.

Reynolds, Aaron. *Back of the Bus.* New York: Philomel Books/Division of Penguin Young Readers Group, 2010.

This is picture book story of a boy and his marble and how he met the woman who changed the way that African Americans rode on buses in the South. When the boy first meets Rosa Parks, she rescues his marble from rolling all the way to the front of the bus and getting lost. When he later learns what she did on that same bus ride by refusing to give up her seat, he feels freedom stirring in his future.

Robinson, Sharon. *Promises to Keep: How Jackie Robinson Changed America.* New York: Scholastic Press, 2004.

In this book, Robinson shows that a sports icon can support the causes that empower others. Using the word "promise," this book emphasizes that a person is valued for keeping his or her word. Jackie Robinson's popularity and his refusal to support segregation and Jim Crow Laws did much to help the African American's quest for equality. With its many photos and interesting story line, this book will be of interest to readers of all ages.

Sirimarco, Elizabeth. *The Civil Rights Movement.* Tarrytown, NY: Benchmark Books/Marshall Cavendish, 2005.

Sirimarco begins her story by helping young readers to understand the definition of a primary source. The text is divided into seven chapters with topics ranging from "The Roots of a Movement" to "We Shall Overcome." The author supports the data by citing references from many prominent leaders and resources. This is an ideal reference for school libraries. It includes a timeline, a glossary, and an index.

Taylor, Kimberly Hayes. *Black Civil Rights Champions.* Minneapolis, MN: The Oliver Press, 1995.

In this book from the Profiles series, Kimberly Taylor has carefully defined the role that African Americans and others played in the Civil Rights movement. The book is divided into eight chapters, covering prominent African Americans who worked diligently to bring about change, establish pride, and build confidence in their community. Advocates such as W. E. B. Du Bois, founder of the NAACP, and others like Thurgood Marshall, became the voices for those who didn't know how to speak for themselves. The author also emphasizes the tremendous role that African American women played in the Civil Rights movement, with Ella Baker being referred to as the "Other Mother of Civil Rights" because of her guidance and direction to young people involved in the events. Black-and-white illustrations, an events timeline, a bibliography, and an index are included.

Wormser, Richard. ***The Rise and Fall of Jim Crow: The African-American Struggle Against Discrimination, 1865–1954.*** **New York: Franklin Watts/A Division of Scholastic, 1999.**

Jim Crow laws were harsh. Leaders in the South were working hard to change the laws. Readers will be surprised to learn that in the state of South Carolina, at one time, African Americans controlled the legislature. Subject content, treatment, and illustrations give readers a vivid description and create a subtle mood for the period described.

Chapter 7

EDUCATION

Dignity and self-respect are the right of every person, but some people try to take those rights away from others. Use the resources in this chapter to introduce students to the concepts of peer pressure, self-discipline, integrity, and the value of education, as well as to individuals in history who, through education, dealt successfully with these issues.

Draper, Sharon. *The Battle of Jericho.* New York: Atheneum, 2003.

About the Author

Welcome to the Official Site of Sharon Draper. n.d. http://sharondraper.com (accessed October 11, 2010).

Literary Elements Clubs Peer Pressure Coretta School King Book Award	**Lexile Range** 700L	**Teacher Resources and Supplies** Books
Reading Level Middle and high school	**Accelerated Reader** Points: 10.0 Book Level: 4.7	
Additional Titles Flake, Sharon G. ***The Skin I'm In.*** Myers, Walter Dean. ***Monster.*** Simmons, Cassandra Walker. ***Becoming Myself: True Stories About Learning from Life.*** **Website** http://parenting.kaboose.com/age-and-stage/teens-development-peer-pressure.html		

Brief Summary

There are good clubs and there are great clubs, and everyone wants to belong to the great clubs. Jericho believes he is about as lucky as a guy could get when he's invited to join a GREAT club. But once he discovers what the club members are really like, he must make an important decision to maintain his integrity.

Focus

- Choices
- Friends
- Clubs
- Self-Discipline, Respect, and Integrity

Teacher Input

- Ask students whether they have ever been excited about joining a school club or sports team.
- Ask students whether a friend or someone else close to them has ever persuaded them to do something they knew was wrong, but they did it anyway to maintain the relationship.
- Discuss with the class the clubs in your school and the requirements for joining them.
- Involve students in a discussion of why they think people sometimes do not accept others, and ask them to offer examples of when this might happen.

Guided Practice

- Have the students create five student club centers in your classroom. Use the following as examples:
    - Be Wise, Stay in School Club (Attendance Club)
    - Hands-On Curriculum Club (Media and Technology Club)
    - Playing My Way Through School Club (Athletic Curriculum)
    - Better Relationship with My Teacher(s) Club (Relationships)
    - Meet My Needs Curriculum Club (Relevance)

Independent Practice

- Suggest that students design a PowerPoint presentation sharing pictures and brief information about the various clubs listed the students made up. Have student volunteers represent each of the clubs. Allow each student to tell why he or she would or would not accept an invitation to join.

Closure

- Survey the students to determine whether they belong to clubs in your school or community.

Assessment

- Student club response cards, student interest, letters, and PowerPoint presentation.

Greenfield, Eloise. *Mary McLeod Bethune.* New York: HarperCollins, 1977.

About the Author

Eloise Greenfield. Scholastic.com. n.d. http://www2.scholastic.com/browse/contributor.jsp?id=3186 (accessed October 22, 2010).

Literary Elements	Lexile Range	Teacher Resources and Supplies
Biography Educator Coretta Scott King Book Award(s)	750L	Books Stick Berry coloring Crate Diploma
Reading Level Grades 2–3	**Accelerated Reader** Points: 0.5 Book Level: 4.9	

Additional Titles

Anderson, Wayne. ***Brown v. Board of Education: The Case Against School Segregation.***
Braun, Eric. ***Booker T. Washington: Great American Educator.***
Morrison, Toni. ***Remember: The Journey to School Integration.***

Websites

http://www.lkwdpl.org/wihohio/beth-mar.htm
http://www.duboislc.org/html/BlackLegacy.html
http://www.tolerance.org/magazine/number-25-spring-2004/brown-v-board-timeline-school-integration-us

Brief Summary

Bethune was born to slave parents, but she refused to allow her childhood memories to dominate her life or to prevent her from thinking and striving to have a productive future. This remarkable woman founded a school to educate others. As a successful educator and advisor to President Theodore Roosevelt, her contributions to education in America were profound.

Focus

- Slavery and Education
- South Carolina
- Giving

Teacher Input

- View the following website to help plan this lesson: http://www.tolerance.org/magazine/number-25-spring-2004/brown-v-board-timeline-school-integration-us.
- Ask the class to define the word "legacy."
- Invite students to state how they would like people to remember them. What would they like people to say about them?
- Ask students what they aspire to be after graduation.
- Ask students if they know what the PSAT and SAT exams are and why they are important. These measurement tools can be explained briefly and equated to successfully passing a spelling test at younger students' grade level.

Guided Practice

- Ask students to think about how people pay for a college education. Do they know how older students go about applying for financial aid for higher education?
- Have students visit the website of Bethune Cookman University and find out what it costs for a student to attend school for one year.
- Divide the class into two teams. Play "***Don't Be a Dropout***" by James Brown using this website: http://www.youtube.com/watch?v=7oczqp8tytQ
- Ask students to list at least five things that make them want to leave school and five that keep them interested in getting an education. View the following website: http://www.suite101.com/content/dropouts-give reasons-a8681.
- Ask students to create a list of issues about education they would discuss if they had the opportunity to advise the president of United States.
- Instruct students to review the lives of Mary McLeod Bethune, Maritcha Remond Lyons, and Booker T. Washington. Have them make lists of the things the educators had in common and the things that were different about them.

Independent Practice

- Suggest that students write an essay titled, "***My Education—What I Have, What I Want, and What I Must Do to Get It.***"

Closure

- Listen to "God Bless the Child" by Billie Holiday and Arthur Herzog, Jr. A CD accompanies Greenfield's book which features the lyrics and Jerry Pinkney's illustrations (2005 Illustrator Honor Book Coretta Scott King Book Awards).

Assessment

- List of advice to president and reports on why students drop out of school.

Hansen, Joyce. *I Thought My Soul Would Rise and Fly: The Diary of Patsy, a Freed Girl.* New York: Scholastic, 1997.

About the Author

Joyce Hansen. n.d. http://www.joycehansen.com/index.htm (accessed October 22, 2010).

Literary Elements	Lexile Range	Teacher Resources and Supplies
Coretta Scott King Book Award Figurative Language History Series: Dear America	820L	Books
Reading Level Grades: 5–8	**Accelerated Reader** Points: 5.0 Book Level: 5.0	
Additional Title Haley, Alex. ***Roots.*** **Websites** http://www.pbs.org/wnet/slavery/teachers/index.html http://www.alex-haley.com/alex_haley_museum.htm http://www.pbs.org/wnet/slavery/experience/education/history2.html http://www.kidskonnect.com/subject-index/20-language-arts/343-figurative-language.html		

Brief Summary

Hansen paints a vivid portrait of Patsy's daily life as a slave. Her description of Patsy and her heartfelt "thirst" to read is deeply touching. This young girl's desire to have then what every American child has today—the opportunity to learn—is an inspiring tool for every reader.

Focus

- Freedom to Read
- Genealogy

Teacher Input

- View the following website with students and then introduce the book: http://www.pbs.org/wnet/slavery/experience/education/history2.html.
- Use the following website to provide students with great examples of figurative language: http://www.kidskonnect.com/subject-index/20-language-arts/343-figurative-language.html.
- Ask students what they know about the history of the South during this time, and provide details of some things students do not know.
- Share a copy of Alex Haley's book ***Roots*** with the class. Talk about the importance of knowing one's family history. People often talk about experiences that changed them. Ask the students to comment on how Alex Haley's literary contribution changed African Americans.
- View and discuss with students the video clip of the Haley Museum at the following website: http://www.alex-haley.com/alex_haley_museum.htm.

Guided Practice

- Have students write a "***My Mind Can Soar***" diary.
- Tell students the definition of a resource and give a few examples. Ask students to consider and list the resources they use in school to support their education.
- Invite students to share stories about the "bad-to-good" events in their lives.
- Have students debate the issue of slaves' desire to learn, why slaves did not have the freedom to become educated, and what price they paid if they were caught trying to read. Have them discuss why they think students today do not have that same eagerness to learn and stay in school.

Independent Practice

- Have students complete a "***I Thought My Soul Would Rise and Fly When . . .***" paper. Allow time for sharing their work with the class.
- Suggest that students create a family genealogy booklet or PowerPoint presentation.

Closure

- The class brainstorms ways to improve student learning.

Assessment

- Student generated diaries.
- Group discussions.
- Production of Genealogy Booklet or PowerPoint presentation.

Littlesugar, Amy. *Freedom School, Yes!* New York: Philomel, 2001.

About the Author

Amy Littlesugar—Books, Biography, Contact Information. 2010. http://www.jacketflap.com/persondetail.asp?person=6588 (accessed October 22, 2010).

Literary Elements Education Synthesis	**Lexile Range** 390L	**Teacher Resources and Supplies** Books Index Cards
Reading Level Grades 3–8	**Accelerated Reader** Points: 0.5 Book Level: 3.4	
Additional Titles Bridges, Ruby. ***Ruby Bridges Goes to School.*** Howard, Elizabeth Fitzgerald. ***Virgie Goes to School with Us Boys.*** **Website** http://www.pbs.org/wgbh/amex/eyesontheprize/story/09_summer.html		

Brief Summary

Learning to read was not always the easiest thing to do, even for those who had the ability to master that skill. You see, in Jolie's day, the South did not believe African Americans should be educated. But some people were determined to learn and willing to endure trials and make sacrifices so that learning became a priority for young and old alike.

Focus

- Fear
- Slavery
- Education
- Faith

Teacher Input

- Ask students: "What does freedom mean to you?" Have them write their answers on index cards. Invite them to share their answers with the class.
- Ask students how they feel on a summer's eve when they gaze up into the sky.
- Ask students what they think what teamwork means. Have them give examples of how they practice teamwork in the classroom.

Guided Practice

- Ask students to tell about themselves by answering the following questions on index cards: Have you ever felt sad? What caused your sadness?

- Ask students to comment on why they think the church was burned.
- Ask students to discuss a time when they felt they were in some type of danger and how they handled the situation.
- Have the class sing a round of "If I Had a Hammer."
- Thinking about "freedom" and creating a better world for all, ask students to complete the following sentence: "If I Had a . . ."
- Have students write about the legacies that Jacob Lawrence, Countee Cullen, and Benjamin Banneker left behind. What impact do the students themselves plan to have on the world?
- Ask students to share in a debate about whether African American history should be celebrated.
- Have students identify three facts or fictions described in *Freedom School, Yes!* compared with what they learn on the following online resource: http://www.pbs.org/wgbh/amex/eyesontheprize/story/09_summer.html.

Independent Practice

- Instruct each student to write an essay titled "Get An Education—Yes, I Can!"
- Students present their version of the song "If I Had a Hammer"
- Invite students to express what freedom means to them.

Assessment

- Student brainstorming, research reports, and debate.

Bibliography

Amy Littlesugar-Books, Biography, Contact Information. 2010. http://www.jacketflap.com/persondetail.asp?person=6588 (accessed October 22, 2010).

BookTalk—Marcia Vaughan. 2010. http://www.leeandlow.com/p/mvaughan.mhtml (accessed October 22, 2010).

Draper, Sharon. *The Battle of Jericho.* New York: Atheneum Books for Young Readers, 2003.

Eloise Greenfield. Scholastic.com. n.d. http://www2.scholastic.com/browse/contributor.jsp?id=3186 (accessed October 22, 2010).

Greenfield, Eloise. *Mary McLeod Bethune.* New York: HarperCollins, 1977.

Grimes, Nikki. *Danitra Brown, Class Clown.* New York: HarperCollins, 2005.

Hansen, Joyce. *I Thought My Soul Would Rise and Fly: The Diary of Patsy, a Freed Girl.* New York: Scholastic, 1997.

Joyce Hansen. n.d. http://www.joycehansen.com/index.htm (accessed October 22, 2010).

Littlesugar, Amy. *Freedom School, Yes!* New York: Philomel, 2001.

Nikki Grimes. n.d. http://www.nikkigrimes.com (accessed October 9, 2010).

Vaughan, Marcia. *Up the Learning Tree.* New York: Lee & Low, 2003.

Welcome to the Official Site of Sharon Draper. n.d. http://sharondraper.com/ (accessed October 11, 2010).

Webliography

The American Experience: Eyes on the Prize. The Story of the Movement. PBS. 1997–2006. http://www.pbs.org/wgbh/amex/eyesontheprize/story/09_summer.html (accessed December 11, 2010).

AR BookFinder US—Quick Search. Renaissance Learning. 2010. http://www.arbookfind.com/Default.aspx (accessed December 7, 2010).

BROWN V. BOARD: Timeline of School Integration in the U.S. Teaching Tolerance. Southern Poverty Law Center. n.d. http://www.tolerance.org/magazine/number-25-spring-2004/brown-v-board-timeline-school-integration-us (accessed December 9, 2010).

Cliques, Peer Pressure, and Teens. How to Deal with School Cliques and Help Teens Keep Peer Influences Positive. Kaboose.com. Disney. n.d. http://parenting.kaboose.com/age-and-stage/teens-development-peer-pressure.html (accessed December 8, 2010).

Desepoli, Darren. *Alex Haley House Museum—Alex Haley Childhood Home.* 2009–2010. http://www.alex-haley.com/alex_haley_museum.htm (accessed December 11, 2010).

Don't Be a Dropout by James Brown. n.d. http://www.google.com/search?sourceid=navclient&aq=3&oq=don%27t+be+a+drop&ie=UTF-8&rlz=1T4TSNA_en___US387&q=don%27t+be+a+dropout+by+james+brown (accessed December 8, 2010).

Dropouts Give Reasons: Why Do Students Leave High School Without a Diploma? Suite 101 Links. November 4, 2006. http://www.suite101.com/content/dropouts-give-reasons-a8681 (accessed December 8, 2010).

Figurative Language. Kids Konnect. 2010. http://www.kidskonnect.com/subject-index/20-language-arts/343-figurative-language.html (accessed December 11, 2010).

Finding Folktales to Tell. Story Arts. 2000. http://www.storyarts.org/classroom/retelling/findingtales.html (accessed December 10, 2010).

James Weldon Johnson. Poets.org-Poetry, Poems, Bios and More. Academy of American Poets. 1997–2010. http://www.poets.org/poet.php/prmPID/72 (accessed October 24, 2010).

The Lexile Framework for Reading. Lexile.com. MetaMetrics. 2010. http://lexile.com/ (accessed November 2, 2010).

Long, John R. *Aesop's Fables—Online Collection—656+ fables.* Star Systems. January 8, 2010. http://aesopfables.com/ (accessed December 11, 2010).

Mary McLeod Bethune Biography. n.d. http://www.lkwdpl.org/wihohio/beth-mar.htm (accessed October 22, 2010).

Mary McLeod Bethune's Legacy. n.d. http://www.duboislc.org/html/BlackLegacy.html (accessed December 8, 2010).

The Pearl Fryar Topiary Garden. n.d. http://www.pearlfryar.com (accessed December 11, 2010).

Slavery and the Making of America. The Slave Experience: Education, Arts, and Culture. PBS, Educational Broadcasting Corporation. 2004. http://www.pbs.org/wnet/slavery/experience/education/history2.html (accessed December 11, 2010).

Slavery and the Making of America. For Teachers. PBS, Educational Broadcasting Corporation. 2004. http://www.pbs.org/wnet/slavery/teachers/index.html (accessed October 22, 2010).

Student Bill of Rights. National Education Servicing. 2005–2010. http://www.nationaled.net/student_bill_of_rights.asp (accessed December 10, 2010).

Trees, by Joyce Kilmer. Poetry-Archive.com. 2002. http://www.poetry-archive.com/k/trees.html (accessed December 11, 2010).

Youth Education at arborday.org. n.d. http://www.arborday.org/kids (accessed October 22, 2010).

Additional Reading Materials

Anderson, Wayne. *Brown v. Board of Education: The Case Against School Segregation.* New York: Rosen Central/Primary Source, 2004.

Integration of African American students into schools where all the students were white was not an easy transition. With Jim Crow laws in southern states, sentiments in favor of separation running high, and inequities in every facet of life, it took the intervention of the Supreme Court in 1954 to mandate reform in education that granted every child the opportunity to receive an equal education. This reference tool reflects the struggles African Americans faced in their quest for education.

Bolden, Tonya. *Maritcha: A Nineteenth-Century American Girl.* New York: Abrams, 2005.

Maritcha has a life-changing experience when she leaves New York because of the riots to live in Rhode Island. She is determined to strive for the best by using her voice to secure a good future. The reader is encouraged to persevere through the actions this young girl takes in pursuit of a better education.

Braun, Eric. *Booker T. Washington: Great American Educator.* Mankato, MN: Capstone Press, 2006.

The life and story of Booker T. Washington, the great educator and founder of the Tuskeegee Institute, is presented in graphic-novel format, appealing even to reluctant readers.

Bridges, Ruby. *Ruby Bridges Goes to School.* New York: Scholastic, 2003.

In this beginning-to-read book, Ruby Bridges describes her turbulent beginning at the William Frantz Elementary School in New Orleans. Young readers are introduced to a little girl who modeled the character traits that students practice in schools today. She has fond memories of the teacher who showed her love and compassion and protected her from verbal abuse as she made this brave transition to improve the quality of education she received. Students will also learn of other famous people who provided encouragement and hope to her during her early years.

Grimes, Nikki. *Bronx Masquerade.* New York: Dial Books, 2002.

Nikki Grimes uses poetry and the topic of youth with problems to attract readers in this award-winning volume of literature. She writes about the wisdom of a caring teacher who used a microphone in an open atmosphere to help young people recognize, identify, and come together to solve their issues. Interwoven throughout this book are many of the same challenges young people face today, such as health, physical abuse, and drug addiction. Through their writings, these youths tell about times in their lives when it was difficult for them to handle their problems, and this book can offer the bibliotherapy that many teens need today to live powerful and effective lives.

Havill, Juanita. *Jamaica and the Substitute Teacher.* New York: Houghton Mifflin, 1999.

Trying to be the perfect student for the substitute teacher stirs up honesty in Jamaica when she confesses that her spelling paper was not perfect and that she had in fact copied the correct spelling of a word from her classmate's work. After making her confession, the teacher tells her that all children matter in the classroom and it isn't necessary for them to be perfect.

Jurmain, Suzanni. *The Forbidden Schoolhouse: The True and Dramatic Story of Prudence Candall and Her Students.* Boston: Houghton Mifflin, 2005.

The author describes the problems that Prudence Crandall faced when she decided to teach African American girls in Canterbury, Connecticut, in the 1800s. Once a teacher who taught only white girls, Crandall is approached by an older African American girl requesting that she teach her so she can teach others of her race. Faced with opposition from the community, she solicits help from William Lloyd Garrison, the abolitionist and editor of the *Liberator* newspaper, to help her recruit enough African American girls so that she can keep her school open when the white parents make the decision to remove their children. Many people had reasons for not wanting her to teach African Americans, and Crandall encountered many obstacles in her life for the decision she made. Before her death, however, the townspeople apologized to her for their cruel behavior and treatment.

Lauture, Denize. *Running the Road to ABC.* New York: Simon & Schuster, 1996.

In this Coretta Scott King Award–winning title, the author describes the eagerness of Haitian students to go to school. She mentions that although some barriers still exist, the students remain focused on learning—something that should be emphasized to students today.

Morrison, Toni. *Remember: The Journey to School Integration.* Boston: Houghton Mifflin Company, 2004.

Today students of all races in public schools learn, work, participate in activities, play sports, and graduate together—with some sharing the highest academic awards. But the road that led to this togetherness was filled with potholes, mud puddles, detours, and some road closings. As Toni Morrison navigates young readers through this book, she reminisces about the past and the strong faith that many had—faith that led to school integration. Some may think the pressures faced in education today are disturbing, but when we consider the terrible conditions African Americans experienced in the past, every student should be encouraged by the entire community to stay in school and strive for academic excellence.

Myers, Walter Dean. *Monster.* New York: Amistad, 2000.

How do you turn a tragedy into a movie script? Steve Harmon knew that he had to remove the stigma attached to his life if he was ever to have a life again. On trial for murder, he knew that a change in his behavior, together with his ability to write, would both be therapeutic and provide a tool for recovery.

Rahaman, Vashanti. *Read for Me, Mama.* Honesdale, PA: Boyds Hill Press, 1997.

Most parents assist their children in learning to read. This book tells the story of a young boy whose love and compassion for his mother are overwhelming. Appreciative of his mother for the long, hard work that she performs daily while still taking time to hear him read—and not knowing how to assist him because she can't read—the boy decides to teach her.

Stuve-Bodeen, Stephanie. *Elizabeti's School.* New York: Lee & Low, 2002.

A young girl's excitement about attending school vanishes when she realizes just how much she misses her mother, baby sister, and other things at home. Still, she learns how to play games with classmates, gather vegetables from the school's garden, and to count. She returns home in the afternoon eager to share her day at school with her family, and once she does, she decides to give school another try.

Walter, Mildred Pitts. *Alec's Primer.* Lebanon, NH: University Press of New England, 2004.

Readers are introduced to Alec Turner, a slave who is taught to read by Zephie, the granddaughter of his mistress, although it is against the law for slaves to read. Told in a humorous way, Walter lures the reader into her story, which is based on an actual event, by describing how this young slave boy bites the head off cookies shaped like soldiers. This amuses Zephie, and after this incident, she seems to understand that what Alec really wants is to be free. She also sees how important a role the ability to read is to truly being free.

Chapter 8

FAITH-BASED DREAMS

Dreams are important to the hope for a better future. Introduce your students to books and activities that emphasize the importance of hope and dreams and of working to accomplish them.

Bryan, Ashley. *Let It Shine: Three Favorite Spirituals.* New York: Atheneum Books for Young Readers, 2007.

About the Author

Artist Profile: Ashley Bryan. NCCIL. n.d. http://nccil.org/experience/artists/bryana/index.htm (accessed October 24, 2010).

Literary Elements	Lexile Range	Teacher Resources and Supplies
Coretta Scott King Book Award Poetry	—	**Book** Flashlight or battery-operated candle Books Worksheet
Reading Level Preschool–Grade 5	**Accelerated Reader** —	
Additional Titles Lewis, E. B. ***This Little Light of Mine.*** Pinkney, Andrea. ***Let It Shine.*** **Websites** http://www.readingrockets.org/books/interviews/bryan http://www.bluebutterflyfund.org/blessings/21004.html http://www.negrospirituals.com http://www.blackgospel.com		

Brief Summary

This little book does a big job of encouraging others to do their best, urging readers to move, march, and use their hands.

Focus

- Attitude
- Discipline
- Perception
- Civil Disobedience

Teacher Input

- Discuss with students the science of light and use the following online resource to "wow" students before presenting the book: http://www.lasertainment.com/laser/festivals.
- Introduce students to this award-winning author by using the following online resource: http://www.readingrockets.org/books/interviews/bryan.
- Divide the class into three groups. Give each group one of the three books listed in this lesson plan and a "***Let It Shine***" Worksheet to record information about the book. Rotate the three books between the groups. Once the rotation is complete, have students report their observations.

Guided Practice

- Have students view Maya Angelou's "I've Got a Little Light" at this website: http://www.bluebutterflyfund.org/blessings/21004.html. Afterward, have them list one or more interpretations of the author's statement and ways that they could use it to help others.
- Ask students why they think light is important.
- Encourage middle and high school students to use this book as a motivational tool. Suggest that they draw or paint pictures reflecting light shining in a place where darkness always seems to dwell. Their pictures can represent a cause, an issue, or a location.
- Have each group examine the book and complete the worksheet.

Independent Practice

- Suggest that students put on a "My Little Light Is Shining" puppet show.
- Have students make their own lights.

Closure

- Have students present their project reports.

Assessment

- Students brainstorming and discussions, completing of projects and project presentations.

Let It Shine Worksheet

Bryan, Ashley ***Let It Shine*** Is this book illustrated? If so, name the illustrator. _______________	Pinkney, Andrea ***Let It Shine*** Is this book illustrated? If so, name the illustrator. _______________	Lewis, E. B. ***This Little Light of Mine*** Is this book illustrated? If so, name the illustrator. _______________
List three things you like about this book. 1. 2. 3.	List three things you like about this book. 1. 2. 3.	List three things you like about this book. 1. 2. 3.
Who are some people or groups that you would recommend read this book? 1. 2. 3. 4. 5.	Who are some people or groups that you would recommend read this book? 1. 2. 3. 4. 5.	Who are some people or groups that you would recommend read this book? 1. 2. 3. 4. 5.
Describe How These Books Are Similar		
How Are They Different?		

Hopkinson, Deborah. *A Band of Angels.* New York: Atheneum Books for Young Readers, 1999.

About the Author

Author Deborah Hopkinson. 2010. http://www.deborahhopkinson.com (accessed October 24, 2010).

Literary Elements Historical Fiction Music	**Lexile Range** 590L	**Teacher Resources and Supplies** Book Worksheet
Reading Level Grades 3–4	**Accelerated Reader** Points: 0.5 Book Level: 4.4	
Additional Titles Bryan, Ashley. ***All Night, All Day: A Child's First Book of African-American Spirituals.*** Nelson, Kadir. ***He's Got the Whole World.*** Pinkney, Gloria Jean, compiler. ***Music from Our Lord's Holy Heaven.*** **Websites** http://www.singers.com/gospel/fiskjubileesingers.html http://www.pbs.org/wgbh/amex/singers/sfeature/songs.html http://www.pbs.org/americanrootsmusic/pbs_arm_saa_fiskjubileesingers.html		

Brief Summary

Traveling back into the past is important to a young girl as she listens to her Aunt Beth weave one of her favorite stories about her great-great-grandmother, Ella. Ella made a great sacrifice, along with other singers, to save Fisk University once she enrolled as a student. After waiting so long to finally get into college after slavery ended, Ella was disappointed to learn from her professor that the school would soon close because of its poor physical condition. Determined to save the school and get a good education, Ella and eight other singers had faith that the school would be saved. Just when it looked like all was lost, Ella allowed her faith to direct her path, and the world became a better place thanks to the melodious sounds of the students who became the Fisk Jubilee Singers.

Focus

- Determination
- Faith
- Jubilee
- Sacrifice

Teacher Input

- Ask students to comment on what the word "sacrifice" means to them.
- Distribute the "***There Were Nine***" ***Worksheet***. Ask students, "Have you ever been willing to make a sacrifice for something you loved or wanted?" Have students visit the following websites: http://www.infoplease.com/spot/bhmheroes1.html; http://tennesseeencyclopedia.net/imagegallery.php?EntryID=J037. Direct students to

use the sites to discover how two different groups of nine people with a "thirst" for basically the same thing made sacrifices clothed in faith.

- Invite students to name their favorite singing groups.
- Introduce the Fisk Jubilee Singers to students.

Guided Practice

- Have students research online and summarize the main occupations of the Jubilee Singers.
- Have students identify their favorite musical groups and describe the genre of their music.
- Ask students to discuss how Ella must have felt and what she thought before she made the decision to bring out a song of her own without first discussing it with her friends.
- Have students compare the similarities and differences between the Fisk Jubilee Singers and their favorite group.
- Instruct students to list other prominent African American leaders who attended Fisk University and describe how they used their gifts to make a difference in the world.
- Have students use online resources to research the Jubilee Singers performing different genres of music.

Independent Practice

- Suggest that students use online resources to locate photos and additional information about the Jubilee Singers and develop a Photo Story or five PowerPoint slides for project presentation.

Closure

- Students present their projects and reports.

Assessment

- Student answers questions about the different genres of music by the Jubilee Singers.

There Were Nine! Worksheet

Getting an Education, Saving an Institution

Historical Fiction	Fisk University—1871 Nashville, Tennessee	
http://tennesseeencyclopedia.net/imagegallery.php?EntryID=J037		
Describe the circumstances of the people listed below		
Isaac Dickerson	Green Evans	Benjamin Holmes
Jennie Jackson	Maggie Porter	Thomas Rutling
Ella Sheppard	Minnie Tate	Eliza Walker
Nonfiction	**Central High School—1957** Little Rock, Arkansas	
http://www.infoplease.com/spot/bhmheroes1.html		
Describe the situation of the people listed below.		
Melba Beals	Minnijean Brown	Elizabeth Eckford
Ernest Green	Gloria Ray Kalmark	Carlotta Walls LaNier
Thelma Mothershed	Terrence Roberts	Jefferson Thomas

McKissack, Patricia, and Fredrick McKissack. *Let My People Go: Bible Stories Told by a Freeman of Color to His Daughter, Charlotte, in Charleston, South Carolina, 1806–16.* New York: Simon & Schuster, 1998.

About the Author

Patricia (L'Ann) C(arwell) McKissack Biography. Answers.com. 2010. http://www.answers.com/topic/patricia-l-ann-c-arwell-mckissack (accessed December 12, 2010).

Literary Elements	**Lexile Range**	**Teacher Resources and Supplies**
Art Character Morals Nonfiction Short Stories	930L	Book
Reading Level Grades 3 and up	**Accelerated Reader** —	
Additional Title Weatherford, Carole Boston. ***Moses: When Harriet Tubman Led Her People to Freedom.*** **Websites** http://www.dltk-bible.com http://www.jamesransome.com http://www.childrensbiblestudy.com		

Brief Summary

In this book a daughter recalls her father's stories, which helped to educate her as well as strengthen her faith and the faith of others. McKissack reminds us of the difference between wanting it and not having it versus having something and not using it to help others and ourselves. In the United States, we enjoy the freedom to read the Bible at any time. We also have the privilege of attending institutions of learning. Many readers will be able to relate to some of the issues in stories found in the Bible. Readers will also learn how those who were deeply rooted in their faith learned to cope with difficult situations.

Focus

- Freedom
- Bible Stories
- Perseverance

Teacher Input

- Share the 13th Amendment to the U.S. Constitution with students.
- Explain the Gullah, South Carolina's Sea Island black culture, to students.

- Discuss the elements of a short story with the class.
- Introduce students to the illustrator James Ransome by using the following website: http://www.jamesransome.com.

Guided Practice

- Assign each story in this collection to a student or group of students to read. Instruct students to read and research additional information about the characters in their story for sharing.
- Ask students to volunteer to tell whether they have a habit that they want to break. Using the theme "Let This Habit Go" ask them to identify the habit and tell why they want to eliminate it.
- Engage students in a discussion about slavery and ask whether they believe it is wrong to hold people against their will.
- Show students a variety of books with covers that feature beautiful, bright, and bold illustrations. Ask students if they would choose to read certain books because of the illustrations.

Independent Practice

- Suggest that students make paper chain links of faith, hope, and love.
- Suggest that students write a movie script about the efforts of Moses and Harriet Tubman as they worked to set captives free from slavery. How were they similar, and how did they differ?
- Have students compose a poem entitled, "***Let Your Children Go!***"

Closure

- Students share the information they found about the book characters.
- Students discuss whether they have been able to eliminate negative habits.
- Students share their poems.

Assessment

- Student brainstorming and presentation of projects.

Tutu, Archbishop Desmond, and Douglas Carlton Abrams. *God's Dream.* Boston: Candlewick Press, 2008.

About the Author

Desmond Tutu Biography. Academy of Achievement. October 14, 2010. http://www.achievement.org/autodoc/page/tut0bio-1 (accessed October 24, 2010).

Literary Elements Point of View Genre	**Lexile Range** —	**Teacher Resources and Supplies** Book Worksheet
Reading Level Grades K–2	**Accelerated Reader** —	
Additional Titles Elster, Jean Alicia. ***I Have a Dream, Too!*** Greenfield, Eloise. ***Africa Dream.*** Kurtz, Jane. ***Martin's Dream.*** **Websites** http://www.npr.org/templates/story/story.php?storyId=1850318 http://www.mlkonline.net/video-i-have-a-dream-speech.html		

Brief Summary

This amazing book reminds children and adults that it is God's dream that we live together in peace and harmony. We are all very important parts of the world that He created without prejudice, even though we're different in gender, race, and where we live.

Focus

- Love
- Caring
- Sharing
- Difference
- Respect
- Faithful

Teacher Input

- Talk with the students about the importance of working together at school, home, and in the community.
- Share the following online resource with the students to help them better understand the afflictions of the National Party of South Africa and apartheid: http://www.npr.org/templates/story/story.php?storyId=1850318.
- Using the following website, discuss the significance of the Nobel Peace Prize which Dr. Desmond Tutu was awarded in 1984: http://nobelpeaceprize.org/en_GB/laureates/laureates-1984.
- Have the class conduct a Dream Study, as described in the Guided Practice, for one week.

Guided Practice

- It's Dream Week! Have students keep a record of all their dreams for one week. Each morning they should record whatever they can remember about their dreams. Have students form a plan for telling others about God's Dream from the book.
- Have students write "Kindness and Caring" quotes.
- Discuss with the students ways to celebrate Kindness Awareness Week using the following website: http://www.kindnessusa.org/kindnessawarenessweek.htm.
- Have students explain the sentence "God's Dream Is Caught, God's Dream Is Taught" by writing a short poem.
- Have the class listen to Dr. King's "I Have a Dream" speech at the following website: http://www.mlkonline.net/video-i-have-a-dream-speech.html.
- Have students write their own speeches using the theme "If It's God's Dream, It's Not Impossible!" Locate and play the song "The Impossible Dream" for the class.

Independent Practice

- Suggest that students design a PowerPoint presentation or design an ***ABC Dream Book*** about their own dream. Archbishop Desmond Tutu wrote about ***God's Dream.*** Dr. Martin Luther King shared his "I Have a Dream" speech.

Closure

- Students present their projects.
- Locate and play the song "***We Are the World.***"

Assessment

- Student brainstorming, project sharing, and reporting.

Bibliography

Artist Profile: Ashley Bryan. NCCIL. n.d. http://nccil.org/experience/artists/bryana/index.htm (accessed October 24, 2010).

Author Deborah Hopkinson. 2010. http://www.deborahhopkinson.com (accessed October 24, 2010).

Bryan, Ashley. *Let It Shine: Three Favorite Spirituals.* New York: Atheneum Books for Young Readers, 2007.

Desmond Tutu Biography. Academy of Achievement. October 14, 2010. http://www.achievement.org/autodoc/page/tut0bio-1 (accessed October 24, 2010).

Hopkinson, Deborah. *A Band of Angels.* New York: Atheneum Books for Young Readers, 1999.

James Weldon Johnson. Poets.org. Academy of American Poets. 1997–2010. http://www.poets.org/poet.php/prmPID/72 (accessed October 24, 2010).

Johnson, James Weldon. *Lift Every Voice and Sing.* New York: Walker Books for Young Readers, 1993.

McKissack, Patricia, and Fredrick McKissack. *Let My People Go: Bible Stories Told by a Freeman of Color to His Daughter, Charlotte, in Charleston, South Carolina, 1806–16.* New York: Simon & Schuster, 1998.

Patricia (L'Ann) C(arwell) McKissack Biography. Answers.com. 2010. http://www.answers.com/topic/patricia-l-ann-c-arwell-mckissack (accessed December 12, 2010).

Tutu, Archbishop Desmond, and Douglas Carlton Abrams. *God's Dream.* Boston: Candlewick Press, 2008.

Webliography

The American Experience: Jublilee Singers: Jubilee Songs. 1999–2000. http://www.pbs.org/wgbh/amex/singers/sfeature/songs.html (accessed October 25, 2010).

Bible Activities. DLTK Sites. 1998–2010. http://www.dltk-bible.com (accessed December 12, 2010).

BlackGospel.com. 1997–2007. http://www.blackgospel.com (accessed October 24, 2010).

The Blue Butterfly Fund—I've Got a Little Light. Butterfly Blessings. February 10, 2004. http://www.bluebutterflyfund.org/blessings/21004.html (accessed December 12, 2010).

Civil Rights Movement Heroes for Kids (Rosa Parks, Martin Luther King Jr.). Infoplease.com. Pearson Education. 2000–2010. http://www.infoplease.com/spot/bhmheroes1.html (accessed December 12, 2010).

Composers Official Site of Negro Spirituals, Antique Gospel Music. n.d. http://www.negrospirituals.com/composers.htm (accessed October 24, 2010).

Desmond Tutu: "God Has a Dream." National Public Radio. 2010. http://www.npr.org/templates/story/story.php?storyId=1850318 (accessed December 11 2010).

The Fisk Jublilee Singers. United Singers International. 2006. http://www.singers.com/gospel/fiskjubileesingers.html (accessed October 24, 2010).

I Have a Dream Speech—full text, audio & video of Dr. Martin Luther King's Most Famous Speech. Stand Out Designs. n.d. http://www.mlkonline.net/video-i-have-a-dream-speech.html (accessed December 11, 2010).

James Weldon Johnson. Poets.org. Academy of American Poets. 1997–2010. http://www.poets.org/poet.php/prmPID/72 (accessed October 24, 2010).

Kindness Awareness Week—Welcome to Kindness USA. Kindness. 2010. http://www.kindnessusa.org/kindnessawarenessweek.htm (accessed December 12, 2010).

Lift Every Voice (acapella). n.d. http://www.youtube.com/watch?v=F0XJPUA5xdI&feature=related (accessed December 12, 2010).

Nobel Peace Prize 1984. Norwegian Nobel Institute. n.d. http://nobelpeaceprize.org/en_GB/laureates/laureates-1984/ (accessed December 11, 2010).

PBS American Roots Music: The Songs and the Artists—The Fisk Jublilee Singers. The Ginger Group. 2001. http://www.pbs.org/americanrootsmusic/pbs_arm_saa_fiskjubileesingers.html (accessed October 24, 2010).

Reading Rockets: A Video Interview with Ashley Bryan. Reading Rockets. 2010. http://www.readingrockets.org/books/interviews/bryan (accessed December 12, 2010).

The Slaves Experiences of the Holidays. The University Library. 2004. http://docsouth.unc.edu/highlights/holidays.html (accessed October 9, 2010).

TN Encyclopedia: Jubilee Singers of Fisk University. Tennessee Historical Society. 2002. http://tennesseeencyclopedia.net/imagegallery.php?EntryID=J037 (accessed December 12, 2010).

Additional Reading Materials

God's Little Instruction Book for African Americans. 2001.

This little book of Bible quotations taken from different chapters of the Bible is a great resource for young readers developing skills of character and integrity.

Grimes, Nikki. _When Daddy Prays._ Eerdmans Books for Young Readers, 2002.

This book describes the feelings, reasons, and results of a father's prayers.

Johnson, James Weldon. _The Creation._ New York: Holiday House, 1994.

James Weldon Johnson's poem "The Creation" is often used as a creative dramatic selection for contestants participating in talent shows. Students interested in reading a powerful speech will find this book to be an appropriate selection.

Ladwig, Tim. _The Lord's Prayer._ Grand Rapids, MI: Eerdman's Books for Young Readers, 2000.

The Lord's Prayer features brilliant, bold, colorful illustrations depicting an African American child as she proudly travels with her father to enjoy the blessings that God has given to His earthly people through the power of prayer. What the illustrator translates to the readers is that we can enjoy God's blessings now.

My Holy Bible for African-American Children. Grand Rapids, MI: Zondervan, 2002.

A remarkable Holy Bible written for African American children with easy-to-read print. Children will find this to be a useful reference for Bible study with its guide words at the top of each page. Throughout this book, stories and passages are accompanied by beautiful illustrations.

Myers, Walter Dean. _One More River to Cross: An African American Photograph Album._ New York: Harcourt Brace & Company, 1995.

Myers has used photos to communicate the message of a popular song so often sung by African Americans whose goals were to triumph over the turbulent river of segregation, prejudice, and Jim Crow laws through faith and prayer.

Newman, Richard. _Go Down, Moses: Celebrating._ New York: Clarkson N. Potter, 1998.

Young and old alike will find this a volume of historic songs that speak of the trials, tribulations, sorrows, and joys of a determined people who found a way to share their messages and feelings through music. Readers will be able to determine through many of these lyrics that music was a way to set the mind free while the body was held in captivity.

Pinkney, Gloria Jean, compiler. _Music from Our Lord's Holy Heaven._ New York: HarperCollins, 2005.

Music lovers will find this volume entertaining as well as informative. The book is beautifully illustrated and consists of many songs supported by Scripture. The songs are divided into three main sections: Adoration, Spiritual Wayfarers, and the Good Shepherd.

Rubright, Lynn. _Mama's Window._ New York: Lee & Low Books, 2005.

This book shares the story of a young boy who is determined to see his late mother's dream of having a stained glass window in the new church fulfilled. He strongly disagrees with the church administrators when they decide to use the money his mother worked hard for to build a brick church and use plain glass windows.

Sebestyn, Ouida. _Words by Heart._ New York: Bantam Doubleday Dell Books for Young Readers, 1981.

A young girl tries hard to impress her father by learning and reciting Bible scriptures. While she is able to recite more scriptures than any of her white counterparts in a contest, her outstanding performance is not recognized because of her gender and race.

Warren, Gwendolin Sims. _Ev'ry Time I Feel the Spirit: 101 Best-Loved Psalms, Gospel Hymns, and Spiritual Songs of the African-American Church._ New York: Henry Holt, 1997.

This is a historical collection of songs reflecting the pain, joy, and jubilation of the African American people as they journey from their homeland of Africa to America.

Who Built the Ark?: Based on an African-American Spiritual. New York: Simon & Schuster Books for Young Readers, 1994.

This is a counting book based on the Bible story of Noah's Ark.

Chapter 9

FAMILY AND FRIENDS

Share books and activities that teach your students that there are many ways to be part of a family and how family members love and support one another.

Cox, Judy. *My Family Plays Music.* New York: Holiday House, 2003.

About the Author

Home-Judy Cox. 2010. http://www.judycox.net (accessed October 26, 2010).

Literary Elements	Lexile Range	Teacher Resources and Supplies
Coretta Scott King Book Award Music Classical Music Musical Instruments Realistic Fiction	—	Book Bongos Cowbell Maracas Pot and pan Worksheets
Reading Level Preschool–Grade 3	**Accelerated Reader** Points: 0.5 Book Level: 2.6	
Additional Title Curtis, Gavin. ***The Bat Boy and His Violin.*** **Websites** http://www.classical.com/charts.php?chart_cat=snglcomp&chart_id=39 http://66.70.148.219/biography (Neville Brothers) http://www.blackmusicamerica.com http://melodyloops.com/music http://www.dsokids.com/listen/instrumentlist.aspx		

Brief Summary

This book introduces readers to a wide variety of music and to musicians who are members of one family. As students begin to develop an appreciation for music genres, Cox provides the teacher with a supplemental tool that can be integrated into any lesson plan related to music or music appreciation.

Focus

- Family Musicians
- Music Genres
- Types of Musical Instruments

Teacher Input

- Ask students to name various musical instruments.
- Conduct a survey of students to determine the type of music they most enjoy.
- Divide the class into three groups to use online resources to research and list musical families and the genre of music that each family performs.

Guided Practice

- Assign students to construct a ***Family Tree*** using the following website: http://www.genealogy.com/genealogy/cgi-bin/tree_gen.cgi?
- Have students write a brief description of their favorite music genre or artist and why.
- Instruct students to count the number of instruments used in the story and draw the one they would most like to learn to play.
- Plan a dance-a-thon using the students' favorite genre of music.
- Have each group of students create an African American Musicians Video designed to introduce families in the music business both past and present.
- Assign students to complete the "***Family Members and Their Ages Math Worksheet.***"

Independent Practice

- Suggest that students use this online website to compose a song for sharing: http://www.iknowthat.com/com/Music.

Closure

- Invite a local musician to perform for the class and to talk about his or her music.

Assessment

- Student interest, project designs, and presentations.

Families and Their Music

Choose the right family member(s) to connect with the artist listed in the table. Please list online references that you consult.

One of the latter three in each of the groups listed below does have a more prominent person with whom most would identify.

Singer	Name the Family Member(s)	Online Reference
Nat King Cole		
Aretha Franklin		
Michael Jackson		
Nicole Richie		
Eddie Levert		
Gladys Knight		
Cissy Houston		

Family Members and Their Ages Worksheet

If you need more space, you can record more family members on the back of this sheet. A survey will be taken to see who has the largest family tree in the class.

	Name of Family Member	Relationship	Age
1			
2			
3			
4			
5			
6			
7			
8			
9			
10			
11			
12			
13			
14			
15			
16			
17			
18			
19			
20			

Flake, Sharon. *Money Hungry.* New York: Hyperion Books, 2001.

About the Author

Sharon G. Flake. 2008. http://www.sharongflake.com (accessed October 26, 2010).

Literary Elements Character Simile	**Lexile Range** 650L	**Teacher Resources and Supplies** Book Play money
Reading Level Grades 6–9	**Accelerated Reader** Points: 4.0 Book Level: 4.2	
Additional Titles Mollel, Tololwa M. ***My Rows and Piles of Coins.*** **Websites** http://www.youtube.com/watch?v=u4ZWngrvm0I http://www.nationalhomeless.org/factsheets/ http://www.bygpub.com/books/tg2rw/chap1excerpt.htm http://www.nationalhomeless.org/projects/awareness/index.html		

Brief Summary

Raspberry Hill loves money! Her ultimate goal is to have enough to afford a house to live in—right now she lives in her mother's old car. So she sells pencils at school without permission from the administration. Raspberry's efforts to end her life as a homeless student backfire and she must face the consequences.

Focus

- Homelessness
- Greed
- Money

Teacher Input

- Discuss barriers that prevent students from learning. Identify homelessness as a major barrier before introducing this book. Use resources from this website: http://www.nationalhomeless.org/projects/awareness/index.html.
- Show the class the following video clip of Homeless to Harvard: http://www.youtube.com/watch?v=u4ZWngrvm0I.
- Lead the class in a discuss about what money is and what it can do.
- Ask students the question "What would you do if you had a million dollars?"

Guided Practice

- Ask students what they think the phrase "Money talks" means.
- Ask students, "What type of value did Raspberry Hill place on money? Do you think that Raspberry was willing to do anything for money?"
- Ask students to list at least five ways they may be able to offer support to the homeless. Allow students to refer to the following website for specific information about the homeless population: http://www.nationalhomeless.org/projects/awareness/index.html.
- Assign students to create graphs and charts showing where the largest numbers of homeless families are located across the United States.
- Have students write an essay supporting "***The Rights of Homeless Students***" to attend the school of their choice: http://www.nationalhomeless.org.

Independent Practice

- Set up a ***Classroom Care Box*** for the homeless shelter in your town.

Closure

- Arrange to have a social worker speak to the class about homelessness and donate your Classroom Care Box to the shelter.

Assessment

- Observation of students working together as a team, student reporting, questions asked of the school social worker, and evidence of research.

Mathis, Sharon Bell. *The Hundred Penny Box.* New York: Puffin Books/Penguin Books USA, 1975.

About the Author

Sharon Bell Mathis. The Brown Book Shelf. February 13, 2010. http://thebrownbookshelf.com/2010/02/13/sharon-bell-mathis/ (accessed October 26, 2010).

<table>
<tr><td>Literary Element
History</td><td>Lexile Range
700L</td><td>Teacher Resources and Supplies</td></tr>
<tr><td>Reading Level
Grades 3–5</td><td>Accelerated Reader
Points: 1.0
Book Level: 3.9</td><td>Book
Container with one hundred pennies
Almanac
Worksheet</td></tr>
<tr><td colspan="3">Additional Title
Bolden, Tonya. Finding Family.
Websites
http://thinkexist.com/quotes/with/keyword/penny/
http://www.npr.org/templates/story/story.php?storyId=1069272</td></tr>
</table>

Brief Summary

This is the heartwarming story of a young boy's love for his Great Aunt Dew. Faced with a dilemma after hearing his mother say that it is time to get rid of the "old wooden box" that houses Aunt Dew's greatest memories, her "hundred pennies," the boy must figure out a way to keep Aunt Dew's treasure while respecting and obeying his mother.

Focus

- Older Generation
- Extended Family
- Historical Events

Teacher Input

- Ask students to name their oldest relatives.
- Ask students to bring twenty-five pennies to class.
- Show the class a map of Atlanta and have students identify the state where the city is located.

Guided Practice

- Lead students in a discussion about why Aunt Dew called Michael by his father's name.
- Have students list two things that Michael's mother did to show she cared for Aunt Dew.
- Allow students to examine their pennies to determine and record the years they were made.

- Assign students to search for information on the composer Tommy Dorsey and his song "Precious Lord" and tell why he wrote the song: http://www.npr.org/templates/story/story.php?storyId=1069272
- Have students compare the differences and similarities between the two musicians named Tommy Dorsey.

Independent Practice

- Suggest that each student create a Penny Chart using at least twenty penny quotes, or quotations that can be found at: http://en.thinkexist.com/quotes/with/keyword/penny.

Closure

- Students share their Penny Charts and quotations.

Assessment

- Student interest, the collection of pennies for individual projects, and presentations.

The Years in My Pocket Worksheet (Learning History Makes Sense)

Bring from five to eight pennies to class for this worksheet exercise. Using online resources, locate and record an important event, historical contribution, or landmark in African American history in the year that each penny was minted.

Year __________

Event:

____

____

____

____

Year __________

Event:

____

____

____

____

Year __________

Event:

____

____

____

____

Year __________

Event:

____

____

____

____

____

Morrison, Toni, and Slade Morrison. *Peeny Butter Fudge.* New York: A Paula Wiseman Book/Simon & Schuster Books for Young Readers, 2009.

About the Author

Toni Morrison Biography-life, family, childhood, children, parents, name, story, death, history. Advameg, Inc. 2010. http://www.notablebiographies.com/Mo-Ni/Morrison-Toni.html (accessed October 30, 2010).

Literary Elements Art Storytelling Poetry and Rhyme	**Lexile Range** —	**Teacher Resources and Supplies** Book Index cards
Reading Level Preschool–Grade 3	**Accelerated Reader** Points: 0.5 Book Level: 1.7	
Additional Titles Belton, Sandra. ***May'naise Sandwiches & Sunshine Tea.*** **Websites** http://www.flash-gear.com/npuz http://www.sackraces.com		

Brief Summary

This is an amusing and realistic story of what it's like to have a grandmother around when the parents are not. Here the writers show us how a grandmother revises a schedule prepared by a parent to reflect what she believes the children would like to do. This book lends itself to a great classroom discussion.

Focus

- Grandmothers
- Grandchildren

Teacher Input

- Introduce the book by polling students to find out who can or cannot eat peanut butter.
- Invite the students to comment on what they like about having their grandmother as sitters. Try to get students to tell whether they get more from their grandmothers when their parents are not around.
- Lead the students in a discussion about the importance of obeying the instructions left on Mom's list.
- Create a set of "Mommy Cards and Nana Cards" for each student.
- Discuss sack racing as a sport, and ask students if they have ever participated in a sack race.
- Show the students how they may download free kitty photos online and generate photo puzzles using http://www.flash-gear.com/npuz.

Guided Practice

- Instruct the students to list three things the children in the story liked doing with Nana.
- Ask students to share some items their parents leave on the list for sitters when they are away.
- Ask students to vote by using their index cards to show how many would prefer Mommy's instructions over doing what Nana planned.
- Have students act out the scene when Nana is in the kitchen baking peanut-butter fudge.
- Lead the class in planning to have a sack race during physical education class or another school event.

Independent Practice

- Have each student write a jingle by using an example found in the book.

Closure

- Hold a ***Jingle in My Pocket Day.*** Walk up to students and teachers on that day and ask, "Would you like to hear the jingle in my pocket?"
- Have students share their creative writing.

Assessment

- Student brainstorming, interests, discussions, and creative writing.

Example of Mommy and Nana Cards

Mommy	Nana

1. I get more from Nana when my parents are present. ___ yes ___ no

2. I get less from Nana when my parents are present. ___ yes ___ no

Smothers, Ethel Footman. *The Hard-Times Jar.* New York: Frances Foster Books/Farrar, Straus & Giroux, 2003.

About the Author

Ethel Footman Smothers (1944–). Biography, Personal, Career, Honors, Awards, Writings, Sidelights. 2010. http://biography.jrank.org/pages/362/Smothers-Ethel-Footman-1944.html (accessed October 26, 2010).

Literary Element Writing	**Lexile Range** AD520L	**Teacher Resources and Supplies** Book Jar Brown paper bags, safety pins or paper rings Crayons and paints
Reading Level K–Grade 4	**Accelerated Reader** Points: 0.5 Book Level: 3.1	
Additional Titles Williams, Sherley Anne. ***Working Cotton.*** **Websites** http://www.nfwm.org/fw/education.shtml http://www.goal-setting-guide.com/goal-setting-tutorials/smart-goal-setting http://center.serve.org/nche/legis_resources.php http://www.freerice.com		

Brief Summary

A young migrant girl's love for reading leads her to write and illustrate her own books using brown paper bags. She attends school for a season, and, to her delight, the teacher shows her the classroom library. She is told to read as many books as she likes while in school, but the books cannot be checked out. However, having that many books proves too much for her and she takes a few home without the teacher's permission. When her mother discovers that she has the books, she must face the consequences.

Focus

- Migrant Workers
- Stealing
- Education and Reading

Teacher Input

- Bring a jar to class and discuss "***Mason and Canning Jars.***"
- Ask students if they know the meaning of the term "***migrant workers***" and what migrant workers do.
- Divide the class into two groups for the "***It Takes a Community***" assignment.

Guided Practice

- Based on the author's story, have students identify some issues that children of migrant workers faced each day.

- Have students participate in the "***It Takes a Community***" activity. Divide students into two groups. Ask Group 1 to list positive and negative aspects of being a migrant worker's child. Ask Group 2 to list ways that educators and schools can support the education of migrant children.
- Allow students to participate in this online activity to support World Hunger: http://www.freerice.com.
- Invite students to share their perspectives on whether the protagonist in the story should have received a stiffer punishment for stealing the books from the teacher's classroom. Why? Why not?
- Assist students in using the goal-setting guide online to identify actions they need to take to achieve goals they have set for themselves: http://www.goal-setting-guide.com/goal-setting-tutorials/smart-goal-setting.
- Engage students in a discussion about whether they are excited to buy books from the bookstore or school book fair.

Independent Practice

- Suggest that students write stories and publish their own books by using large brown paper bags, safety pins, and paper rings.

Closure

- Students sponsor a "***Show and Tell.***" Discuss how some people may experience economic problems at home and cannot afford to buy books. Make books for the "We Made Our Own Books for the Brown Paper Book Fair."

Assessment

- Student brainstorming, discussions, reports, and projects.

Bibliography

http://thebrownbookshelf.com/2010/02/13/sharon-bell-mathis/ (accessed October 26, 2010).

Cox, Judy. *My Family Plays Music.* New York: Holiday House, 2003.

English, Karen. *The Baby on the Way.* New York: Farrar, Straus & Giroux, 2005.

Ethel Footman Smothers (1944–). Biography, Personal, Career, Honors, Awards, Writings, Sidelights. 2010. http://biography.jrank.org/pages/362/Smothers-Ethel-Footman-1944.html (accessed October 26, 2010).

Flake, Sharon. *Money Hungry.* New York: Hyperion Books, 2001.

Jacqueline Woodson: Author of books for children and young adults. 2002-2010. http://www.jacquelinewoodson.com/ (accessed 10 11, 2010).

Judy Cox (homepage). 2010. http://www.judycox.net/ (accessed October 26, 2010).

Karen English. Macmillan Books. 2008. http://us.macmillan.com/author/karenenglish (accessed October 26, 2010).

Mathis, Sharon Bell. *The Hundred Penny Box.* New York: Puffin Books/Penguin Books USA, 1975.

Morrison, Toni, and Slade Morrison. *Peeny Butter Fudge.* New York: A Paula Wiseman Book/Simon & Schuster Books for Young Readers, 2009.

Sharon Bell Mathis. The Brown Book Shelf. February 13, 2010.

Sharon G. Flake. 2008. http://www.sharongflake.com (accessed October 26, 2010).

Smothers, Ethel Footman. *The Hard-Times Jar.* New York: Frances Foster Books/Farrar, Straus & Giroux, 2003.

Toni Morrison Biography. Advameg. 2010. http://www.notablebiographies.com/Mo-Ni/Morrison-Toni.html (accessed October 30, 2010).

Woodson, Jacqueline. *Locomotion.* New York: Penguin Group, 2003.

Webliography

Freerice.com. World Food Programme. 2007–2010. http://www.freerice.com (accessed December 12, 2010).

grandchildren.com. n.d. http://grandchildren.com (accessed October 26, 2010).

Grandparents.com—For Grandparents, Parents and Grandchildren. 2007–2010. http://www.grandparents.com/gp/home/index.html (accessed October 26, 2010).

Homeless to Harvard—Part 1. n.d. http://www.youtube.com/watch?v=u4ZWngrvm0I (accessed December 12, 2010).

Locomotion Little Eva—MP3 Search & Free Mp2 Downloads. Beemp3.com. n.d. http://beemp3.com/index.php?q=locomotion+little+eva (accessed December 12, 2010).

National Coalition for Homeless. National Coalition for the Homeless. n.d. http://www.nationalhomeless.org/ (accessed December 12, 2010).

National Farm Worker Ministry. July 16, 2008. http://www.nfwm.org/fw/education.shtml (accessed October 26, 2010).

National Foster Care Month. n.d. http://www.fostercaremonth.org/Pages/default.aspx (accessed October 26, 2010).

National Hunger and Homeless Awareness Week. National Coalition for the Homeless. n.d. http://www.nationalhomeless.org/projects/awareness/index.html (accessed December 12, 2010).

NCHE—Legislative Resources. SERVE. n.d. http://center.serve.org/nche/legis_resources.php (accessed December 12, 2010).

Penny quotes and quotations. ThinkExist. 1999–2010. http://en.thinkexist.com/quotes/with/keyword/penny (accessed December 12, 2010).

"*Take My Hand, Precious Lord.*" National Public Radio. 2010. http://www.npr.org/templates/story/story.php?storyId=1069272 (accessed December 12, 2010).

The Teenager's Guide to the Real World Online. 1997. http://www.bygpub.com/ (accessed October 22, 2010).

Additional Reading Materials

Banks, Sara Harrell. *A Net to Catch Time.* New York: Alfred A. Knopf, 1997.

A young boy describes the joy of having a loving family and the excitement of going crabbing to earn money to be able to one day buy his own boat.

Battle-Lavert, Gwendolyn. *Papa's Mark.* New York: Holiday House, 2003.

A boy is determined to help his father learn how to write his name on the day that he travels into town to cast his vote for the first time. Determined not to allow an "X" to represent his political rights, Samuel T. Blow is learning how to write his name as well as to recognize it on paper.

Best, Cari. *Red Light, Green Light, Mama and Me.* New York: Orchard Books, 1995.

Red means stop and green means go. This book gives young readers the opportunity to read about a young girl who goes to work with her mother at the downtown public library one day. Her travels to the library are humorous as she describes her ride on the subway to downtown, being able to only look at shoes and toes. She stops with her mother to get a treat before arriving at the library. Upon her arrival, she is greeted by her mother's friends and invited to lunch. She helps her mother with story time, recommends a book to a reader, and she searches for an answer to a "why" question. What a day she has in the city! Young readers will get to share their experiences in big cities and how they use their public libraries.

Bradby, Marie. *More Than Anything Else.* New York: Orchard Books, 1995.

Nine-year-old Booker's family is very poor. His dream is to learn how to read, but he has no books—plus he must work with his father and brother in the salt mine. The work is very hard and wearing on Booker's body. He gets cuts on his hands, feet, and arms, but his passion to read is far greater than his pain. One day after they finish work, a crowd gathers around a brown man in a wagon reading a newspaper. Booker daydreams and visualizes the brown man being him one day, reading to the crowd. The next day after work, he goes home and tells his mother, "I want to read." She has known for a long time that this is his passion. One night she gives him a blue book. He takes the book and begins to try to understand the words. He looks for the brown man to help him. Once he figures out the words, he is very happy.

Caines, Jeannette. *Just Us Women.* New York: Scholastic, 1982.

A young girl and her aunt decide to take a scenic tour across North Carolina, leaving everyone else behind.

Fradin, Dennis Brindell. *My Family Shall Be Free! The Life of Peter Still.* New York: HarperCollins, 2001.

Peter Still was determined to free his family from the degradation of slavery. He was always looking for a way to set them free. Leaving his wife Vina and the children behind was the hardest thing he had ever done. Although he made several attempts to free her, she succumbed to the harsh environment when the lives of her children were threatened. Finally after much persuasion, Peter is told that he may buy his family's freedom for $5,000. Faced with countless obstacles, he would always rejuvenate himself by discovering new ways to earn the money necessary to free his family. Students will be able to use their math skills while tracking Peter as his travels take him to earn the money to purchase his family's freedom.

Gray, Libba Moore. *Little Lil and the Swing-Singing Sax.* New York: Simon & Schuster Books for Young Readers, 1996.

Little Lil, her mother Mama Lil, and Uncle Sudi, a saxophone player, all live together in a small apartment. The family is very poor. Uncle Sudi plays his sax by night to make people both happy and sad. When Mama Lil becomes ill, Uncle Sudi must pawn his saxophone for money to buy medicine for her. Without his instrument, Uncle Sudi wears a sad face, and Mama Lil shows no joy. Little Lil knows that she must do something to bring life and joy back to their little apartment. So she paints a picture and takes it to the owner of the pawn shop, Honest Dan, hoping to trade the picture for Uncle Sudi's sax. But what Honest Dan is most interested in is the ring that Mama Lil gave her that belonged to her great-grandmother. Little Lil must make a very important decision.

Greenfield, Eloise. *She Comes Bringing Me That Little Baby Girl.* New York: HarperCollins, 1993.

In this award-winning book, a young boy is disappointed with the baby sister his mother brings home from the hospital after he specifically asked for a little brother.

Grimes, Nikki. *What Is Goodbye?* New York: Hyperion Books for Children, 2004.

Nobody likes to discuss death. It's very hard to know exactly what to say to a grieving family during such a difficult time. In this book, Grimes finds a way to describe the feelings that most would find relevant to the pain and sorrow. Told from both the brother's and sister's points of view, the two siblings must find a way to cope with their feelings as well as those shared and those kept inside by other members of the immediate family.

Herron, Carolivia. ***Always an Olivia: A Remarkable Family History.*** **Minneapolis, MN: Kar-Ben, 2007.**

Families are special, and a young girl learns just how special and unique she is from the conversation she and her grandmother have about her diverse culture. Many children today come from blended families. This book describes just how unique individuals are.

Howard, Elizabeth Fitzgerald. ***Aunt Flossie's Hats (and Crab Cakes Later).*** **New York: Clarion Books/Houghton Mifflin, 1991.**

Two sisters look forward to visiting with their Great-Great-Aunt Flossie because they get to hear many interesting stories about her hats. Once Aunt Flossie tells her stories and makes the trip back from Memories Past, she takes the girls out for crab cakes.

Howard, Elizabeth Fitzgerald. ***What's in Aunt Mary's Room?*** **New York: Clarion Books, 1996.**

Readers will once again meet the two sisters and their Great-Great-Aunt Flossie. This time, they wonder what's behind the door in her house that had at one time belonged to Aunt Mary. Their uncertainty leads to an ABC game that they create, until the day comes to turn the lock and walk into the room. Howard's intriguing story keeps the reader determined to read every page carefully.

Johnston, Tony. ***Angel City.*** **New York: Philomel Books, 2006.**

Readers will learn that true love has no barriers—no matter the race, creed, or color. Often it is hard to imagine how people form relationships in life. Such is the case between an old black man who finds an abandoned child and raises him to develop an appreciation for both the Mexican American and African American cultures.

Kroll, Virginia. ***Africa Brothers and Sisters.*** **New York: Simon & Schuster Children's Publishing, 1993.**

Through a conversation between a young boy and his father as to why he doesn't have brothers or sisters, readers will learn much about the various tribes in Africa and what they're known to produce. This informative book cleverly identifies various African tribes and allows readers to use their imaginations to learn how they contribute to artistic and cultural craftsmanship.

Kroll, Virginia. ***Masai and I.*** **New York: Simon & Schuster Books, 1992.**

A young heroine daydreams of the transformation she would make if she and her family were part of the Masai people and lived in East Africa. The author allows the reader to travel with this young heroine as she ventures through the day-to-day activities common to this African cultural background. This book offers young people the chance to see a different world and spend time with a people whose cultural heritage is different from their own.

McKissack, Patricia C. ***Ma Dear's Aprons.*** **New York: Atheneum Books for Young Readers, 1997.**

What a clever way to teach children their colors and days of the week! This delightful book uses a small boy's description of his mother's daily work schedule. With a special job performed each day represented by a specific color, readers soon learn their colors and days of the week. Teacher and students can develop their own special work schedules by using the author's style.

Moss, Thylias. ***I Want to Be.*** **New York: Dial Books for Young Readers, 1993.**

The world is big and full of many choices that a young girl must consider as she seeks to determine her life's goals and ambitions. She observes many people and their daily occupations and decides to look for the best and for beauty in others, to be thoughtful of others, and to be active and ready to help and serve others.

Neasi, Barbara J. ***Listen to Me.*** **New York: Children's Press, 2001.**

Grandmothers will take the time to listen to their grandchildren. In this beginning-to-read book, it pleases a young boy to have so much time with his grandmother who allows him to talk as much and for as long as he desires.

Porter, Connie. ***Addy's Little Brother.*** **Middleton, WI: Pleasant, 2000.**

This historical fiction novel is part of the American Girl series that will also appeal to male readers. Addy is disappointed with her brother once he returns home from the war because he chooses to spend more time with a friend than with her.

Schertle, Alice. *Down the Road.* New York: Browndeer Press, 1995.

Hetty is given the responsibility of going into town for eggs. Excited to have such a big assignment from her parents, she purchases the eggs and heads for home. On the way, she avoids one catastrophe, but when she stops to pick wild apples, the unthinkable happens. The eggs roll from the basket, leaving her devastated. After a while, her father finds her high in the apple tree, where he decides to join her as they think things over. Realizing that her daughter and husband are both missing, Hetty's mother goes in search of her family. When she decides to join them in the tree, they climb down with new ideas. So instead of the eggs they wanted to have for breakfast, they have apple pie!

Tate, Eleanora E. *Celeste's Harlem Renaissance.* New York: Little, Brown and Company, 2007.

What would you do if you were told that you would be relocating without even having the opportunity to discuss the matter? This is the situation in which CeCe finds herself. After her mother's death and her father's illness, Aunt Society, who CeCe thinks dislikes her because of her skin color, ships CeCe off to New York to live with her Aunt Val. Upon her arrival, she learns that Val is not as successful as she thought, and CeCe is forced to work to help earn her keep. While in New York, she becomes part of the Renaissance explosion. When she returns back to the South to care for her now-ill Aunt Society, the flavor of the times, talents, and taste of this exciting period in New York follows her to fill the void.

Taylor, Mildred. *Song of the Trees.* New York: The Yearling, 1989.

This book is one of a series that can be used when students are assigned to do a comprehensive author study in elementary, middle, or secondary schools. Taylor uses her skills to tell the stories told to her by family members of the Logan family. She shares the courageous actions of Stacey, Cassie, Christopher-John, Little Man, their parents, and Big Mama living in the South during a time of unrest. Told by Cassie, the children are exposed to racism, discrimination, and segregation. They never waver from the strong bond and teachings of their parents and Big Mama. Cassie manages to escape many of the negative things around her by tuning into the songs led by the trees. While these books lend themselves to the challenges this family faced, readers will be able to identify elements in them that they have seen, heard, or experienced themselves.

Woodson, Jacqueline. *Peace, Locomotion.* New York: G. P. Putnam's Sons, 2009.

Orphaned from a fire that claimed the lives of both his parents, Lonnie T. Motion stays in constant touch with his sister, Lili. While both live in different foster homes, Lonnie makes an effort each day to keep his sister in his life no matter who else may open up their hearts to him.

Chapter 10

GROWING GIRLS

Share these self-esteem–building books and activities with your class and all students will benefit, particularly your female students. The activities provided will help students build self-confidence, learn ways to triumph over disappointment, and respect and tolerate differences.

Draper, Sharon M. *Sassy: Little Sister Is Not My Name!* New York: Scholastic, 2009.

About the Author

The Official Site of Sharon Draper. n.d. http://sharondraper.com (accessed October 11, 2010).

Literary Elements Parent's Choice Award Storytelling	**Lexile Range** 630L	**Teacher Resources and Supplies** Book Large Scarf Storytelling Bag Noise Makers
Reading Level 630L	**Accelerated Reader** Points: 3.0 Book Level: 3.8	
Additional Title Latifah, Queen. ***Queen of the Scene.*** **Websites** http://www.grandparents.com/gp/content/opinions/grand-perspectives/article/the-african-american-grandparenting.html http://42explore.com/story.htm http://www.childrenslibrary.org/icdl/ExhibitionPage?exhibition=4&ilang=English		

Brief Summary

This story is great bibliotherapy for young readers of every size because the author's words are encouraging to those who may lack self-confidence because of their body types. After reading this book, the reader will be convinced that size has nothing to do with one's ability to perform and that having the skills to get things done is of far greater importance than physical stature.

Focus

- Family Life
- Grandmothers
- Genres
- Storytelling

Teacher Input

- Introduce this book by telling the class a story about a character who lacked self-confidence because she was small.
- Ask the students to comment on whether they think that having the support of family members is important to people believing they can accomplish something.

Guided Practice

- Have the students discuss why it was easy for Sassy to identify with her Grammy.
- Assign students to write and tell about one way in which size did matter when they wanted to get involved in an event.
- Ask students to share their views by telling what they liked and disliked about Sabin and Sadora, Sassy's siblings.
- Have students select a good story for telling based on their research from the following website: http://42explore.com/story.htm.
- Have students write a poem titled "This Is Who I Am."
- Have students debate why they should or should not wear school uniforms.

Independent Practice

- Suggest that students design and make crafts for ***"It's in the Bag" and "Let's Make Some Sounds Up in Here" Day.***

Closure

- Host a Student Bag and Storytelling Day. Allow students to invite their grandmothers to participate in the event.

Assessment

- Student interest and involvement, project design, and presentations.

Greenfield, Eloise. *Me & Neesie.* New York: HarperCollins/Amistad, 1975.

About the Author

Eloise Greenfield. Scholastic.com. n.d. http://www2.scholastic.com/browse/contributor.jsp?id=3186 (accessed October 22, 2010).

Literary Element Reading Aloud	**Lexile Range** —	**Teacher Resources and Supplies** Book Worksheet
Reading Level Preschool–Grade 3	**Accelerated Reader** Points: 0.5 Book Level: 2.8	
Additional Title Stuve-Bodeen, Stephanie. ***Elizabeti's Doll.*** **Websites** http://www.familyresource.com/parenting/character-development/imaginary-friends-should-you-be-concerned		

Brief Summary

Janelle enjoys the friendship of her imaginary friend Neesie—until she goes to school! Janelle's Aunt Bea realizes that Janelle may be seeing a ghost and takes her walking stick to get rid of it. Janelle's invisible friend doesn't want to go to school, so while Janelle is in school, Neesie meets some new friends and disappears. Janelle is unable to find Neesie when she returns home. Janelle decides not to tell her school friends about Neesie.

Focus

- Imaginary Friend
- Parents, Grandmothers
- School Friends

Teacher Input

- Invite students to tell whether they ever had an imaginary friend.
- Distribute the worksheet "***Drawing My Imaginary Friend Contest Forms and The Friend Game Cards***" to each student.

Guided Practice

- Invite students with imaginary friends to participate in the contest by drawing a picture of their imaginary friend. Students without such friends can serve as judges to determine the "largest, most unusual, best looking, and the imaginary friend they would like to adopt."
- Have students discuss and provide reasons why Aunt Bea used her cane to get rid of the ghost she thought might be on the sofa.
- Ask students to assess Aunt Bea's reaction to Neesie and to determine whether they think Aunt Bea already knew about the imaginary friend. If so, who do they think told her this information? Why?
- Have students list five reasons why they feel Janelle needed Nessie.

- Ask students to discuss and give reasons why they believe Neesie couldn't be found when Janelle returned home from school.

Independent Practice

- Suggest that each student participate in "The Friend Game." For Show and Tell, have students bring their blankets, stuffed animals, or whatever other items they cuddled and loved as a young child.

Closure

- Hold a "***My Best Friend Day***" to give students the opportunity to share things about their friends. Also, this is a great time for students to meet new friends.

Assessment

- Student interest, discussions, classroom, and project presentations.

Harper, Hill. *Letters to a Young Sister: Define Your Destiny.* New York: Gotham Books, 2008.

About the Author

Hill Harper—Letters to a Young Sister (interview). http://www.youtube.com/watch?v=ZPwu10m0Vyw
http://www.manifestyourdestiny.org

Literary Elements Guidance Storytelling Writing	**Lexile Range** —	**Teacher Resources and Supplies** Book Stationery Worksheet
Reading Level Grades 6 and up	**Accelerated Reader** Points: 16.0 Book Level: 6–9	
Additional Titles Flake, Sharon G. ***Who Am I Without Him?*** Harper, Hill. ***Letters to a Young Brother: MANifest Your Destiny.*** **Websites** http://www.youtube.com/watch?v=ZPwu10m0Vyw http://www.youtube.com/watch?v=s9ZSlWDXyJE http://www.bet.com/specials/blackgirlsrock/		

Brief Summary

Many people are familiar with Mary McLeod Bethune's written legacy, *My Last Will and Testament.* In addition to this great educator's passion for learning, she wanted to share her "principles and policies" for leading a productive life with others as inspiration. Hill Harper's book is a contemporary version of Bethune's philosophy. This resource provides great words of wisdom from men and women representing every walk of life. Young African American girls connect with and are encouraged by the advice given in these letters by the role models featured in the book.

Focus

- Girls
- Self-Esteem
- Role Models

Teacher Input

- Introduce this book by presenting some of these online resources:
    - http://www.youtube.com/watch?v=ZPwu10m0Vyw
    - http://www.youtube.com/watch?v=s9ZSlWDXyJE
    - http://www.bet.com/specials/blackgirlsrock/
- Discuss how important it is to an individual to have the support of family, civic and community leaders, and social groups.

Guided Practice

- Have students discuss and identify the characteristics of a positive role model.
- Have the class debate the following statement: "Being a successful man or woman does not mean someone is successful at being a great role model."
- Have the students use Google to research additional information about one person in each of the five chapters found in Harper's book. Have them then tell why they chose these characters.

Independent Practice

- Have students write letters to one of the people they chose.

Closure

- Have the students present their letters.

Assessment

- Student interest and involvement, project design, and presentations.

Letters Full of Hope

Part One: **Empowerment 3.0**		Michelle Obama Tavis Smiley Eve Alfre Woodard Ciara Sanaa Lathan Nikki Giovanni
Part Two: **Relationships, Family, Friends, and Boys**		Jasmine Guy Shar Jackson Chanel Iman Nia Long Kim Porter Blair Underwood Terri J. Vaughn Shahdae Janelle Holland Ruby Dee
Part Three: **Overcoming Obstacles**		Niecy Nash Kenya Moore Devynity Cathy Hughes Dr. S. Elizabeth Ford Chariesse Griffin Bishop Noel Jones
Part Four: **Your Future**		Dr. Melissa Nobles Marvet Britto Christina M. Gomes Angela Basset Nicole Loftus Candace Bond McKeever Sharla Crow
Part Five: **The Wonderment of Life**		Congresswoman Carolyn Cheeks Kilpatrick Malinda Williams Tatyana Ali Zoe Saldana

Johnson, Angela. *Heaven.* New York: Simon & Schuster, 1998.

About the Author

Angela Johnson. AALBC.com. 1997–2010. http://aalbc.com/authors/angela.htm (accessed October 10, 2010).

Literary Elements	Lexile Range	Teacher Resources and Supplies
ALA Best Book for Young Adults Coretta Scott King Book Award Heaven Trilogy	790L	Book
Reading Level Grades 6 and up	**Accelerated Reader** Points: 3.0 Book Level: 4.7	
Additional Title Childress, Alice. ***Rainbow Jordan.*** **Websites** http://www.youtube.com/watch?v=2enmrczF0oc http://books.simonandschuster.com/Heaven/Angela-Johnson/9780689822292/reading_group_guide http://www.squidoo.com/about-sunflowers		

Brief Summary

Knowing the truth can hurt, especially when you feel like you've been betrayed by someone you once admired for his or her bravery and bold expeditions. Much to her surprise, a fourteen-year-old must face these facts while putting together the pieces of her life, realizing that she was living with people she loved but who were not her biological parents.

Focus

- Adopted Families
- Uncles
- Expeditions

Teacher Input

- Introduce Shirley Caesar's song "Heaven" Using the following website: http://www.youtube.com/watch?v=2enmrczF0oc.
- Ask students to share what they know about heaven.
- Share additional information about Johnson's book by using the following resource: http://books.simonandschuster.com/Heaven/Angela-Johnson/9780689822292/reading_group_guide.
- Ask students to explain how Marley and her family settled in Heaven, Ohio.
- Invite students to discuss and name extended family members who have made a difference in their lives.
- Invite students to tell what they enjoy about hanging out with their families.
- Assign students to define the word "expedition" and use online resources to locate maps of where Uncle Jack's travels took him.

Guided Practice

- Have students discuss how Marley's mother decided they would make their home in Heaven, Ohio.
- Suggest that students use online resources to find additional information about the beauty and many uses of the sunflower: http://www.squidoo.com/about-sunflowers.
- Have students write an essay titled "Why I Like Hanging Out With My Family."
- Have students discuss what they liked best about "Shoogy" and explain why she needed counseling.
- Invite students to express their feelings about Uncle Jack's not telling Marley the truth about who he was and whether her adopted parents should have told her about her past before she found out on her own.

Independent Practice

- Suggest that students take photos of their dogs or use online graphics and sponsor a "Photographic Silent Dog Show." The silent show must consist of a flip chart or PowerPoint of five slides that include describing the dog, identifying the breed, and caring for dog.

Closure

- Have students share writings and projects.

Assessment

- Student discussions, brainstorming, and project designs.

McKissack, Patricia C. *Loved Best.* New York: Aladdin Paperbacks/An Imprint of Simon & Schuster Children's Publishing, 2005.

About the Author

Patricia C. McKissack. http://authors.simonandschuster.com/Patricia-C-McKissack/1763349/biography

Literary Element Drama	**Lexile Range** 560L	**Teacher Resources and Supplies**
		Book Yardstick and rulers
Reading Level Grades 1–5	**Accelerated Reader** Points: 1.0 Book Level: 3.6	
Additional Title Smith, Patricia. ***Janna and the Kings.*** **Websites** http://pbskids.org/itsmylife/family/sibrivalry/ http://raisingchildren.net.au/articles/sibling_rivalry_video.html/context/1105		

Brief Summary

In this book, a young girl tries to justify why age should be the main reason for her parents loving her more since she is the oldest of the three children. The author takes the reader on a humorous and sometimes disappointing journey to teach the young protagonist a valuable lesson about true love, which can never be measured or found in history books but must come from the heart.

Focus

- Sibling Rivalry
- School Play, Drama
- Family Support System

Teacher Input

- Bring a yardstick and rulers to class. Give each student a ruler to participate in a measurement activity.
- Ask students to discuss their families and share how they spend time together.

Guided Practice

- Have students list words that mean someone is strong and important.
- Invite students to discuss Carolyn's performance in the school play and tell why it was not her best.
- Have students tell what Carolyn's father did to restore her confidence.
- Ask students to determine whether Carolyn was a good example for her siblings. Was she jealous of them? If so, provide examples.
- Have students list ways that Carolyn tried to lure her entire family into her selfish way of thinking.

- Invite students to measure their love for family members. Students should brainstorm whether they will be able to make such an assessment.

Independent Practice

- Suggest that students develop a news bulletin on one of these topics: "**What's It Like to Have Siblings**" ***or*** "***What's It Like Being an Only Child.***" http://www.kidzworld.com/article/5950-siblings-in-sports

Closure

- Invite students to share their news bulletins.

Assessment

- Student discussions, classroom sharing, and project presentation.

Smith, Jada Pinkett. *Girls Hold Up This World.* Photographs by Donyell Kennedy-McCullough. New York: Scholastic, 2005.

About the Author

Jada Pinkett Smith: Biography. Answers.com. 2010. http://www.answers.com/topic/jada-pinkett-smith (accessed October 29, 2010).

Literary Element Self-esteem	**Lexile Range** —	**Teacher Resources and Supplies**
Reading Level Grades 1–3	**Accelerated Reader** Points: 0.5 Book Level: 2.3	Book Still camera Flip camera Video camera

Additional Titles
Fornay, Alfred. ***Born Beautiful: The African American Teenager's Complete Beauty Guide.***
Johnson, Jen Cullerton. ***Seeds of Change.***
Simmons, Cassandra Walker. ***Becoming Myself: True Stories About Learning from Life.***

Website
http://www.studentphoto.com/i4a/pages/index.cfm?pageid=1

Brief Summary

This is a book of praise and encouragement for girls in the twenty-first century. Each page depicts at least one photo of a beautiful girl accompanied by empowering and inspiring text. The author allows the reader to enjoy the colorful illustrations while opening the doors for girls to claim their rightful place in history during various stages of growth.

Focus

- Self-esteem
- Gender—Girls
- Discipline

Teacher Input

- Show and discuss different types of cameras with the class.
- Demonstrate how different cameras are used to record various events.
- Introduce the word "discipline" to class and give its meaning, along with examples.
- Distribute index cards to each student and have each list ways of showing kindness and why it is important to show kindness daily.
- Group students into two or more teams. Assign each team a writing task.

Guided Practice

- Have students discuss why the author wrote that "Kindness takes hard work."
- Ask students to explain what the word "blessing" means to them.

- Allow students to choose from one of the two writing prompts below. Each report must include two photos taken by a member on the team to support their writing project:
    1. "I Am Beautiful Because . . ." (Self-esteem)
    2. "I See the Beauty That You Wear." (The way that you present yourself)
- Lead students in assessing how the new generation of girls differs from girls of long ago. Consider race, culture, social involvement, and school integration.
- Allow students to choose the best color of construction paper for making hearts to show love.

Independent Practice

- Suggest that each student create a PowerPoint "***Photo Biography***" consisting of at least five photos taken using a digital or flip camera. The biography can be titled, "Here's My Heart."

Closure

- Invite the school's photographer or a newspaper or television photographer to discuss types of careers in photography with the class.

Assessment

- Student interests in writing and project design and project presentation.

Woodson, Jacqueline. *Feathers.* New York: G. P. Putnam's & Sons/The Penguin Young Readers Group, 2007.

About the Author

Jacqueline Woodson: Author of Books for Children and Young Adults. 2002–2010. http://www.jacquelinewoodson.com/ (accessed October 11, 2010).

Literary Element Reading Aloud	**Lexile Range** —	**Teacher Resources and Supplies** Book Feathers
Reading Level Grades 6–8	**Accelerated Reader** AR points: 4.0 Book Level: 4.4	
Additional Title English, Karen. ***Francie.*** **Websites** http://www.stopbullyingnow.hrsa.gov/kids http://academic.brooklyn.cuny.edu/English/melani/cs6/hope.html		

Brief Summary

This encouraging book tells its readers never to lose hope in the midst of a struggle. Frannie's life and surroundings are typical until she meets the Jesus Boy. This new boy manages to give hope to those who have none; to give those who are afraid of the classroom bully a chance to stand up; and to give those with prejudices and seem too blind to see the real person an opportunity to see that people can be kind, gentle, and forgiving.

Focus

- Hope
- Bullying
- Faith

Teacher Input

- Read aloud Emily Dickinson's poem "***Hope Is the Thing With Feathers***" available at http://academic.brooklyn.cuny.edu/english/melani/cs6/hope.html.
- Lead the class in a discussion about ways that individuals can enhance their self-esteem.
- Invite students to share what they understand about ***Hope.***
- Define the terms "surreal" and "bilingual" for the students and ensure they understand their meaning.

Guided Practice

- Ask students to comment on why a person should not be judged by his or her skin color.
- Have students describe Trevor's behavior and determine whether the new boy was afraid of him.
- Assign students to write a poem about feathers.
- Have students brainstorm about the "One Thing They Have in Common."

Independent Practice

- Suggest that students write their life stories for sharing by creating a brochure or producing a Photo Story or PowerPoint presentation titled "***My Life Story.***"

Closure

- Allow the students to share their poems and projects.

Assessment

- Student participation, interest, and projects.

Bibliography

Angela Johnson. AALBC.com. 1997–2010. http://aalbc.com/authors/angela.htm (accessed October 10, 2010).

Draper, Sharon M. *Sassy: Little Sister Is Not My Name!* New York: Scholastic, 2009.

Eloise Greenfield. Scholastic.com. n.d. http://www2.scholastic.com/browse/contributor.jsp?id=3186 (accessed October 22, 2010).

Greenfield, Eloise. *Me & Neesie.* New York: HarperCollins/Amistad, 1975.

Harper, Hill. *Letters to a Young Sister: Define Your Destiny.* New York: Gotham Books, 2008.

Hill Harper—Letters to a Young Sister (Interview). n.d. http://www.youtube.com/watch?v=ZPwu10m0Vyw (accessed December 14, 2010).

Hill Harper—Letters to a Young Sister (Interview). ForRealSolutions.com. October 18, 2008. http://www.manifestyourdestiny.org/HillHarper/videos/view/8?item=19&type=Video (accessed December 14, 2010).

Jacqueline Woodson: Author of Books for Children and Young Adults. 2002–2010. http://www.jacquelinewoodson.com/ (accessed October 11, 2010).

Jada Pinkett Smith: Biography. Answers.com. 2010. http://www.answers.com/topic/jada-pinkett-smith (accessed October 29, 2010).

Jeanette Winter. Macmillan Books. 2008. http://us.macmillan.com/author/jeanettewinter (accessed October 29, 2010).

Johnson, Angela. *Heaven.* New York: Simon & Schuster, 1998.

McKissack, Patricia C. *Loved Best.* New York: Aladdin Paperbacks/An Imprint of Simon & Schuster Children's Publishing, 2005.

Patricia C. McKissack Biography. Simon & Schuster. n.d. http://authors.simonandschuster.com/Patricia-C-McKissack/1763349/biography (accessed October 29, 2010).

Queen Laifah. DBurns Designs. n.d. http://www.queenlatifah.com/ (accessed October 29, 2010).

Queen Latifah. *Queen of the Scene.* New York: HarperCollins, 2006.

Smith, Jada Pinkett. *Girls Hold Up This World.* New York: Scholastic, 2005.

Welcome to the Official Site of Sharon Draper. n.d. http://sharondraper.com (accessed October 11, 2010).

Winter, Jeanette. *Wangari's Trees of Peace.* Florida: Harcourt, 2008.

Woodson, Jacqueline. *Feathers.* New York: G. P. Putnam's & Sons/The Penguin Young Readers Group, 2007.

Woodson, Jacqueline. *The Other Side.* New York: G. P. Putnam's Sons, 2001.

Webliography

The African American Grandparenting Experience. Grandparents.com. 2007-10. http://www.grandparents.com/gp/content/opinions/grand-perspectives/article/the-african-american-grandparenting.html (accessed November 1, 2010).

AR BookFinder US—Quick Search. Renaissance Learning. 2010. http://www.arbookfind.com/Default.aspx (accessed December 7, 2010).

August Wilson (biography). http://www.gale.cengage.com/free_resources/bhm/bio/wilson_a.htm

The Beauty and Benefits of Sunflowers. Squidoo. 2010. http://www.squidoo.com/about-sunflowers (accessed December 12, 2010).

Black Girls Rock 2010. BET Networks. 2010. http://www.bet.com/specials/blackgirlsrock (accessed December 15, 2010).

Books: Heaven: Reading Group Guide. Simon & Schuster. n.d. http://books.simonandschuster.com/Heaven/Angela-Johnson/9780689822292/reading_group_guide (accessed December 12, 2010).

Caesar, Shirley. "*Heaven.*" n.d. http://www.youtube.com/watch?v=2enmrczF0oc (accessed December 12, 2010).

Denzel Back on Broadway in "Fences" Revival. Liquida Video. n.d. http://www.liquida.com/video/a596ab93e/denzel-back-on-broadway-in-fences-revival (accessed December 16, 2010).

Dickinson, Emily. *Hope.* http://academic.brooklyn.cuny.edu/english/melani/cs6/hope.html (accessed December 17, 2010).

Exhibition: Strong Women and Girls Make the World Go Round. n.d. http://www.childrenslibrary.org/icdl/ExhibitionPage?exhibition=4&ilang=English (accessed December 15, 2010).

Lamb, Annette, and Larry Johnson. *Storytelling.* October 2002. http://42explore.com/story.htm (accessed December 12, 2010).

The Lexile Framework for Reading. Lexile.com. MetaMetrics. 2010. http://lexile.com/ (accessed November 2, 2010).

May All Your Fences Have Gates. n.d. http://books.google.com/books?id=9J7DW-lXBp8C&pg=PA86&lpg=PA86&dq= building+racial+fences&source=bl&ots=r7s-pabTek&sig=RfHrQPLvUtfFnsAXXs3eyWlkFrk&hl=en&ei=En0KTa_ZFIOdlgeWtvXaAQ&sa=X&oi=book_result&ct=result&resnum=4&ved=0CC4Q6AEwAw#v=onepage&q&f=false (accessed December 16, 2010).

The O'Jays. *She's Only a Woman.* n.d. http://www.youtube.com/watch?v=s9ZSlWDXyJE (accessed December 15, 2010).

Sibling Rivalry. Raising Children Network. 2006–2010. http://raisingchildren.net.au/articles/sibling_rivalry_video.html/context/1105 (accessed December 16, 2010).

"Sibling Rilvary, You vs. Them." *It's My Life.* PBS Kids GO! CastleWorks Inc. 2005. http://pbskids.org/itsmylife/family/sibrivalry (accessed November 3, 2010).

Siblings in Sports. Serena & Venus Williams. Bonde & Tiki Barber. Eli & Pe. Kidzworld. 2010. http://www.kidzworld.com/article/5950-siblings-in-sports (accessed December 16, 2010).

Stop Bullying Now! n.d. http://stopbullyingnow.hrsa.gov/kids/ (accessed October 10, 2010).

Additional Reading Materials

Armstrong, Stephanie Covington. *Not All Black Girls Know How to Eat: A Story of Bulimia.* Chicago: Lawrence Hill Books, 2009.

In this book, the author discusses an eating disorder she had for many years before finally coming to grips with it and writing to help others with the same problem. Readers will readily identify with the trials and issues some black girls face as they transition from being a girl to a young woman.

Greenfield, Eloise. *Sister.* New York: Random House, 1974.

In this book, Greenfield shows how two sisters handle the death of their father very differently. While the older sister, Alberta, is free to go and do as she pleases, the younger girl, Sister, dreams of staying out of trouble and wishes the same for Alberta. As she grows older, Sister realizes that she has some of the same traits as Alberta. Alberta is no longer staying in the home, and Sister longs to have her return so she can talk with her, share her thoughts that she has recorded in a diary, and get the guidance and advice from her that could keep her out of trouble.

Hamilton, Virginia. *Dustland.* New York: Scholastic Inc., 1998.

What if you were different from other kids your age? What if you had powers that only you and your siblings could control? What would you do, and who would you tell? In this book, Hamilton provides another great science fiction read for loyal readers. Unlike Madeleine L'Engle's characters in ***A Wrinkle in Time***, who were caught in a "tesseract," Virginia Hamilton's sibling characters are in ***Dustland*** which is Book Two of the Justice Trilogy. Arriving in Dustland could lead to their end. However, with Justice's extrasensory powers, she saves their lives from the evil one and they're able to return home.

Harrington, Janice N. *The Chicken Chasing Queen of Lamar County.* New York: Farrar, Straus & Giroux, 2007.

How would you like to be queen for a day? Many young girls long to have such an opportunity. Lamar County had its own unique queen, known as the Queen of Chickens. While Grandma tells her to leave the chickens alone, she waits for her chance to go chasing after the barnyard birds. Even chasing chickens can be a challenge when the fastest chicken, Miss Hen, is never caught and disappears from the barnyard. Determined to catch Miss Hen at any cost, she finds the chicken and much more. Now she can hardly wait for her little surprises to grow up so that she can teach them how to run across the barnyard and never get caught.

Sanders, Dori. *Clover.* Chapel Hill, NC: Algonquin Books, 1990.

A young African American girl named Clover must come to grips with the fact that her father has married a white woman. Then her father dies, and although Clover was resentful of her stepmother before that event, she comes to defend Sara Kate because she realizes that true love is color blind and that people whose hearts are not open to truth often miss seeing it.

Smith, Patricia. *Janna and the Kings.* New York: Lee & Low Books, 2003.

Janna's trips with her granddaddy to the barbershop on Saturday mornings, where she becomes Princess Sugarlump, are very special because they share greetings and kind words with people along the way. In fact, the author's words begin to build excitement and expectations for the reader as soon as she leaves the house with her granddaddy. Always respectful of what Janna has to contribute to whatever conversation they have, Janna's self-esteem is high. But one morning, Janna's mother has to share some very sad news with her about her granddaddy. Hearing the words "Granddaddy's heart has gone to sleep" is terribly painful. Trying hard to ease the pain of her loneliness and grief, one morning Janna decides to walk, not knowing exactly where she is going. She finds herself at Terrell's Barbershop. The Kings see her lingering outside and invite her in, calling her by that familiar name of Princess Sugarlump. As the Kings involve her in their conversations once again, she feels the spirit of her granddaddy very near.

Woodson, Jacqueline. *I Hadn't Meant to Tell You This.* New York: Laurel Leaf, 1995.

An African American girl named Marie and a white girl named Lena become friends when their personal circumstances are more important than racial division and cultural differences. Both girls are without their mothers. Marie's mother seems too busy for her and Lena's is deceased. Lena tells Marie a secret about her father and what he does to her that she can no longer keep to herself, hoping that one day her life will change. Thinking of a way out for Lena, Marie is often distracted. Readers will discover that this friendship makes it easier for both girls to be more tolerant because they rely on each other. Woodson wrote this book at a time when many found it difficult to discuss issues such as incest.

Chapter 11

HISTORIC SITES, LANDMARKS, AND PLACES

Teach students about the wonders of traveling in their own United States. These books and activities cover historic places, events, and happenings and the geographic locations where they occurred. Students will learn how to read a map and plan a trip and how the library can open up a world of adventure to its visitors.

Curtis, Nancy C. *Black Heritage Sites: The North.* New York: The New Press, 1990.

Literary Elements	Lexile Range	Teacher Resources and Supplies
African American Studies Choice Outstanding Academic Book Award Guidebooks History Nonfiction Regions Travel United States	—	Book
Reading Level Grades: K–12	**Accelerated Reader** —	
Additional Title Curtis, Nancy C. ***Black Heritage Sites: The South.*** **Websites** http://creativefolk.com/travel/canada.html http://www.ferris.edu/jimcrow		

Brief Summary

In this volume, students will learn many interesting facts about people and events, as well as the geographic location where these historic happenings occurred. Included in this book are black-and-white photos and map shapes. This is a great reference tool to supplement the teaching of social studies and map skills.

Focus

- Historic Sites and Landmarks
- Churches and Museums
- Map Skills and Geographic Regions

Teacher Input

- Ask students to name local parks and recreation centers in their communities. Have them tell how those parks were named and why.
- Show online resources of African American historic sites and places, located in both the United States and Canada. Use the following website to assist in this activity: http://creativefolk.com/travel/canada.html.

Guided Practice

- Have students examine the contents of this book and use its format as a guide for writing a description of their communities. Have them list the contributions that African Americans have made to the school, churches, and community.
- Have students develop plans for a Peace Park reflecting the dreams and unity of people working together. In this design, students will draw pictures or use five images of African Americans who worked for harmony and peace.
- Instruct students to write a speech titled "We Carry Their Legacies—No Matter the Color."
- Take students on a virtual trip to the Jim Crow Museum to discover how the word "Jim Crow" originated and to learn more about the origin and contents of the museum.

Independent Practice

- Suggest that students create slideshows consisting of pictures, articles, and maps and then identify historic sites.

Closure

- Students give their speeches to the class and present their projects.

Assessment

- Student collaboration, discussions, and project presentation.

Duncan, Alice Faye. *The National Civil Rights Museum Celebrates Everyday People.* Mahwah, NJ: Bridgewater Books, 1995.

About the Author

Alice Faye Duncan. n.d. http://www.alicefayeduncan.com/bio/index.htm (accessed October 29, 2010).

Literary Elements	Lexile Range	Teacher Resources and Supplies
Art Biography Civil Rights Music Nonfiction Religious United States History	—	Book
Reading Level All grades	**Accelerated Reader** —	
Additional Title Parker, Toni Trent. ***Sienna's Scrapbook.*** **Websites** http://www.thekingcenter.org http://www.civilrightsmuseum.org/home.htm (Memphis, Tennessee) http://www.sitinmovement.org (Greensboro, North Carolina) http://www.bcri.org/index.html http://www.mlkonline.net/video.html http://school.discoveryeducation.com/lessonplans/programs/freeatlast		

Brief Summary

The historical account of how the Lorraine Motel became a museum is both heartbreaking and inspiring—heartbreaking because it provides a vivid description of an ordinary man whose life became extraordinary because of his unselfish work for humankind. Dr. Martin Luther King, Jr. lived a life for people he did not know, and his work and actions provided hope for all who knew him. From the bus ride with Rosa Parks to the Lorraine Motel to march with sanitation workers, he rode, walked, talked, and preached nonviolence.

Focus

- Lorraine Motel, Memphis, Tennessee
- Dr. Martin Luther King, Jr.
- Activists, Everyday People

Teacher Input

- Show a bus, plasticware, and a schoolbook to present this lesson to students.
- Ask the students to identify a "peace sign" and to define the word "synergy."

- Lead students in a discussion about ways they can serve as peacemakers and problem solvers in today's world.
- Introduce and discuss other African American personalities who stayed at the Lorraine Motel. Refer to this site for educational resources: http://school.discoveryeducation.com/lessonplans/programs/freeatlast.

Guided Practice

- Assign students to analyze the information about people featured in this book—from Dr. King to the sanitation workers in Tennessee—to determine that "everyday people" made a difference.
- Allow students to listen to and interpret what Dr. King is saying to ordinary people about service at this website: http://www.thekingcenter.org.
- Assign students to work in seven teams to collect facts about the activists and describe in their own words information about Rosa Parks, the Montgomery Bus Boycott, the Little Rock Nine, student sit-ins, the Freedom Riders, the March on Washington, and other protests.
- Invite students to evaluate and/or debate whether Presidents John F. Kennedy and Lyndon B. Johnson supported the protestors.

Independent Practice

- Suggest that the seven student groups develop a ***Travel Guide*** using PowerPoint for promoting the National Civil Rights Museum.

Closure

- Invite the curator to share additional information about the museum with the students through e-mail or a brief online video.

Assessment

- Student discussions, brainstorming, student participation, and project design.

Robinson, Wayne C. *The African-American Travel Guide*. Walpole, MA: Hunter Publishing, 1998.

About the Author

Wayne Robinson. IndieGoGo. n.d. http://www.indiegogo.com/wayne2 (accessed December 14, 2010).

Literary Elements	Lexile Range	Teacher Resources and Supplies
Geographic Regions Guides Social Science Travel Math	—	Book Paper Digital camera Worksheet
Reading Level Grades 6 and up	**Accelerated Reader** —	
Additional Title Hansen, Joyce. ***Breaking Ground, Breaking Silence: The Story of New York's African Burial Ground*** (Coretta Scott King Author Honor Book). **Websites** http://www.nps.gov/history/nr/feature/afam http://www.soulofamerica.com http://www.suite101.com/content/general-geographic-regions-of-the-united-states-a219525		

Brief Summary

This guide takes the reader to various historical African American sites across North America. The eighteen chapters—two of which cover provinces in Canada—provide readers and travelers with information about historic sites and landmarks, museums, exhibits, and a lot more.

Focus

- Historic Sites and Landmarks, Museums and Exhibits
- Educational Institutions, Historic Churches

Teacher Input

- Introduce this book by showing students an online resource of African American historical landmarks in the United States.
- Talk about the formation of the United States and show students how it is divided into regions.
- Define and discuss the various types of guidebooks available to researchers and travelers.

Guided Practice

- Have students identify and select the correct geographic regions for each state listed in Robinson's book by using online map resources.

- Ask students to explain why the King Center is relevant to the Civil Rights movement.
- Have students develop an outline explaining why the Mary McLeod Bethune Statue in Washington, DC, was erected.
- Assign students to collect data about the Harriet Tubman House and tell why Harriet Tubman was called the "Black Moses."
- Allow students to review the travel guide and plan at least three trips for tourists to one of three cities in the United States, as well as a trip to one of the provinces in Canada. Have students follow the directions listed on the ***"I'll Take You There" Worksheet.***

Independent Practice

- Suggest that each student design and develop a travel guide for an interesting site or landmark in their town, city, or state.

Closure

- Present student reports and projects.

Assessment

- Student discussions, student group participation, and project reporting.

"I'll Take You There" Worksheet

Location:	http://www.ny.com/museums/schomburg.center.for.research.in.black.culture.html List one fact:
Location:	http://www.nps.gov/nr/travel/atlanta/kin.htm List one fact:
Location:	http://www.louisarmstronghouse.org/visiting/overview.htm
List the name and location of African American museums by viewing this website: http://www.blackmuseums.org.	
Location:	Museum Type
	1.
	2.
	3.
	4.
	5.

Use the travel guide to plan three trips. The following website will serve as a reference: http://www.suite101.com/content/general-geographic-regions-of-the-united-states-a219525.

Name of city and geographic region:

Starting point and end of destination:

Number of miles and travel time:

Name of city and geographic region:

Starting point and end of destination:

Number of miles and travel time:

Name of city and geographic region:

Starting point and end of destination:

Number of miles and travel time:

Bibliography

African American Historic Places. National Register of Historic Places, National Park Service. Edited by Beth L. Savage. Washington, DC: The Preservation Press/John Wiley & Sons, 1994.

Curtis, Nancy C. *Black Heritage Sites: The North.* New York: The New Press, 1990.

Duncan, Alice Faye. *The National Civil Rights Museum Celebrates Everyday People.* Mahwah, NJ: Bridgewater Books, 1995.

McKissack, Patricia C. *Goin' Someplace Special.* New York: Atheneum Books for Young Readers, 2001.

Robinson, Wayne C. *The African-American Travel Guide.* Walpole, MA: Hunter Publishing, 1998.

Webliography

African American Historic Places. Google Books. n.d. Go to http://books.google.com and insert the book title in the search field (accessed December 18, 2010).

Association of African American Museums. 2008. http://www.blackmuseums.org (accessed December 19, 2010).

Birmingham Civil Rights Institute. 2010. http://www.bcri.org/index.html (accessed December 16, 2010).

Black Travel Guides, Photos, Videos, Reviews, Deals, Community, Maps, Events. Soul of America. 1997–2010. http://www.soulofamerica.com (accessed November 6, 2010).

The Civil Rights Movement—Lesson Plan Library. Discovery Education. 2010. http://school.discoveryeducation.com/lessonplans/programs/freeatlast (accessed December 19, 2010).

eFieldTrips. Distance Learning Integrators. 2002–2009. http://www.efieldtrips.org/dredscott (accessed December 18, 2010).

Field Trips—African American History and Education Underground. The Gist of Freedom. 2009–2010. http://www.thegistoffreedom.com/Field_Trips.html (accessed Decembeer 18, 2010).

Gribi, Gerri. *Black Heritage Travel—Canada.* African American Heritage.com. January 30, 2009. http://creativefolk.com/travel/canada.html (accessed December 18, 2010).

International Children's Digital Library. n.d. http://en.childrenslibrary.org (accessed December 19, 2010).

The International Civil Rights Center and Museum. December 11, 2010. http://www.sitinmovement.or (accessed December 16, 2010).

ipl2: Information You Can Trust. College of Information Science and Technology. The iSchool at Drexel. 2009. http://www.ipl.org (accessed December 19, 2010).

Jim Crow Museum of Racist Memorabilia at Ferris State University. n.d. http://www.ferris.edu/jimcrow (accessed November 4, 2010).

K–12 School Libraries Directory. Yahoo. 2010. http://dir.yahoo.com/Reference/libraries/school_libraries (accessed December 19, 2010).

The King Center. n.d. http://www.thekingcenter.org (accessed December 7, 2010).

Library of Congress for Teachers. n.d. http://www.loc.gov/teachers (accessed December 15, 2010).

List of Museums Focused on African Americans. Wikipedia, the Free Encyclopedia. September 12, 2010. http://en.wikipedia.org/wiki/List_of_museums_focused_on_African_Americans (accessed December 19, 2010).

Louis Armstrong House Museum. 2008. http://www.louisarmstronghouse.org/visiting/overview.htm (accessed December 19, 2010).

Martin Luther King Video: Watch Full Length Videos of Dr. King's I Have a Dream Speech. Stand Out Designs. n.d. http://www.mlkonline.net/video.html (accessed December 16, 2010).

Martin Luther King, Jr., National Historic Site. Atlanta: A National Register of Historic Places Travel Itinerary. n.d. http://www.nps.gov/nr/travel/atlanta/kin.htm (accessed December 19, 2010).

National Register of Historic Places Official Website—Part of the National Park Service. http://www.nps.gov/history/nr/feature/afam February 2010. (accessed December 17, 2010).

Outline Maps of USA—Printouts. EnchantedLearning.com. 2003–2010. http://www.enchantedlearning.com/geography/outlinemaps/usa.shtml (accessed December 19, 2010).

Schnaubelt, Maria. *United States General Geographic Regions: Nicknames for Cultural Regions of U. S.* March 29, 2010. http://www.suite101.com/content/general-geographic-regions-of-the-united-states-a219525 (accessed December 16, 2010).

Schomburg Center for Research in Black Culture. MediaBridge Infosystems. 1994–2010. http://www.ny.com/museums/schomburg.center.for.research.in.black.culture.html (accessed December 19, 2010).

U.S. States Fast Facts and Trivia. Marchex. 2010. http://www.50states.com/facts (accessed December 19, 2010).

USA Geography—Map Game. Geography Online Games. Sheppard Software. n.d. http://www.sheppardsoftware.com/web_games.htm (accessed December 18, 2010).

Welcome to the Website of the National Civil Rights Museum. National Civil Rights Museum. 2010. http://www.civilrightsmuseum.org/home.htm (accessed November 6, 2010).

Why Teach Preservation? National Trust for Historic Preservation. 2009. http://www.preservationnation.org/resources/teaching-preservation/why-teach-preservation.html (accessed December 18, 2010).

Additional Reading Materials

Curtis, Nancy C. *Black Heritage Sites: The South.* New York: New Press, 1998.

A practical and useful resource for use in the classroom as an additional resource for teaching social studies. This book is also a great reference guide when planning historic trips for travelers of all ages.

Gates, Henry Louis, Jr. *Wonders of the African World.* New York: Alfred A. Knopf, 1999.

This travel guide was written to highlight the richness of Africa, from its vast resources to its resilient people. Gates helps readers travel to the Motherland to see more than slaves leaving on slave ships. His discussion of Africa offers readers a deeper understanding of the continent's vast resources, history, and monuments and gives insight into the education, perseverance, and determination of its people. This extended knowledge of what Africa has been and is today, should give our young African American citizens a new appreciation of African pride.

Myers, Walter Dean. *Here in Harlem: Poems in Many Voices.* New York: Holiday House, 2004.

This is a book of poetry expressing the opinions of men and women in various occupations that share their lives and desires for opportunity in this historic place.

Tarpley, Natasha Anastasia. *Destiny's Gift.* New York: Lee & Low, 2004.

This is a great book for readers because the author takes the reader beyond the home, school, or public library and prepares them for lifelong learning by introducing a bookstore where literacy seekers may purchase their own resources. Told in a way that involves the reader in community matters, this is the story of a young girl named Destiny who is told that her favorite place will be closing. She is determined to save this establishment that empowered her with new words and the opportunity to meet authors. Devastated upon hearing the news from the storekeeper, her friend Mrs. Wade, Destiny immediately goes to work to save the bookstore.

Williams, Karen Lynn. *When Africa Was Home.* New York: Orchard Books, 1991.

This book is included as part of this unit because it's a loving description of a young white boy's longing to return to his home in Africa. In the text, the author describes the innocence of children before they are exposed to the ills that cause barricades and spread hatred. Although the boy's mother shares something positive about living in America each time he refers to Africa as home, he cannot seem to adjust and think of the United States as his home. But he hears the best news ever when his father says that once again they will be going to Africa.

Chapter 12

LINKS TO LITERATURE

Teach your students to love literature using classic songs, poems, and stories, along with activities that encourage creative writing.

Clinton, Catherine. *I, Too, Sing America: Three Centuries of African American Poetry.* New York: Houghton Mifflin, 1998.

About the Author

CatherineClinton.com. n.d. http://www.catherineclinton.com (accessed October 30, 2010).

Literary Elements	Lexile Range	Teacher Resources and Supplies
Patriotism Poems Poetry	—	Book Paper for rhyming activity
Reading Level Grades 5 and up	**Accelerated Reader** —	
Additional Title Medina, Tony. ***Love to Langston.*** **Websites** http://www.poemhunter.com/poem/mother-to-son http://www.poetryfoundation.org/bio/langston-hughes http://teacher.scholastic.com/writewit/poetry/poetry_engine.htm		

Brief Summary

This book provides readers with twenty-five poets and poems covering multi-interest subjects. Included in this collection are protest, motivational, spiritual, encouraging, and biographical poems—and much more. With such a large variety to choose from, readers will be motivated to use this book as an important resource.

Focus

- Poets, Poetry, and Poems

Teacher Input

- Play the song "America" to the class before introducing this book. Then instruct students to brainstorm and share what the lyrics mean to them.

- Read Langston Hughes's "I, Too, Sing America." http://www.poemhunter.com/poem/mother-to-son.
- Discuss rhyming and make certain that students know what it means. Then write the following words on the board and ask students to list words that rhyme with each one on a sheet of paper distributed at the start of class.
    - Book, School
    - Chair, Table, and Bus
- Introduce students to rhymezone.com, an online resource that can be used to assist students with the composition of poems.
- Invite students to comment on the works presented in Clinton's book and examine their attitudes toward the subject matter and its value to the literary world.

Guided Practice

- Give students an assignment to write a poem about their families using http://www.rhymezone.com to assist with rhyming.
- Have students create an "***It's in the Zone!***" game to discover who found the largest number of words by using rhymezone.com.
- Instruct students to select and meditate on one of the poems from this book. On a scale from one to five, with five being the highest, have them tell why they like or dislike the poet's point of view.
- Have students reflect on Hughes's poem and write an interpretation of it to share.

Independent Practice

- Allow each student to choose a poem for reading aloud. Students may also develop a PowerPoint presentation or flip chart of the poet to explain his or her work.

Closure

- Invite students to share their original poems on the school television network or work with a news team to sponsor a ***Poetry Live! Fest.***

Assessment

- Student creativity, brainstorming, involvement, projects.

Greenfield, Eloise. *Honey, I Love and Other Love Poems.* New York: Harper Trophy/A Division of HarperCollins, 1978.

About the Author

Eloise Greenfield. Scholastic.com. n.d. http://www2.scholastic.com/browse/contributor.jsp?id=3186 (accessed October 22, 2010).

Literary Elements Poetry National Poetry Month Music	**Lexile Range** —	**Teacher Resources and Supplies** Book Worksheet
Reading Level Grades 1–3	**Accelerated Reader** Points: 0.5 Book Level: 2.4	
Additional Title Greenfield, Eloise. ***Nathaniel Talking.*** **Websites:** http://home.cogeco.ca/~rayser3/poetry.htm http://www.jackson5abc.com http://www.earthwindandfire.com		

Brief Summary

Greenfield has captured the innocence of childhood through her reminiscence of fond memories told from a child's perspective. This collection of fifteen poems lends itself to a wide range of discussions on topics from music to physical education.

Focus

- Poetry
- Poems
- Childhood Memories

Teacher Input

- Introduce the musicians described in the poem, "*Way Down in the Music.*"
- Ask students to name their favorite musicians and tell what they like about their music.

Guided Practice

- Have students list their fondest memories of their early childhoods.
- Invite students to read their lists to the class. Instruct students to compare their similarities and differences while listening to the oral reports.
- Ask students to add up the number of cousins on both their mothers' and fathers' sides of the family and give the total number.

- Have students use online resources to access information about musicians discussed in the poem "Way Down in the Music" and cite one interesting fact about each one (see http://myplay.com/audio_player/michael_jackson/195/459768/461780?allowBrowsing=1).
- Ask students to name one humanitarian event that the group Earth, Wind and Fire supported (see http://www.earthwindandfire.com).
- Have students compose an original song after distinguishing the sound made by a bass guitar using the following online resource: http://mostplays.com/play/Virtual_Bass_Guitar_25454.
- Instruct students to write a poem titled "Honey" or "Still Got It!"
- Have students explain the difference between a bass instrument and piano.

Independent Practice

- Suggest that students compile poems and create a poetry video.

Closure

- Allow students to share their original poems with the class.

Assessment

- Student discussions, worksheets, and poems.

"My Fondest Memories"

Discussion and Worksheet

1. What I remember about my childhood.

____

____

____

2. How many boys and girls are there on both your mother's and your father's side of the family?

Boys: ________________ (Mother's Side) ________________ (Father's Side)

Girls: ________________ (Mother's Side) ________________ (Father's Side)

Total Number of Cousins: ______________________________

Here's what I found about the musicians listed below.

The Jackson Five
Earth, Wind & Fire

4. How was Earth, Wind & Fire involved with the island nation of Haiti in 2010?

____

____

5. Write a poem titled "*Honey*" or "*Still Got It!*" (Use a separate sheet of paper for your poem.)

6. Explain the difference between a bass instrument and piano.

Bass Instrument	Piano

Hamilton, Virginia. *The Girl Who Spun Gold.* New York: The Blue Sky Press/An Imprint of Scholastic, 2000.

About the Author

Virginia Hamilton—America's Most Honored Writer of Children's Literature. Hamilton Arts. 2009. http://www.virginiahamilton.com/biography (accessed October 20, 2010).

Literary Elements Fairy Tale Multicultural Stories	**Lexile Range** —	**Teacher Resources and Supplies**
		Book Worksheet
Reading Level Grades 3–6	**Accelerated Reader** Points: 0.5 Book Level: 3.3	
Additional Title Pinkney, Brian. ***Thumbelina.*** **Websites** http://www.webrary.org/kids/jbibfairytalevariations2.html#RUMPELSTILTSKIN http://news.nationalgeographic.com/news/2002/08/0829_020829_wirstrawgold.html		

Brief Summary

What a magical West Indian tale Hamilton spins in this retelling of Rumplestiltskin. Instead of hearing a father brag about his gifted daughter, she chose a mother to tell the king that her daughter, Quashiba, can spin golden threads from straw. Revealing his greed for gold—and lots of it—Big King asks Quashiba to become his wife. Because she only knows how to spin plain thread, Quashiba is sad and scared. Now, hiding in the bushes when the king rides up is Lit'mahn, an ugly little man who admires the girl and promises to help her—if she agrees to a nearly impossible task. After the marriage, the king places the girl in a room to spin golden threads. When read aloud, this story weaves the students into a room of mesmerized listeners, waiting to find out what happens next.

Focus

- Fairy Tales, African American Fairy Tales, Rumplestiltskin, Greed

Teacher Input

- Introduce students to Hamilton's book and discuss other variations of this tale that can be found at http://www.webrary.org/kids/jbibfairytalevariations2.html#RUMPELSTILTSKIN.
- Share the online *National Geographic* article about spinning straw into gold with students.http://news.nationalgeographic.com/news/2002/08/0829_020829_wirstrawgold.html
- Divide the class into teams for planning and developing a ***Poster Board Theater***, and work with the art teacher or art department to plan the production.

Guided Practice

- Have students draw or paint a picture based on the author's description of "Lit'mahn."
- Ask students to explain what is meant by "all over ugly."

- Have students recall names the queen gives to Lit'mahn and design a ***Name Guessing Game*** by using them all.
- Have students write, illustrate, and produce a poster board version of Rumplestiltskin.

Independent Practice

- Assign student teams to locate, read, and share another variation of the Rumplestiltskin Fairy Tale: http://www.webrary.org/kids/jbibfairytalevariations2.html.

Closure

- Presentation of "***Our Variation of Lit'mahn***" story summaries.

Assessment

- Students interests, group participation, worksheets, and project report.

The Girl Who Spun Gold Worksheet

Word Problems

1. According to the author's description, how many items were served at the wedding feast?

2. Lit'mahn gave Queen Quashiba three days to guess his name. Each day he would allow the Queen to guess three times. How many guesses did she have before he would make her small?

3. How long did it take Queen Quashiba to forgive Big King for being so greedy?

Draw a picture of Lit'mahn in the box below.

The Variation of Rumplestiltskin My Summary

4. Explain what the term "all over ugly" means.

5. What names does the queen use for Lit'mahn?

Watts, Jeri Hansel. *Keepers.* New York: Lee & Low, 1997.

About the Author

Jeri Hanel Watts (1957–). Biography, Personal, Career, Member, Writings, Work in Progress, Sidelights. Net Industries. 2010. http://biography.jrank.org/pages/2322/Watts-Jeri-Hanel-1957.html (accessed October 2–30, 2010).

Literary Elements Culture Storytelling Writing	**Lexile Range** —	**Teacher Resources and Supplies** Book
Reading Level Grades 2–4	**Accelerated Reader** Points: 0.5 Book Level: 3.7	
Additional Title Cameron, Ann. ***Stories Julian Tells.*** **Websites** http://www.blackbooksdirect.com/children.html http://www.storyarts.org http://www.angelfire.com/pa5/kotc		

Brief Summary

A young boy works hard to become the "Keeper" of the family's tradition of keeping and telling stories. While trying hard to convince Little Dolly, the grandmother who will be ninety her next birthday, that he should have this task, the lad learns that the Keeper has always been a girl. But his birthday present to Little Dolly convinces her that the tradition will be in good hands if he becomes the Keeper. What does he give Little Dolly? Let the readers enjoy the surprise.

Focus

- Storytelling
- Grandmothers

Teacher Input

- Define what Little Dolly meant by the word "*Keeper.*"
- Use this online resource to introduce students to additional resources related to storytelling: http://www.storyarts.org.
- Develop a "Grandmothers Survey" for students to use as a guide when interviewing their grandmothers. Include the following questions:
    1. Do you have a nickname? If so, what is it, who gave it to you, and why?
    2. Are you a "Keeper"?
- Have students complete an index card that provides the name, date, and time that grandmothers may be able to participate in a school news show, "***Grandmothers and Their Stories.***"

Guided Practice

- Have students identify the "Keepers" in their families.
- Give students an assignment of conducting a survey with their grandmothers.
- Allow students to use the following website to investigate and learn more about the "Keepers of Culture" and storytelling: http://www.angelfire.com/pa5/kotc.
- Have students identify the states with towns or cities called Lexington.
- Ask students to assess Kenyon's feelings when told by Little Dolly that she needs a girl "Keeper." After the celebration of her ninetieth birthday, Little Dolly changes her mind. How do you think this made Kenyon feel? See if you can describe his feelings.

Independent Practice

- Assign students a project using the title, "***I'm My Grandmother's Keeper.***"

Closure

- Host a day when students invite their grandmothers to share stories with their class.

Assessment

- Student interest, participation, involvement, the number of grandmothers recruited to participate in the activities, and projection of projects.

Pinkney, Jerry. *The Lion & the Mouse.* New York: Little, Brown and Company, 2009.

About the Illustrator

Jerry Pinkney Studio. n.d. http://www.jerrypinkneystudio.com (accessed October 30, 2010).

Literary Elements	Lexile Range	Teacher Resources and Supplies
Caldecott Book Award Fable Wordless Book	—	Book
Reading Level Preschool–Grade 2	**Accelerated Reader** —	
Additional Title Pinkney, Jerry. ***Aesop's Fables.*** **Websites** http://www.jerrypinkneystudio.com/frameset.html http://www.pacificnet.net/~johnr/aesop http://www.nga.gov/kids/zone/zone.htm http://www.princetonol.com/groups/iad/links/artgames.html		

Brief Summary

Author and illustrator Jerry Pinkney was the first African American winner of the Caldecott Medal. His book is a beautifully illustrated, wordless text that provides incentive for anyone who may be interested in creating his or her own version of this or another fable.

Focus

- Caldecott Award
- Illustrators, Illustrations, and Artists

Teacher Input

- Introduce students to the Caldecott Award by using this online resource: http://www.embracingthechild.org/caldecott.html.
- Introduce the following online resource which provides information about illustrators for children: http://www.childrensillustrators.com.
- Ask students to describe how illustrators communicate with their audience.
- Have students list ways they find joy through painting or drawing.
- Collaborate with the art teacher or art department to plan an exhibit using the theme "***I See, You See—We Show Art Expo.***"

Guided Practice

- Using the following resource, show students what a Venn diagram is and ask them to differentiate between an artist and an illustrator: http://www.eduplace.com/graphicorganizer/pdf/venn.pdf.

- Have students use the following online resource to learn terms related to art: http://www.artincanada.com/arttalk/arttermsanddefinitions.html.
- Suggest that students view and study tutorials online for beginners interested in learning how to paint or illustrate.
- Have students identify people in their community who are artists or illustrators.

Independent Practice

- Suggest that students select one of the Caldecott Medal and Honor Books for the year, study the style of art and mediums used, and write a biography of illustrators. Have them read their biographies to the class.

Closure

- Have a "***Show and Tell About Jerry***" Illustrator's Day. Use the school's automated library catalog or online resources to locate additional books written and illustrated by Jerry Pinkney.

Assessment

- Student artwork, team planning, and project presentation.

Bibliography

Eloise Greenfield. Scholastic.com. n.d. http://www2.scholastic.com/browse/contributor.jsp?id=3186 (accessed October 22, 2010).

Greenfield, Eloise. *Honey, I Love and Other Love Poems.* New York: Harper Trophy/A Division of HarperCollins, 1978.

Hamilton, Virginia. *The Girl Who Spun Gold.* New York: The Blue Sky Press/An Imprint of Scholastic, 2000.

Jerry Pinkney Studio. n.d. http://www.jerrypinkneystudio.com (accessed October 30, 2010).

Myers, Walter Dean. *Here in Harlem: Poems in Many Voices.* New York: Holiday House, 2004.

Pinkney, Jerry. *The Lion & the Mouse.* New York: Little, Brown and Company, 2009.

Virginia Hamilton—America's Most Honored Writer of Children's Literature. Hamilton Arts. 2009. http://www.virginiahamilton.com/biography (accessed October 20, 2010).

Walter Dean Myers Author. n.d. http://www.walterdeanmyers.net (accessed October 10, 2010).

Webliography

Career Exploration Guides and Resources for Younger Students. Vocational Information Center. March 29, 2010. http://www.khake.com/page64.html (accessed December 28, 2010).

Children Arts Resources: Child Arts and Crafts Projects Ideas & Coloring Pages: Art Development. AllFreeLance. 2000–2009. http://www.princetonol.com/groups/iad/links/artgames.html (accessed November 6, 2010).

Fairytale Variations, Part 2. Morton Grove Public Library. November 11, 2010. http://www.webrary.org/kids/jbibfairytalevariations2.html (accessed December 29, 2010).

Family Reunion, Sack Racing Burlap Sacks, Picnics, Church Social, Backyard Games, Picnic. Info@sackraces.com. n.d. http://www.sackraces.com (accessed December 29, 2010).

The Fifty States (maps, flags, geography, population, statistics). Infoplease.com. Pearson Education. 2000–2010. http://www.infoplease.com/states.html (accessed December 29, 2010).

Jackson5abc.com: Jackson Five Portal. n.d. http://www.jackson5abc.com (accessed November 6, 2010).

Jerry Pinkney Studio. n.d. http://www.jerrypinkneystudio.com (accessed October 30, 2010).

Michael Jackson: The King of Pop. http://www.michaeljackson.com/us/home. Sony Music Entertainment. 2010. (accessed December 29, 2010).

NGAKids Art Zone. National Gallery of Art, Washington, DC. 2010. http://www.nga.gov/kids/zone/zone.htm (accessed November 6, 2010).

The Official Earth, Wind & Fire Website. Kalimba Entertainment. 2009–2011. http://www.earthwindandfire.com (accessed December 29, 2010).

Outta Ray's Head Poetry Lessons. n.d. http://home.cogeco.ca/~rayser3/poetry.htm (accessed December 29, 2010).

Pacific Review of Ethnomusicology: MAYS—Some Liked It Hot: Jazz Women in Film and Television. Regents of the University of California. 2009. http://www.ethnomusic.ucla.edu/pre/Vol14/Vol14html/V14Mays.html (accessed November 8, 2010).

Photography Puzzle Maker. n.d. http://www.flash-gear.com/npuz (accessed December 29, 2010).

Play Virtual Bass Guitar—Online Game. MostPlays Online Games. 2007–2010. http://mostplays.com/play/Virtual_Bass_Guitar_25454 (accessed December 29, 2010).

Researchers Spin Straw Into Gold. National Geographic Society. 1996. http://news.nationalgeographic.com/news/2002/08/0829_020829_wirstrawgold.html (accessed December 29, 2010).

Additional Reading Materials

***African-American Children's Stories: A Treasure of Traditional Tales.* Lincolnwood, IL: Publications International, 2001.**

This is a proven resource for sharing the oral tradition. The stories and poems listed in this volume should be included in every reference collection. They are short, witty, and funny and teach a lesson on why one should never judge a person by size, race, or ability.

Belton, Sandra. *May'naise Sandwiches & Sunshine Tea.* New York: Macmillan, 1994.

A grandmother shares with her granddaughter how she learned to love may'naise sandwiches and sunshine tea. As a young girl, her playmate Betti Jean's mom would make lunch for them. They would have "pile high sandwiches with delicious in between." When Betti Jean came to her house, she wanted her mom to do something special, although she knew they couldn't afford such expensive foods. So her mother brought out baskets and glasses of water. She called this a special lunch for two little girls. The girl's mother told her and Betti Jean to enjoy the sandwiches, and if they looked through their glasses, they would see the sun dancing, which is why their special lunch drink was called sunshine tea.

Greenfield, Eloise. *Nathaniel Talking.* New York: Black Butterfly Children's Books, 1988.

Nathaniel raps about everything. This is a motivational book for reluctant readers who may want to rap instead of read.

Hurston, Zora Neal. *The Six Fools.* New York: HarperCollins, 2006.

This is the retelling of an old story heard years ago. In Hurston's version of the tale, readers submerge themselves into the text quickly to see what's going to happen next. Tanksley's bright, bold illustrations help to draw the reader into the story. This is a great introduction for presenting Hurston's book ***Their Eyes Were Watching God*** to high school students.

***Many Colors of Mother Goose.* Adapted by Cheryl Willis. East Orange, NJ: Just Us Books, 1997.**

In a very creative and amusing way, Cheryl Willis Hudson has developed a unique style for retelling one of the most popular and beloved collections of rhymes—Mother Goose. Excitement can be heard in the classroom as the teacher introduces young listeners and readers to many of these well-known rhymes.

Myers, Walter Dean. Illustrated by Christopher Myers. *Harlem.* New York: Scholastic, 1997.

Walter Dean Myers and son Christopher have created a powerful story and description of people migrating from the South, looking for hope in what they believe they will find in Harlem. They didn't come empty-handed; they brought music and poetry to fill the air. They brought love in their hearts to share. And, to surround all of that, they brought a peace of mind.

Chapter 13

MEN OF HONOR

Share with your students books and activities that profile African Americans advocates, activists, leaders, educators, and now a president.

When I think of a portrait, I think of a picture, a photograph, and a reflection. But for the past three hundred years, the black man's portrait, along with his reputation, has been scarred.

From kings and queens in Africa to slavery in America. To physical freedom but mental subjugation. From the era of segregation and discrimination to the present times, the black man has seen it all.

The black man has been a figure of the devastation in this country. Every time I turn on the television news, 90 percent of black people shown or mentioned have done something wrong. A murder here, a beating there, a black man's face everywhere. This is the kind of picture I see every day for a black man—negative, hateful, and despicable.

But, all that I just said is what others want us to believe—and live up to. The black man's portrait is totally different from that. There's hope, love, peace, charity, and opportunity.

The hope that one day the black man, along with his race, can rise above all disparities and conquer anything he wants to conquer, like being doctors, lawyers, businessmen, even the first black president of the United States. Instead of being drug pushers, sellers, and users, the black man can build up communities, making them strong and safe, instead of weak and dangerous. The forty-fourth president of the United States is an African American—Barack Obama.

The black man has the love, peace, and charity to raise a family without ending in divorce and separation. The black man has love to respect every fellow man and every race, even those that discriminate against him. The black man knows peace—that one has to solve problems with the mind's mental capability, not with a handgun. The black man has charity in taking care of others and supporting others not just with money but love, kindness, goodness, and heart.

And with support and unity, the black man will be able to survive in a whole new world, by going to school, building up the mind's power, tearing down the power of bad choices, and getting a good job that will take him places, not push him back. For the black man, doors are opening every minute; we've just got to be there to walk through them. The black man knows who to lean on, the leadership of God.

So, if you ask me about the portrait of a black man, I'll tell you that it's bright, powerful, amazing, joyous, and magnificent. With God in front, we will make it and conquer all.

—Bobby Guthrie ("BeeGee"), the author's son

Bolden, Tonya. *Strong Men Keep Coming: The Book of African American Men.* New York: John Wiley & Sons, 1999.

About the Author

Tonya Bolden Books—Tonya Bolden . . . An Author for the Ages. 2007–2010. http://www.tonyaboldenbooks.com.

Literary Elements	Lexile Range	Teacher Resources and Supplies
Biography	—	Book Worksheet
Reading Level Grades 6 and up	**Accelerated Reader** —	

Additional Titles
Nelson, Marilyn. ***A Wreath for Emmett Till.***
Tillman, Leon. ***Leon's Story.***

Websites
http://photo2.si.edu/mmm/mmm.html
http://law.jrank.org/pages/5251/Civil-Rights-Movement-Million-Man-March.html
http://www.pbs.org/thisfarbyfaith/people/thomas_dorsey.html
http://www.poemhunter.com/poem/million-man-march-poem

Brief Summary

Bolden has once again reached back into the past to uncover men whose work deserves to be recognized. As historians, writers, and illustrators try to help readers discover the benefits of knowing more about black history and its champions, this reference book will help students access that information. This volume covers a vast amount of information from Jamestown to the Million Man March.

Focus

- Advocates and Activists
- Careers and Occupations

Teacher Input

- Show an online video of the Million Man March (see http://www.c-spanvideo.org/program/67630-1) and lead a discussion about African American men and the methods and strategies they used to improve living and working conditions for their race.
- Ask the students to list the known issues, problems, and controversies that have plagued African American men, from the degradation of slavery until now.
- Distribute the "***Honoring and Recognizing Their Services***" worksheet to the class.
- Assign an online research project focusing on African American men who have made noteworthy contributions to the United States.
- Divide the class into two groups. In Group 1, students will read and discuss ***The Story of Emmett Till*** on page 229. In group 2, students will read and discuss ***Leon's Story*** by Leon Walter Tillage.
- Students compare the differences and similarities between the story of Emmett Till and *Leon's Story.*

Guided Practice

- Have students research and list men whose contributions and achievements in life continued to be influential via ***Youth Book Awards.***
- Assign Maya Angelou's poem "Million Man March Poem" for students to read. It can be found at http://www.poemhunter.com/poem/million-man-march-poem.
- Have students name the men in Bolden's book whom she called the "Father of Black History," "Father of Gospel Music," and "Father of Afrocentricity."

Independent Practice

- Suggest that each student select a personality from this book about whom to develop a slide show or PowerPoint presentation for the class to view.

Closure

- Students share projects with the class.

Assessment

- Student discussions, interest in subject, and project presentations.

"Honoring and Recognizing Their Services"

Discussion and Worksheet

1. My list of issues, problems, and controversies that have plagued African American Men.

a.

b.

c.

d.

e.

2. Who was the first black person in America to earn a medical degree?

____

3. What made James Boon unique?

____

____

How did Boon connect with John Hope Franklin, a professor at Duke University?

____

____

4. List books for young people featuring African American heros who have won an award (such as the Caldecott Medal, Newbery Medal and Honor Books, or Coretta Scott King Book Awards).

Book Title	Award

5. Who was Father of Black History? ______________________

6. Who was Father of Gospel Music? ______________________

7. Who was Father of Afrocentricity? ______________________

A Wreath for Emmett Till http://www.youtube.com/watch?v=TjY8_1An1KY http://www.pbs.org/wgbh/amex/till Poetry, Michael L. Printz Award, Coretta Scott King Honor Book, Narrative	Leon's Story Social Studies, Biography, Jim Crow Boston Globe-Horn Book Award, ALA Best Book for Young Adults, Memoir
The Story:	**The Story:**
Compare the Similarities and Differences	

Englar, Mary. *Colin Powell.* Chicago: Heinemann-Raintree, 2006.

About the Author

Mary Englar—Books, Biography, Contact Information. Jacketflap.com. 2010. http://www.jacketflap.com/persondetail.asp?person=106821 (accessed October 30, 2010).

Literary Element Biography	**Lexile Range** —	**Teacher Resources and Supplies** Book Worksheet
Reading Level Grades 4 and up	**Accelerated Reader** Points: 1.0 Book Level: 6.5	
Additional Titles Fletcher, Marvin E. ***America's First Black General: Benjamin O. Davis, Sr. 1880–1970.*** Wheeler, Jill C. ***Colin Powell.*** **Websites** http://www.achievement.org/autodoc/page/pow0bio-1 http://www.youtube.com/watch?v=IxFhjQautq0		

Brief Summary

This biography reviews the many achievements and accomplishments of Colin Powell, a man whose career was critical to the management and safety of the United States. In this book, the author's description of Powell's legacy includes stories of appointments with, commitments to, and expectations of leaders who recognized the quality of his leadership skills. After reading this biography, which is a part of the African-American Biographies series, young people will be motivated to find their place in life.

Focus

- Leadership
- U.S. Army General
- World Affairs

Teacher Input

- Ask students to define "leadership." What words describe a good leader? Direct students to use the online graphic organizer wheel to record their answers.
- Distribute the "***Power to Powell!***" worksheet.
- Have students list how they believe Powell raised the low morale of the soldiers.
- Discuss Powell's role in Operation Desert Storm; September 11, 2001; the War with Iraq; and the capture of Saddam Hussein.

Guided Practice

- Instruct students to record their descriptions of a good leader.
- Have students identify the services Powell performed by matching him with the correct U.S. Army fort and its location.
- Instruct students to examine Powell's educational background and his interest in education, and brainstorm what he is doing today to improve school attendance: http://www.americaspromise.org/News-and-Events/News-and-Features/APB-2010/Vol-34/Education-Nation.aspx.
- Suggest that students write General Powell a letter explaining why they would consider dropping out of school.
- Lead students in a discussion of the concept that African Americans have to work twice as hard to keep a position or job. Ask students whether they believe this is a true statement. Ask students what evidence they can provide to prove or disprove this statement.

Independent Practice

- Allow students to search online, sketch, and identify various medals awarded to General Powell throughout his career.
- Have students create a portfolio or PowerPoint presentation explaining Powell's involvement in one of the wars and how and why such medals were given. They may use the following web resource: http://www.britannica.com/facts/5/137659/Persian-Gulf-War-as-discussed-in-Colin-Powell-United-States-general-and-statesman. Students may refer to the following website to listen to a chat between President Barack Obama and General Colin Powell: http://www.youtube.com/watch?v=lxFhjQautq0.
- Assign a research project to determine the number of veterans in your community. Establish a Veterans Week, and encourage students to get involved and encourage other classes to honor veterans by writing letters of appreciation, drawing pictures, or writing poems of gratitude.

Closure

- Invite a veteran to speak to your class.
- Invite students to make project presentations to the class.

Assessment

- Student discussions, worksheet completion, and project reports.

The Power of Powell

Discussion and Worksheet

1. Define "leadership."

2. Complete the following chart, giving the fort's location and what Colin Powell did there.

Fort	Location	Services Performed
Fort Bragg		
Fort Benning		
Fort Devens		
Fort McPherson		
Fort Meyer		

3. What does "ROTC" stand for?

   R

   O

   T

   C

4. List ways that Powell raised the morale of students.

   1.

   2.

   3.

   4.

   5.

5. Research and summarize Operation Desert Storm. List website(s) you consulted.

6. Locate a map of ***Afghanistan.*** In your opinion, what issues caused the conflict, which is now a war that arose there?

7. When Powell resigned as Secretary of State, who did President Bush appoint to this position?

McKissack, Patricia, and Fredrick McKissack. *Carter G. Woodson: The Father of Black History* (Great African Americans Series). Berkeley Heights, NJ: Enslow, 2002.

About the Author

Patricia C. McKissack Biography. Simon & Schuster. n.d. http://authors.simonandschuster.com/Patricia-C-McKissack/ 1763349/biography (accessed October 29, 2010).

Literary Element Biography	**Lexile Range** —	**Teacher Resources and Supplies** Book Worksheet
Reading Level Grades 3 and up	**Accelerated Reader** Points: 0.5 Book Level: 3.0	
Additional Title Bader, Bonnie. ***Who Was Martin Luther King, Jr.?*** **Websites** http://www.youtube.com/watch?v=jkBEjJH1j5U http://www.asalh.org/woodsonbiosketch.html http://www.africawithin.com/bios/carter_woodson.htm http://www.america.gov/st/diversity-english/2005/June/20080207153802liameruoy0.1187708.html http://www.youtube.com/watch?v=D2CaRaXrzro		

Brief Summary

Many people celebrate Black History Month but are not aware how it began. In this easy reader, readers of all ages will learn historical information on the how and why as well as the origin of the celebration by a person who dedicated his life to researching the facts, securing the resources, and developing a way to captivate the public's attention to the importance of celebrating.

Focus

- Founding Father of Black History
- Black History
- Education

Teacher Input

- Ask students to explain why black history is celebrated.
- Ask students to describe how black history is recognized or celebrated in their school or community.
- Introduce Dr. Carter G. Woodson, a humble man who believed that "***It's never too late to learn.***" See http://www.africawithin.com/bios/carter_woodson.htm.
- Ask students to explain why Woodson was called "***The Father of Black History.***"
- Distribute the "***Let Me Know, Help Me Know***" ***Worksheet.***

Guided Practice

- Instruct students to summarize on the worksheet how black history is celebrated in their school and community.
- Have students define "humility."
- Ask students to identify a person who they think is humble and give their reasons for naming this person.
- Have students tell why Dr. Woodson felt that students in the Philippines were not learning.
- Have students to draw a picture of Dr. Carter G. Woodson.
- Assign a reading about Dr. Woodson from the following website: http://www.america.gov/st/diversity-english/2005/June/20080207153802liameruoy0.1187708.html. After reading, students write and deliver a speech titled "Why We Don't Learn!"

Independent Practice

- Have each student create a trifold brochure of ***Black History Facts***, create a PowerPoint slideshow of notable facts and photos of African Americans, or develop a timeline of historical events in the history of black America from 1865 to 2010.

Closure

- Invite a notable African American from your community to speak to your class. Show the video of Carter G. Woodson from YouTube: http://www.youtube.com/watch?v=D2CaRaXrzro

Assessment

- Student questions and discussions, worksheet completion, and project design.

"Let Me Know, Help Me Know"

Discussion and Worksheet

1. Tell what you know about black history.

____

____

____

2. How is black history celebrated in our school and community?

At School	In the Community

3. Explain in your own words why Dr. Woodson is known as "The Father of Black History."

____

____

____

4. List reasons given in the book for why students living in the Philippines were not learning.

a. ____

b. ____

c. ____

5. Do you think that any of those reasons exist today? Why or why not?

____

____

____

6. Define "humility."

____

____

____

7. Explain why Dr. Woodson believed it was necessary for him to learn the language of the people of Philippines.

____

____

____

8. Why do you think he taught his students their history and about their national heroes?

____

____

____

____

Wheeler, Jill C. *Barack Obama.* Edina, MN: ABDO, 2009.

About the Author

Jill C. Wheeler—Books, Biography, and Contact Information. Jacketflap.com. 2010. http://www.jacketflap.com/persondetail.asp?person=74322 (accessed October 30, 2010).

Literary Elements	Lexile Range	Teacher Resources and Supplies
Biography United States History	—	Book Worksheet
Reading Level Grades 1–5	**Accelerated Reader** Points: 0.5 Book Level: 5.4	
Additional Titles Edwards, Roberta. ***Who Is Barack Obama?*** Winter, Jonah. ***Barack.*** **Websites** http://www.whitehouse.gov/contact http://www.whitehouse.gov		

Brief Summary

This book provides young readers with a great description of the life and history of the first African American president of the United States. This book shares information about his interracial parents, his grandparents, his wife and children, and a series of events leading up to his inauguration as forty-fourth president. In addition, the author provides the learner with special information about the branches of government that surround the president and how the government functions.

Focus

- First African American President of the United States of America
- Life of President Barack Obama
- Forty-Fourth President of United States

Teacher Input

- Ask students the question "What is significant about President Barack Obama's election?"
- Distribute the "***Yes, He Did!***" worksheet.
- Ask students to define the word "homonym."
- Have the students list the positions Barack Obama held before he was elected president.
- Divide the class into three groups. Each should create a list of concerns that they would like to see the president address.

Guided Practice

- Have students research and define what "***Barack***" means in Swahili.

- Lead students in a discussion about how President Obama didn't allow ***race*** to interfere with his ***race*** to excellence.
- Ask students to list reasons why President Obama's election was special.
- Invite students to comment on their ethnicity and tell what makes them proud of their heritage.
- Ask students to name the title of President Obama's first book.
- Have students list the name of President Obama's running mate and vice president.
- Have students list the name of the Republican candidates for president and vice president who campaigned against President Obama.

Independent Practice

- Allow each team to share the questions generated from their discussions about what they would like the president to address. Suggest that they write to the president using the following e-mail: http://www.whitehouse.gov/contact.

Closure

- Have the groups share their questions for the president with the class.

Assessment

- Student interest, group work, and worksheet completion.

Yes, He Did! Worksheet

1. Why do you feel the election of President Obama was special? List at least three reasons.

   a. ______________________________

   b. ______________________________

   c. ______________________________

2. What positions did Barack Obama hold before becoming president?

____

____

____

____

3. In Swahili, the name "Barack" means ______________________________.

4. What is a homonym?

____

____

____

____

5. President Obama didn't allow ***race*** to interfere with his ***race*** to excellence.

My evidence: ______________________________

____

____

____

____

6. Complete the following sentences with things you can do!

   a. I can ______________________________.

   b. I can ______________________________.

   c. I can ______________________________.

   d. I can ______________________________.

   e. I can ______________________________.

Bibliography

Bolden, Tonya. *Strong Men Keep Coming: The Book of African American Men.* New York: John Wiley & Sons, 1999.

Englar, Mary. *Colin Powell.* Chicago: Heinemann-Raintree, 2006.

Jill C. Wheeler—Books, Biography, and Contact Information. Jacketflap.com. 2010. http://www.jacketflap.com/persondetail.asp?person=74322 (accessed October 30, 2010).

Kids@Random/Catalog/Patricia McKissack. n.d. http://www.randomhouse.com/kids/catalog/author.pperl?authorid=20049 (accessed October 9, 2010).

Mary Englar—Books, Biography, Contact Information. Jacketflap.com. 2010. http://www.jacketflap.com/persondetail.asp?person=106821 (accessed October 30, 2010).

McKissack, Patricia, and Fredrick McKissack. *Carter G. Woodson: The Father of Black History* (Great African Americans Series). Berkeley Heights, NJ: Enslow, 2002.

Myers, Walter Dean, and Bill Miles. *The Harlem Hellfighters: When Pride Met Courage.* New York: HarperCollins, 2006.

Tonya Bolden Books—Tonya Bolden . . . An Author for the Ages. 2007–2010. http://www.tonyaboldenbooks.com (accessed October 10, 2010).

Walter Dean Myers Author. n.d. http://www.walterdeanmyers.net (accessed October 10, 2010).

Wheeler, Jill C. *Barack Obama.* Edina, MN: ABDO, 2009.

Webliography

American Experience: The Murder of Emmett Till. Corporation for Public Broadcasting. 1996–2009. http://www.pbs.org/wgbh/amex/till (accessed December 19, 2010).

America's Promise Alliance—General and Mrs. Colin Powell to Address Dropout Crisis During NBC. America's Promise Alliance. 2009. http://www.americaspromise.org/News-and-Events/News-and-Features/APB-2010/Vol-34/Education-Nation.aspx (accessed December 19, 2010).

AR BookFinder US—Quick Search. Renaissance Learning. 2010. http://www.arbookfind.com/Default.aspx (accessed December 7, 2010).

Carter G. Woodson—African American Trailblazers. May 10, 2009. http://www.youtube.com/watch?v=jkBEjJH1j5U.

Carter G. Woodson, Father of Black History. America.gov. June 6, 2005. http://www.america.gov/st/diversity-english/2005/June/20080207153802liameruoy0.1187708.html (accessed December 19, 2010).

Carter G. Woodson, Father of Black History. Association for the Study of African American Life and History. January 3, 2008. http://www.asalh.org/woodsonbiosketch.html (accessed November 6, 2010).

Civil Rights Movement: Million Man March. 2010. http://law.jrank.org/pages/5251/Civil-Rights-Movement-Million-Man-March.html (accessed November 7, 2010).

Colin Powell Biography. American Academy of Achievement. November 11, 2010. http://www.achievement.org/autodoc/page/pow0bio-1 (accessed December 19, 2010).

Dr. Carter G. Woodson, Father of the African American History Month. n.d. http://www.youtube.com/watch?v=D2CaRaXrzro (accessed December 19, 2010).

Harlem Hellfighters. n.d. http://www.youtube.com/watch?v=Cy1c_xjGvy8 (accessed December 19, 2010).

Jim Europe's 369th Infantry "Hellfighters" Band. n.d. http://www.redhotjazz.com/hellfighters.html (accessed November 6, 2010).

The Lexile Framework for Reading. MetaMetrics, Inc. 2010. http://lexile.com/ (accessed November 2, 2010).

Million Man March. C-SPAN Video Library. October 16, 1995. http://www.c-spanvideo.org/program/67630-1 (accessed December 19, 2010).

Million Man March. Smithsonian Institution. 1995. http://photo2.si.edu/mmm/mmm.html (accessed November 7, 2010).

Million Man March Poem by Maya Angelou. PoemHunter.com. December 19, 2010. http://www.poemhunter.com/poem/million-man-march-poem (accessed December 19, 2010).

Photographs of the 369th Infantry and African Americans During World War 1. The US National Archives and Records Administration. n.d. http://www.archives.gov/education/lessons/369th-infantry (accessed November 6, 2010).

President Obama Meets with General Colin Powell. n.d. http://www.youtube.com/watch?v=lxFhjQautq0 (accessed December 19, 2010).

The Story of Emmett Till. n.d. http://www.youtube.com/watch?v=TjY8_1An1KY (accessed December 19, 2010).

Tales from Ghana. n.d. http://www.africawithin.com/tour/ghana/ghtales.htm (accessed October 9, 2010).

This Far by Faith: Thomas Dorsey. The Faith Project. PBS. 2003. http://www.pbs.org/thisfarbyfaith/people/thomas_dorsey.html (accessed November 7, 2010).

The White House. n.d. http://www.whitehouse.gov (accessed November 6, 2010).

The White House President Barack Obama. n.d. http://www.whitehouse.gov/administration/president-obama (accessed October 10, 2010).

Additional Reading Materials

Bader, Bonnie. *Who Was Martin Luther King, Jr.?* New York: Grosset & Dunlap, 2008.

This is an easy-to-read chapter book for young readers. This book is aimed at those who always request "chapter books" and consists of black-and-white illustrations, a timeline, and bibliography of other books about this unsung hero. From the series: Who Was . . .?

Edwards, Roberta. *Who Is Barack Obama?* New York: Grosset & Dunlap, 2010.

Once again the reader is given a vivid portrait of the life of America's first African American president. This is an easy-to-read chapter book for young readers. The text is large print with black-and-white illustrations. Readers will find a timeline and bibliography at the end of the book. From the series: Who Was . . .?

Gibson, Karen Bush. *Thurgood Marshall: A Photo Illustrated Biography* (Photo-Illustrated Biographies). Mankato, MN: Bridgestone Books, 2002.

Thurgood Marshall's role in history was crucial to African Americans because he was dedicated to issues affecting the poor and needy. Experiencing racism while growing up, he was never afraid to use his voice to help improve legal conditions.

Gillis, Jennifer Blizin. *Scott Joplin: The King of Ragtime.* Chicago: Heinemann Library, 2006.

Joplin was a composer, musician, and performer whose genre of music is unique, based on the author's description of how it was created. Many music lovers will find Joplin's music entertaining and worthy of sharing.

Myers, Walter Dean. *Fallen Angels.* New York: Scholastic, 1988.

Walter Dean Myers' riveting fictional reflection on the Vietnam War describes seventeen- and eighteen-year-old young men who go into war without ever having truly experienced life itself. This award-winning novel is exceptional because the young men it features volunteered even though the draft was in place. When they looked at their future, they saw futility, hopelessness, and the possibility of an early death from unhealthy community circumstances. And so they enlisted and went to war.

Myers, Walter Dean. *Sunrise over Fallujah.* New York: Scholastic, 2009.

Myers has once again created a book expressing the desires of young people to defend their country. In addition to being part of the American military presence in the Iraq War, these young people must create ways to help bring peace and stability to a country torn by unrest.

Nelson, Marilyn. *A Wreath for Emmett Till.* Boston: Houghton Mifflin, 2005.

This Coretta Scott King Book Award winner is a poem about a fourteen-year-old boy who was murdered for being accused of talking to and whistling at a white woman. The final laying of this wreath is an expression of the pain readers will feel as they learn his story.

Simon, Charnan. *Jesse Jackson: I Am Somebody.* New York: Children's Press/Grolier Publishing, 1997.

This is a book about a Civil Rights activist who continues to advocate for those in need. His contributions to black America and world affairs are evidence that his wisdom, guidance, and love are gifts from God.

Strazzabosco, Jeanne. *Learning About Forgiveness from the Life of Nelson Mandela.* New York: Rosen, 1996.

The author uses an easy format to share the facts about a man who dedicates himself to improving the lives of others. Persecuted for trying to do what was right for his people and searching for equality, this man has encountered an array of hardships, yet he continues to this day to press forward.

Tillage, Leon. *Leon's Story.* New York: Farrar, Straus & Giroux, 2000.

There are people who tell stories, and there are stories that tell people. Leon's story tells about him. It tells of a young boy who at an early age witnessed a tragic act. And it tells how he persevered through the years to muster enough strength to allow his story to tell him when to share it with others. While readers may develop a sense of pain for Leon's much-too-young-to-see-so-much life, Leon's story tells how he, too, worked to create a better life for younger African Americans.

Winter, Jonah. *Barack.* New York: HarperCollins, 2008.

Winter takes the reader on a journey to learn more about the first African American president of the United States, Barak Obama. With its bold, crisp illustrations, this book is an attractive read for all young readers.

Chapter 14

SCIENTIFIC IN THEIR THINKING

Introduce your students to renowned African American inventors, doctors, and business professionals who overcame the challenges that confronted them, and, through their contributions, improved the quality of life for all.

Blue, Rose, and Corinne J. Naden. *Ron's Big Mission.* New York: Dutton Children's Books, 2009.

About the Author

Rose Blue (1931–). Biography—Personal, Addresses, Career, Member, Honors Award, Writings, Adaptations, Sidelights. New Industries. 2010. http://biography.jrank.org/pages/1978/Blue-Rose-1931.html (accessed October 30, 2010).

Literary Elements	**Lexile Range**	**Teacher Resources and Supplies**
Biography Historical Fiction Read-Aloud Science	440L	Book Library card Model airplane Paper
Reading Level Grades 1–3	**Accelerated Reader** Points: 0.5 Book Level: 2.9	
Additional Title McKissack, Patricia. ***Goin' Someplace Special.*** **Websites** http://www.youtube.com/watch?v=y3_VMPkzl8A http://video.tvguide.com/The+Early+Show/Astronaut+Ron+McNair%27s+Legacy/2459408 http://space.about.com/cs/deceasedastronaut/a/ronmcnair.htm http://www.ilovelibraries.org/lovemylibrarian/home.cfm		

Brief Summary

In this book, a young boy is determined to walk out of his favorite place with books he has checked out in his name. Tired of always reading in the library and disappointed that he had to search for a very long time before locating books about people like him, he questioned the system. What a triumph!

Focus

- Libraries and Books
- Discrimination

Teacher Input

- Use the online video about building a paper airplane (http://www.youtube.com/watch?v=y3_VMPkzI8A) or show a library card to introduce this book.
- Ask students which of them like to fly.
- Ask students whether they are library card holders and use the following online resource to provide information to students: http://www.ilovelibraries.org/lovemylibrarian/home.cfm.
- Invite the public librarian or the school librarian to speak to the class about library cards and Library Card Sign-Up Month observed in September.
- Ask students to define what goals are and what it means to set goals.
- Discuss Ron's question "***Why can't I check out books like everyone else?***" with the class. Ask students to reflect on student rights given to some but not to others.
- Instruct each student to write an essay titled "***Why Can't I?***"

Guided Practice

- Have students create an outline of their future goals.
- In a "Flying with Ron" project, have students design a paper airplane or create a plane from craft sticks and list the steps Ron took to develop skills and achieve his goals.
- Invite students to discuss the behavior of the library clerk who ignored Ron when he went to the desk to check out his books. Ask students if they think such behavior is prevalent today.
- Ask students to comment on how they use the public library.
- Have students judge whether Ron's big mission was his exploration in the sky as an astronaut or at the library when he challenged the system to acquire a library card.
- Divide the class into homogeneous groups; assign Blue's book for the boys to read and discuss and McKissack's book to the girls. Ask each group to record information gathered from reading. Have the groups exchange books and follow the same instructions.

Independent Practice

- Suggest that each group make a comparison chart between McKissack's and Blue's books and characters for group sharing.

Closure

- Invite a librarian from the public library to speak about services to schools.
- Exhibit aircraft projects in the school library.

Assessment

- Student discussion about public libraries, and project reports.

Kraske, Robert. *Mae Jemison: Space Pioneer.* Mankato, MN: Capstone Press, 2007.

About the Author

Robert Kraske—Books, Biography, Contact Information. Jacketflap.com. 2010. http://www.jacketflap.com/persondetail.asp?person=133099 (accessed October 30, 2010).

Literary Element Biography	**Lexile Range** 680L	**Teacher Resources and Supplies** Book Model of spaceship Worksheet
Reading Level Grades K–4	**Accelerated Reader** Points: 0.5 Book Level: 4.2	
Additional Title Borden, Louise, and Mary Kay Kroeger. *Fly High!: The Story of Bessie Coleman.* Lindbergh, Reeve. *Nobody Owns the Sky: The Story of "Brave Bessie" Coleman.* **Websites** http://www.jemisonfoundation.org/whatistews.htm http://www.omniglot.com/language/phrases/swahili.php http://www.facthound.com http://www.youtube.com/watch?v=6Vy0ncmUvUw		

Brief Summary

This book provides the bibliotherapy that many of our children need to push them forward. The author clearly states that Jemison had dreams she had wanted to fulfill, and she set high goals for herself. Jemison's dreaming would remain just that—dreaming—if she had failed to adequately prepare herself for the task. In a series of events, she accomplished everything she wanted to in her life and reached back to clear the deck for others to launch their dreams.

Focus

- African American Female Astronauts

Teacher Input

- Introduce Mae Jemison's biography with this online video: http://www.youtube.com/watch?v=6Vy0ncmUvUw.
- Introduce students to this book by placing a toy spaceship on the desk and introducing the following website: http://www.facthound.com.
- Distribute an "***It's on Record***" activity sheet to students.
- Brainstorm with students about the importance of staying focused and committed to the goals they formulate.
- Discuss with students how people leave legacies or memories and how we honor a deceased person so that others may learn from his or her good example. Ask students to explain why the James McCosh Elementary School was renamed the Emmett Till Math and Science Academy.

Guided Practice

- Ask students to show examples of their record keeping. Have students list the type of records they want the teacher to keep.
- Have students prioritize what they want in life.
- Have students research Emmett Till online for information to support the decision to rename McCosh Elementary School.
- Instruct students to use the website on the worksheet to learn five Swahili words or phrases to record on index cards and share.

Independent Practice

- Suggest that each student write an informative paper, develop a chart, or create a PowerPoint presentation from one of the websites listed below to share with classmates.
    - The Peace Corps: http://www.peacecorps.gov/index.cfm?shell=about.pctoday
    - Sickle Cell Anemia: http://kidshealth.org/teen/diseases_conditions/blood/sickle_cell_anemia.html
    - The Jemison Group: http://myhero.com/go/hero.asp?hero=M_jemison

Closure

- Have students explain how and why the desire to fly was different for Mae Jemison compared with Bessie Coleman.

Assessment

- Student interest, brainstorming, worksheet completion, and project sharing.

"It's on Record" Worksheet

1. When did Mae Jemison become the first African American woman astronaut?

____

2. Go to this link to learn more about the Adler Planetarium: http://www.adlerplanetarium.org.

   What is the planetarium's primary focus? ________________________________

3. What is record keeping? With the class, discuss the following:

   a. Why do people keep records?

   b. Give examples of important records that are kept.

   c. Where does your family keep their family records?

4. Who was Madeline L'Engle? Which book by L'Engle encouraged Jemison to pursue her goal? ____________

____

5. What course did Jemison take in high school to prepare her for a career in aviation?

____

6. Define "nerd." Do you think Jemison was a "nerd"? Why or why not?

____

____

____

____

7. Can you speak a different language? If so, what language? ____________________________

____

Use this online site to learn Swahili phrases: http://www.omniglot.com/language/phrases/swahili.php:

Bessie and Mae	
What About That Bessie?	Tell Me About Mae!

Bibliography

Blue, Rose, and Corinne J. Naden. *Ron's Big Mission.* New York: Dutton Children's Books, 2009.

Carson, Ben. *Gifted Hands: The Ben Carson Story.* Grand Rapids, MI: Zondervan, 1990.

Dr. Ben Carson—The Gifted Hands Interview. AALBC.com. 1997–2010. http://aalbc.com/reviews/ben_carson.htm (accessed December 20, 2010).

Kraske, Robert. *Mae Jemison: Space Pioneer.* Mankato, MN: Capstone Press, 2007.

Laura Purdie Salas. Winding Oak. 2007–2010. http://www.laurasalas.com.

Lisa Yount—Books, Biography, Contact Information. Jacketflap.com. 2010. http://www.jacketflap.com/persondetail.asp?person=96140 (accessed December 21, 2010).

Robert Kraske—Books, Biography, Contact Information. Jacketflap.com. 2010. http://www.jacketflap.com/persondetail.asp?person=133099 (accessed October 30, 2010).

Rose Blue (1931–). Biography: Personal, Addresses, Career, Member, Honors Award, Writings, Adaptations, Sidelights. New Industries. 2010. http://biography.jrank.org/pages/1978/Blue-Rose-1931.html (accessed October 30, 2010).

Salas, Laura Purdie. *Charles Drew: Pioneer in Medicine.* Mankato, MN: Capstone Press, 2006.

Yount, Lisa. *Black Scientists.* New York: Facts on File, 1991.

Webliography

Biography of Ronald E. McNair (PhD), NASA Astronaut. The New York Times Company. 2010. http://space.about.com/cs/deceasedastronaut/a/ronmcnair.htm (accessed November 6, 2010).

Black Scientists. Google Books. 2010. http://books.google.com/books?id=SFbhAAAAMAAJ&dq=black%20scientists%20yount&source=gbs_book_other_versions (accessed December 20, 2010).

Blood Types. American National Red Cross. 2010. http://www.redcrossblood.org/learn-about-blood/blood-types (accessed December 20, 2010).

Changing the Face of Medicine. Dr. Jane Cooke Wright. National Library of Medicine. n.d. http://www.nlm.nih.gov/changingthefaceofmedicine/physicians/biography_336.html (accessed December 21, 2010).

Charles Drew—The Blood Bank. About.com—The New York Times Company. 2010. http://inventors.about.com/library/inventors/bldrew.htm (accessed December 21, 2010).

Daniel Hale Williams—Black Inventor Online Museum. Adscape International. 1998–2009. http://www.blackinventor.com/pages/danielwilliams.html (accessed December 21, 2010).

Dr. Ben Carson—The Gifted Hands Interview. AALBC.com. 1997–2010. http://aalbc.com/reviews/ben_carson.htm (accessed December 20, 2010).

Dr. Charles Drew—Black Inventor Online Museum. Adscape International. 1998–2009. http://www.blackinventor.com/pages/charlesdrew.html (accessed November 6, 2010).

Ernest Everett Just. Infoplease.com. Pearson Education. 2000–2010. http://www.infoplease.com/ipa/A0775692.html (accessed December 21, 2010).

Forgotten Genius: Library Resource Kit—Bibliography. NOVA. PBS. n.d. http://www.pbs.org/wgbh/nova/julian/lrk-biblio.html (accessed December 20, 2010).

Fraser-Reid, Bertram O. (1934–). The Black Past: Remembered and Reclaimed. 2007–2009. http://www.blackpast.org/?q=aah/fraser-reid-bertram-o-1934 (accessed December 21, 2010).

Games. American Red Cross. n.d. http://www.redcrossblood.org/donating-blood/donor-community/games (accessed December 20, 2010).

Gifted Hands: The Ben Carson Story—About the Movie. TNT Movies, Turner Broadcasting System. 2010. http://www.tnt.tv/movies/giftedhands/ (accessed November 6, 2010).

Gifted Hands, A Small Group Discussion by Charlene Davis. Teachers Network. 2010. http://www.teachersnetwork.org/ntny/nychelp/manage/giftedhands1.htm (accessed December 20, 2010).

Grade Selection. FactHound. 2009. http://www.facthound.com (accessed December 21, 2010).

How to Build the Best Paper Airplane in the World. n.d. http://www.youtube.com/watch?v=y3_VMPkzI8A (accessed December 21, 2010).

ilovelibraries.org/lovemylibrarian/home.cfm. American Library Association. 2009. http://www.ilovelibraries.org/lovemylibrarian/home.cfm (accessed November 6, 2010).

Inventor George Washington Carver Biography. The Great Idea Finder. 1997–2007. http://www.ideafinder.com/history/inventors/carver.htm (accessed December 21, 2010).

John P. Moon Apple Computers. DirectHit.com. 2010. http://www.directhit.com/ansres/John-P-Moon-Apple-Computers.html (accessed December 21, 2010).

Mae Jamison on Teaching Arts and Sciences Together. n.d. http://www.youtube.com/watch?v=6Vy0ncmUvUw (accessed December 28, 2010).

The My Hero Project—Mae Jemison. March 19, 2007. http://myhero.com/go/hero.asp?hero=M_jemison (accessed December 20, 2010).

The Mysterious Human Heart. Endlessly Beating. PBS. Educational Broadcasting Corporation. 2007. http://www.pbs.org/wnet/heart/episode1/index.html (accessed December 21, 2010).

The Official Home for Dr. Ben Carson and The Carson Scholars Fund. Carsons Scholars Fund. 2009. http://carsonscholars.org (accessed November 6, 2010).

Peace Corps Today. About Us. December 14, 2009. http://www.peacecorps.gov/index.cfm?shell=about.pctoday (accessed December 20, 2010).

Percy Julian—Black Inventor Online Museum. Adscape International. 1998–2009. http://www.blackinventor.com/pages/percyjulian.html (accessed December 21, 2010).

Sasson, Remez. *The Power of Positive Thinking and Attitude.* Success Consciousness.com. 2001-2010. http://www.successconsciousness.com/index_000009.htm (accessed December 21, 2010).

Science Projects—Peanut Power. California Energy Commission. 2006. http://www.energyquest.ca.gov/projects/peanut.html (accessed November 6, 2010).

Sickle Cell Anemia. The Nemours Foundation. 1995–2010. http://kidshealth.org/teen/diseases_conditions/blood/sickle_cell_anemia.html (accessed December 20, 2010).

Useful Swahili Phrases. Simon Ager. 1998–2010. http://www.omniglot.com/language/phrases/swahili.php (accessed November 6, 2010).

Watch the Early Show Astronaut Ron McNair's Legacy—Online Video Guide. July 1, 2009. http://video.tvguide.com/The+Early+Show/Astronaut+Ron+McNair%27s+Legacy/2459408 (accessed December 20, 2010).

Welcome to Adler Planetarium! Adler Planetarium. 2005. http://www.adlerplanetarium.org (accessed December 21, 2010).

What Is Blood Plasma? November 12, 2010. http://www.wisegeek.com/what-is-blood-plasma.htm (accessed December 20, 2010).

What Is TEWS? TEWS. 2004. http://www.jemisonfoundation.org/whatistews.htm (accessed December 21, 2010).

Additional Reading Materials

Borden, Louise, and Mary Kay Kroeger. *Fly High! The Story of Bessie Coleman.* New York: Scholastic, 2001.

Bessie Coleman was a remarkable young woman who learned how to persevere while "walking" to attain her goal. The reader will find this book motivational and encouraging.

Brodie, James Michael. *Created Equal: The Lives and Ideas of Black American Innovators.* New York: William Morrow, 1993.

This book provides students with information about those African Americans who worked diligently "***to heal the wounds, preserve their inventions and press out the wrinkles of prejudice***" for all humankind. It is a powerful reference consisting of brief biographies of the struggles, achievements, accomplishments, celebrations, and, finally, recognitions of African Americans.

Burns, Khephra, and William Miles. *Black Stars in Orbit.* Orlando, FL: Harcourt Brace, 1995.

Based on a screenplay documentary, Burns and Miles produced a primary resource of names, data, and black-and-white photos of African Americans who learned to fly above the earth. The flights begin with Colonel Guion S. Bluford on August 30, 1983. This book captures the resiliency of a group of men and women who refused to allow their dreams to be grounded.

Carson, Ben. ***Think Big.*** **Grand Rapids, MI: Zondervan, 2006.**

Carson's willingness to "think big" is evident in his professional success today. He faced many challenges—low self-esteem, poverty, a dysfunctional family—and he could have let this hold him back. But his mother was his battleship. She encouraged Carson and his brothers to overcome their challenges by using their minds.

Taylor, Gaylia. ***George Crum and the Saratoga Chip.*** **New York: Lee & Low Books, 2006.**

This book will be therapeutic for any person who sometimes feels as though life's problems are coming from every side. George Crum didn't have the best memories of childhood because of his speech difficulties and other family issues. He found comfort spending time outdoors alone. While making plans to teach someone a lesson, he never realized that success was "chipping" its way toward him, making history.

Hayden, Robert C. ***Eight Black American Inventors.*** **Reading, PA: Addison-Wesley, 1972.**

This book offers information about important African American inventors and their contributions to America's success. The text is informative, easy to read, and a worthwhile reference tool.

Hendersen, Susan K. ***African-American Inventors.*** **Mankato, MN: Capstone Press, 1998.**

This biographical resource offers young readers the opportunity to learn how African American scientists have worked to discover and invent technologies to enhance scientific exploration. From Dr. Patricia Bath and her medical invention to Philip Emeagwali, known as a computer guru, these men and women have brought about change for a better future.

Krohn, Katherine. ***Madam C. J. Walker and New Cosmetics.*** **Mankato, MN: Capstone Press, 2007.**

Hair sculpture is beautiful, and African American styles are diverse, with some styling requiring much time. This book tells of a woman who transitioned her way from poor to rich through determination, assertiveness, and hard work. Although troubled at times with problems at home, gender discrimination, and segregation, she rose to the top and reached out to help others. Her story can inspire young minds to strive to develop and reach their goals.

Lassieur, Allison. ***Benjamin Banneker: Astronomer and Mathematician.*** **Mankato, MN: Capstone Press, 2006.**

Benjamin Banneker was an African American man born in the eighteenth century who devoted his life to studying the sky and stars. He took advantage of his freedom and used it to improve the quality of life for others. Many were surprised that a black man could be smart, intelligent, and productive, and it is thus that Banneker won respect through "the content of his character."

McKissack, Patricia C. ***Goin' Someplace Special.*** **New York: Atheneum Books for Young Readers, 2001.**

Tricia Ann is disappointed by the way she is treated on her journey to that special place—a library—where she would have the freedom to travel anywhere through the pages of a book.

Miller, Raymond H. ***George Washington Carver.*** **Detroit, MI: Thomson/Gale, 2005.**

Readers will discover that George Washington Carver's life was more than just experimenting with the peanut. Carver left a legacy for young scientists to follow.

Sullivan, Otha Richard. ***Black Stars: African American Inventors.*** **New York: John Wiley & Sons, 1998.**

This is a collected biography of African American men and women whose contributions to America, from health to hair care, helped shape and mold the lives of all people.

Welch, Catherine A. ***Benjamin Banneker.*** **Minneapolis, MN: Lerner, 2008.**

The word "freedom" does not always mean the same thing to everyone. Although as a freeman Benjamin Banneker was free from the chains of slavery, he didn't take his freedom for granted. And he became one of the greatest astronomers and mathematicians of all time. As the grandson of a slave, there were times in his life when "freedom" was only a word—he still battled discrimination because of the color of his skin. Throughout his life, though, he was determined to achieve his goals, even amid segregation and prejudice. As a clock maker and mathematician, he earned the respect of those who at one time loathed him.

Wyckott, Edwin Brit. ***Heart Man: Vivien Thomas, African-American Heart Surgery Pioneer.*** **Berkeley Heights, NJ: Enslow Elementary, 2008.**

The book will be an inspiration to all readers. It tells of a young man whose life ambition was to become a physician. Having no money but strong faith, he became not only a physician but a great one, who contributed significantly to what doctors know about the cardiovascular system.

Chapter 15

SISTERS

Through these books and activities, students are introduced to strong African American women who worked to improve not only their own lives but those of all people. Learn about Oseola McCarty, Maya Angelou, Sojourner Truth, Coretta Scott King, Michelle Obama, and many others.

Hansen, Joyce. *Women of Hope: African Americans Who Made a Difference.* New York: Scholastic, 1998.

About the Author

Joyce Hansen. n.d. http://www.joycehansen.com/index.htm (accessed October 22, 2010).

Literary Element Collected Biographies	**Lexile Range** 1140L	**Teacher Resources and Supplies** Book Worksheet
Reading Level Grades 3 and up	**Accelerated Reader** Points: 1.0 Book Level: 7.8	
Additional Title Colbert, David. *Michelle Obama: An American Story.* **Websites** http://joycehansen.com/index.htm http://www.youtube.com/watch?v=s9ZSIWDXyJE http://womenshistory.about.com/od/africanamerican/a/black_women.htm http://www.youtube.com/watch?v=gW7z5ASa4W0&feature=related http://stlouiswalkoffame.org/inductees/willie-smith.html		

Brief Summary

Contained in this book are twelve powerful stories told about African American women who sacrificed their time and talents to improve the social, political, and moral standards of other African Americans in areas from child welfare to space travel. Also included is a resource list of other great women who made contributions in an array of vocations. This book is an excellent resource to use for Women's History Month or for lesson plans throughout the year, for all grades.

Focus

- African American Women
- Advocates

Teacher Input

- Ask students how they define the word "hope."
- Divide the class into seven groups. Distribute the ***Sistas' Tell All Worksheet.*** Direct the students to use the websites provided to locate and learn more about the historical contributions of these women.

Guided Practice

- Instruct students to complete the worksheet by working in their assigned groups.
- Have students search online to discover African American journalists and explain the role they play in communicating with people. See, for example:
    - http://www.washingtonpost.com/wp-dyn/content/article/2009/07/01/AR2009070103938.html.
    - Go to books.google.com and insert *Raising Her Voice: African-American Women Journalists Who Changed History* in the search field.
- Instruct students to compare the type of coverage Ida B. Wells-Barnett provided as a journalist to what journalists cover today.
- Assign students the task of identifying the first female African American to have a book of poetry published in the United States.
- Have students locate and play music by Willie Mae Ford Smith, known as the "Mother of Gospel Music," by using the following websites:
    - http://www.youtube.com/watch?v=gW7z5ASa4W0&feature=related
    - http://stlouiswalkoffame.org/inductees/willie-smith.html.

Independent Practice

- Suggest that student groups search online for quotes from the women featured in this book and then share some of their group's favorite quotes in "***They Said It, We'll Share It.***" The groups may also create a poster, flip chart, brochure, or PowerPoint slides sharing noteworthy information about the women with the rest of the class.
- Ask students to read and explain this commentary in their own words: http://www.essence.com/entertainment/fortyfierceandfab/commentary_why_i_am_a_fierce_black_woman.php.

Closure

- Students present their projects and discuss them.

Assessment

- Group participation, interest, and project development.

My Hope Is Built on Women Blessed

Discussion and Open-Ended Response Worksheet

Define "hope." ____

____

Search for similarities and differences among the following writers.

Sistas' Tell All
Maya Angelou (Uses simile) Locate examples of these literary devices. http://www.studyworld.com/newsite/reportessay/biography/literaryauthors%5Cmaya_angelou__the_person_and_poet-225.htm What is the title of her autobiographical series?
Toni Morrison (Real and Unrealistic Text) http://tech.mit.edu/V112/N24/morrison.24a.html Which of Morrison's books did Oprah Winfrey purchase the rights to, then make and star in the movie?
Marian Wright Edelman (Social Reform, Women's History, Children's Advocate) http://www.childrensdefense.org/about-us/leadership-staff/marian-wright-edelman/ Name and describe the organization founded by Edelman. Describe Edelman's Freedom Schools.
Alice Walker (Letter Writing, Descriptive Language, Poet; Author of *The Color Purple*) http://www.youtube.com/watch?v=fjiZe4zUxQM View the movie on YouTube and brainstorm with other students. Can you analyze and give reasons why Walker penned this book? What did you see, and what did you want to see? What didn't you like seeing?
Zora Neale Hurston (Author of *Their Eyes Were Watching God*) Go to books.google.com and enter *Their Eyes Were Watching God* in the search field. Visit http://www.gradesaver.com/their-eyes-were-watching-god/study-guide/major-themes. List some of the literary elements found in this acclaimed volume of literature. 1. 2. 3. 4. 5.

Student teams work together to locate one African American woman in each of the categories listed below.

Independent Research

Students will locate on their own online resources to obtain information for subjects listed below. Students must remember to cite their resource.

The Sista'	The Job—Provide Information
Aviator	Cite Website:
Artists, Writers, etc.	Cite Website:
Musicians	Cite Website:
Caregivers	Cite Website:
Educators	Cite Website:
Activists	Cite Website:
Athletes	Cite Website:

Rockwell, Anne. *Only Passing Through: The Story of Sojourner Truth.* New York: Albert A. Knopf, 2000.

About the Author

Anne Rockwell. 2008. http://www.annerockwell.com/ (accessed October 30, 2010).

Literary Elements	Lexile Range	Teacher Resources and Supplies
Biography Coretta Scott King Book Award Winners Women's Rights	AD790L	Book Bible Worksheet
Reading Level Grades and 2 up	**Accelerated Reader** Points: 0.5 Book Level: 5.2	
Additional Titles McGovern, Ann. ***"Wanted Dead or Alive:" The True Story of Harriet Tubman.*** McKissack, Patricia. ***Ain't I a Woman?*** Pinkney, Andrea. ***Sojourner Truth's Step-Stomp Stride.*** **Websites** http://www.sojournertruth.org http://www.blackpast.org/?q=african-american-history-major-speeches		

Brief Summary

Sojourner Truth passed through life leaving a favorable impression on many people. Relying on the strength of her faith, she felt it was her duty to help those who could not help themselves. Seeking to buy her own freedom and that of her son, she spoke out against slavery and other oppressive issues. With her fearless and powerful speeches, she did much to change the rights of all women. Truth is noted for her famous speech, "Ain't I a Woman?"

Focus

- Abolitionists
- African American Women
- Coretta Scott King Book Award

Teacher Input

- Write on the board, "Did you tell the 'Truth' about that?" Allow students to comment on what they think the statement means before introducing the book.
- Ask students how they would interpret the title "Only Passing Through" without reading the book.
- Ask students to comment on the question: "When you pass through a town on your way to someplace else, does it mean anything to you?"
- View the following website with the class: http://www.sojournertruth.org.

Guided Practice

- Assign students the task of finding and reading a famous speech made by an African American and to summarize in their own words what it means. Ask students how they might be able to use their voices to encourage and provide hope for people. Speeches can be found at: http://www.blackpast.org/?q=african-american-history-major-speeches.
- Have students scan the news media and identify issues facing women today. They may then identify and list ways that society can assist women to overcome these issues.

Independent Practice

- After identifying issues facing women, suggest that each student write and deliver a speech based on one critical issue that appealed to him or her personally during their research. Encourage students to emphasize points about this issue that will touch the hearts of listeners.

Closure

- Students deliver speeches and share quotes.

Assessment

- Student brainstorming, discussions, research, and project presentations.

Only Passing Through: Greatness and Perseverance Worksheet

List issues some women face today. Use the following website to identify five such issues and provide a summary of your concerns: http://www.globalissues.org/article/166/womens-rights.

Define the word "slave." Do you think that slavery exists today? Why or why not? Where?

Is change always good for you? Isabella Baumfree changed her name to Sojourner Truth. She felt that it would help in her journey to sojourn whenever needed, always telling the truth. Explain what "sojourn" means.

List two things that affect you in a negative way that you would like to see changed.

What are you willing to work hard for? Make a list of those things that you will work hard to achieve.

In what ways did Sojourner Truth's advocacy help African American people?

What is "character"? In what way did Truth's character influence you?

If Sojourner Truth were alive today, do you think that she would be pleased with the condition of our country? Why or why not? Let's brainstorm.

Ain't That the Truth?

Design a TRUTH Bingo Card Game using the template on the next page. Students will learn about famous African- American women by developing and playing this game.

Give students worksheets to complete. Each student will be responsible for finding answers to an assigned set of numbers based on the number of students in your class.

	Woman's Name	List One Fact	Reference
T1	Sojourner Truth		
T2	Biddy Mason		
T3	Harriet Tubman		
T4	Shirley Chisholm		
T5	Fannie Lou Hamer		
T6	Rosa Parks		
T7	Dorothy Irene Height		
T8	Ella Josephine Baker		
T9	Mary McLeod Bethune		
T10	Ida B. Wells-Barnett		
T11	Carole Boston Weatherford		
T12	Henrietta M. Smith		
T13	Eloise Greenfield		
T14	Jackie "Moms" Mabley		
T15	Hattie McDaniel		
R16	Sallie Martin		
R17	Zora Neale Hurston		
R18	Maya Angelou		
R19	Aretha Franklin		
R20	Ida B. Wells-Barnett		
R21	Marian Anderson		
R22	Leontyne Price		
R23	Mae C. Jemison		
R24	Bessie Coleman		
R25	Alice Walker		
R26	Patricia McKissack		
R27	Andrea Pinkney		
R28	Cheryl Hudson		
R29	Gloria Jean Pinkney		
R30	Mahalia Jackson		
U31	Nina Simone		
U32	Debbie Allen		
U33	Michelle Obama		
U34	Oprah Winfrey		
U35	Nikki Giovanni		
U36	Alfre Woodard		

Ain't That the Truth?

U37	Hazel Johnson-Brown		
U38	Barbara Jordan		
U39	Johnnetta Cole		
U40	Florence Griffith-Joyner		
U41	Jackie Joyner-Kersee		
U42	Debi Thomas		
U43	Sherian Grace Cadoria		
U44	Sharon Draper		
U45	Althea Gibson		
T46	Wilma Rudolph		
T47	Gwendolyn Brooks		
T48	Ann Gregory		
T49	Charlemae Rollins		
T50	Daisy Bates		
T51	Toni Stone		
T52	Camilla Williams		
T53	Pearl Bailey		
T54	Crystal Bird Fauset		
T55	Ella Fitzgerald		
T56	Madam C. J. Walker		
T57	Maggie Lena Walker		
T58	Ethel Waters		
T59	Maxine Waters		
T60	Dinah Washington		
T61	Condoleezza Rice		
T62	Valerie Jarrett		
T63	Dorothy Powell		
T64	Leslie Uggams		
T65	Carol Moseley-Braun		
T66	Alma Littlejohn—Bonus Chip		
T67	Nannie Helen Burroughs		
T68	Mary Lucinda Cardwell Dawson		
T69	Katherine Dunham		
T70	Selma Burke		
T71	Oseola McCarty		
T72	Nancy Wilson		
T73	Phillis Wheatley		
T74	Mamie Smith		
T75	Susie King Taylor		

Shange, Ntozake. *Coretta Scott.* New York: Amistad/Katherine Tegen Books/Harper-Collins, 2009.

About the Author

Ntozake Shange. AALBC.com. 1997–2010. http://aalbc.com/authors/ntozake.htm (accessed October 30, 2010).

<table>
<tr><td>Literary Elements
Coretta Scott King Book Awards
Named in Her Honor
Literacy
Poetry
Reading
Biography</td><td>Lexile Range
—</td><td rowspan="2">Teacher Resources and Supplies
Book
Coretta Scott King Book Awards Titles
Worksheet</td></tr>
<tr><td>Reading Level
Grades and 2 Up</td><td>Accelerated Reader
Points: 0.5
Book Level: 4.9</td></tr>
<tr><td colspan="3">Additional Title
Coretta Scott King Book Awards

Websites
http://www.ala.org/ala/mgrps/rts/emiert/cskbookawards/index.cfm
http://usliberals.about.com/od/peopleinthenews/p/CorettaKing.htm
http://www.achievement.org/autodoc/page/kin1bio-1</td></tr>
</table>

Brief Summary

This is a beautifully illustrated book told in poetic form about a woman who dedicated her life to her family and the people of the United States.

Focus

- Women
- Education
- Role Models
- Civil Rights

Teacher Input

- Take students on a virtual journey to learn more about the life of Coretta Scott King at the following site: http://usliberals.about.com/od/peopleinthenews/p/CorettaKing.htm.
- Ask the students if they know of women in their community who have made noteworthy contributions. Start them off with an example.
- Invite students to comment on why they think education is important.
- Discuss nonviolence with the class and ask students if they know what it means to be nonviolent. Visit the following website for more information on nonviolence: http://www.mkgandhi.org.

- Discuss with the class what it means to realize the sacrifices made by our forefathers. Cite examples.
- Discuss the three special Coretta Scott King Book Awards and why these awards are given.

Guided Practice

- Have students read about Gandhi and his philosophy and views on life.
- Using online quotes from Gandhi, have students write their own quotes.
- Have students list the things the author mentioned in the story that inspired perseverance.
- Ask the class to imagine our forefathers saying, "***There's no need to fuss, it's happened to the best of us.***" Ask them to explain what is meant by this statement.
- Have the students create a list of causes that led to Bloody Sunday in Selma, Alabama.
- Have students listen to the freedom song "***Ain't Gonna Let Nobody Turn Me Round, Turn Me Round.***" Ask students to explain what they think is the song's meaning. See http://www.youtube.com/watch?v=c5Z1trynEHs.
- Suggest that students create and design an award for women in their community whose work is outstanding.
- Have students list at least three guidelines for establishing the Coretta Scott King Awards based on what they know about Mrs. King.

Independent Practice

- Suggest that students research the Coretta Scott King Book Awards. Have them find another book written by Ntozake Shange and illustrated by Kadir Nelson.

Closure

- Students use the following online resource to hear the freedom song "***We Shall Overcome***"***:*** http://www.youtube.com/watch?v=CnzmPrsLXn8&feature=related.
- Direct students to use this resource to read lyrics and then write changes they would make to keep the song alive in the hearts and minds of people: site http://www.k-state.edu/english/nelp/american.studies.s98/we.shall.overcome.html.

Assessment

- Student research, completed reports, and project design.

"She Kept His Dream Alive" Worksheet

Use this online site to listen to a news story about the life and legacy of Coretta Scott King: http://www.npr.org/templates/story/story.php?storyId=5180053.

What did Coretta Scott King and Ghandi have in common?

____

____

____

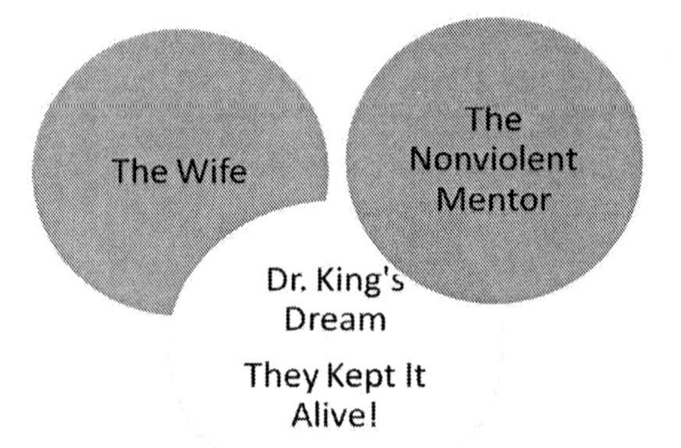

Use Google Images to locate, cut and paste a photo of Coretta Scott King

HERE

Design and create your Sista' Award here.

Use Google Images to locate, cut and paste a photo of Coretta Scott King

HERE

Define "criteria."

____

What criteria will you use to present your award?

____

____

Identify the artist singing "We Shall Overcome" in this YouTube video: http://www.youtube.com/watch?v=CnzmPrsLXn8&feature=related. Explain the lyrics.

____

____

____

Do you agree with Dr. King's and Ghandi's nonviolent approach to violence? Why or why not?

____

____

____

Name the book written by Shange and illustrated by Nelson that won the Coretta Scott King Book Award.

____

____

Bibliography

Andrea Davis Pinkney. n.d. http://www2.scholastic.com/browse/contributor.jsp?id=2861 (accessed October 9, 2010).

Anne Rockwell. 2008. http://www.annerockwell.com (accessed October 30, 2010).

Coleman, Evelyn. *The Riches of Oseola McCarty.* Chicago: Albert Whitman, 1998.

Hanson, Joyce. *Women of Hope: African Americans Who Made a Difference.* New York: Scholastic, 1998.

Joyce Hansen. n.d. http://www.joycehansen.com/index.htm (accessed October 22, 2010).

Ntozake Shange. AALBC.com. 1997–2010. http://aalbc.com/authors/ntozake.htm (accessed October 30, 2010).

Pinkney, Andrea Davis. *Let It Shine: Stories of Black Women Freedom Fighters.* New York: Gulliver Books/Harcourt, 2000.

Rockwell, Anne. *Only Passing Through: The Story of Sojourner Truth.* New York: Albert A. Knopf, 2000.

Shange, Ntozake. *Coretta Scott.* New York: Amistad/Katherine Tegen Books/HarperCollins, 2009.

Welcome to Evelyn Coleman's Children's Books. n.d. http://www.evelyncoleman.com/Welcome.htm (accessed October 30, 2010).

Webliography

African American History: Major Speeches. The Black Past: Remembered and Reclaimed. 2007–2009. http://www.blackpast.org/?q=african-american-history-major-speeches (accessed November 5, 2010).

African American Women's History—Black Women's History. New York Times Company. 2010. http://womenshistory.about.com/od/africanamerican/African_American_Womens_History.htm (accessed November 5, 2010).

African American Women's Organizations. National Council of Negro Women. n.d. http://www.ncnw.org/ (accessed December 22, 2010).

"*Ain't Gonna Let Nobody Turn Me 'Round*" by Sweet Honey in the Rock. n.d. http://www.youtube.com/watch?v=c5Z1trynEHs (accessed December 22, 2011).

Children and Saving—Teaching Children to Save. Kid Stuff. About.com. 2010. http://banking.about.com/od/childrenandsaving/Children_and_Saving.htm (accessed December 21, 2010).

The Color Purple (Movie, part 1 of 15). n.d. http://www.youtube.com/watch?v=fjiZe4zUxQM (accessed December 21, 2010).

"Commentary: I Am a Fierce Black Woman." *Essence.* 2010. http://www.essence.com/entertainment/fortyfierceandfab/commentary_why_i_am_a_fierce_black_woman.php (accessed December 21, 2010).

Coretta Scott King Biography. American Academy of Achievement. 1996–2010. http://www.achievement.org/autodoc/page/kin1bio-1 (accessed November 10, 2010).

The Coretta Scott King Book Awards for Authors and Illustrators. American Library Association. 2010. http://www.ala.org/ala/mgrps/rts/emiert/cskbookawards/recipients.cfm (accessed November 10, 2010).

Famous African American Women—Women of Black History. About.com. 2010. http://womenshistory.about.com/od/africanamerican/a/black_women.htm (accessed November 10, 2010).

Finance Lessons Exhibit. The Women's Museum. 2010. http://www.thewomensmuseum.org/womens_museum/exhibits/EXB_ve_exhibit1.asp (accessed November 9, 2010).

How to Make Soap. eHow. 1999–2010. http://www.ehow.com/how_2027286_make-soap.html (accessed November 9, 2010).

I'll Never Turn Back. n.d. http://www.youtube.com/watch?v=gW7z5ASa4W0&feature=related (accessed December 21, 2010).

Jacobs, Nancy. *Oseola McCarty, Mississippi Writer from Hattisburg, Mississippi.* 1999. http://www.mswritersandmusicians.com/writers/oseola-mccarty.html (accessed December 21, 2010).

King, Donnell. *We Shall Overcome.* November 22, 1999. http://www.k-state.edu/english/nelp/american.studies.s98/we.shall.overcome.html (accessed December 22, 2010).

Marian Edelman Wright. Children's Defense Fund. 2010. http://www.childrensdefense.org/about-us/leadership-staff/marian-wright-edelman (accessed December 22, 2010).

Maya Angelou—The Person and Poet. Oakwood Management. 1996–2010. http://www.studyworld.com/newsite/reportessay/biography/literaryauthors%5Cmaya_angelou__the_person_and_poet-225.htm (accessed December 22, 2010).

Miss Ola, The Mississippi Giver by the Austin Church (http://austinchurchmusic.com). n.d. http://www.youtube.com/watch?v=FUf_ZCla51U (accessed December 21, 2010).

"Morrison Discusses Her Novel and Shares Her Ideas." *The Tech—MIT's Oldest and Largest Newspaper.* 2010. http://tech.mit.edu/V112/N24/morrison.24a.html (accessed December 22, 2010).

The National Organization for African-American Women. 2008. http://www.noaw.org (accessed December 22, 2010).

Oseola McCarty. Google Images. n.d. See http://www.google.com/images and enter "Oseola McCarty" in the search field.

"Oseola McCarty." *Chicken Bones: A Journal for Literary and Artistic African-American Themes.* June 10, 2008. http://www.nathanielturner.com/oseolamccarty.htm (accessed December 21, 2010).

Profile of Coretta Scott King, Human Rights Advocate & Civil Rights Activist. About.com. 2010. http://usliberals.about.com/od/peopleinthenews/p/CorettaKing.htm (accessed December 22, 2010).

Raising Her Voice: African American Women Journalists Who Changed History. n.d. See http://books.google.com and enter book title in the search field.

Shah, Anup. *Women's Rights—Global Issues.* July 20, 1998. http://www.globalissues.org/article/166/womens-rights (accessed December 22, 2010).

Sojourner Truth.org Home Page. Michigan Humanities Council. n.d. http://www.sojournertruth.org (accessed December 22, 2010).

Their Eyes Were Watching God. n.d. See http://books.google.com and enter book title in the search field (accessed December 22, 2010).

Their Eyes Were Watching God: Major Themes (study guide). GradeSaver LLC. 1999-2010. http://www.gradesaver.com/their-eyes-were-watching-god/study-guide/major-themes (accessed December 22, 2010).

This Little Light of Mine by the Cedarmont Kids (free download). abmp3.com. n.d. http://abmp3.com/download/3532191-this-little-light-of-mine.html (accessed December 22, 2010).

"*This Little Light of Mine*" song and lyrics. KIDiddles. 1998–2010. http://www.kididdles.com/lyrics/t029.html (accessed November 10, 2010).

Tuition, Campus Housing & Meal Plans. The University of Southern Mississippi. 1995–2010. http://www.usm.edu/admissions/tuition-campus-housing-meal-plans (accessed December 22, 2010).

We Shall Overcome (sung by Diana Ross). n.d. http://www.youtube.com/watch?v=CnzmPrsLXn8&feature=related (accessed December 22, 2010).

Willie Mae Ford Smith. St. Louis Walk of Fame. 1997–2008. http://stlouiswalkoffame.org/inductees/willie-smith.html (accessed December 21, 2010).

Additional Reading Materials

Angelou, Maya. *I Know Why the Caged Bird Sings.* New York: Random House, 1970.

This book is part of Maya Angelou's autobiographical series in which she describes what her life was like growing up in the South. In a dysfunctional family, Maya developed low self-esteem and couldn't seem to cope until she challenges herself to be more than the leaders expect from African American students. With her Mommy and brother's encouragement, she overcame adversity, and today readers have her literary stories.

Birtha, Becky. *Grandmama's Pride.* Chicago: Albert Whitman, 2005.

This is a story that recalls the unfair laws that existed in the South in the past. Today those laws no longer exist because of the successful boycotting, protests, and demands made by voices of both races. The author's powerful story begins with how things were and how Sarah Marie and her family endured segregation, which ultimately led to a strong sense of hope and pride that grew out of the struggle for integration.

Bolden, Tonya. *Take-Off: American All-Girl Bands During WWII.* New York: Alfred A. Knopf, 2007.

American women—they've been singing and playing music for years. This interesting and information-filled book reflects on the significant role of female bands, both black and white, and how their musical genius was a part of the World War II era.

Brenza, Corona. ***Sojourner Truth's "Ain't I a Woman?" Speech: A Primary Source Investigation.*** **New York: Rosen, 2005.**

This book is a primary source defining the impact that an ex-slave had on the Women's Rights movement and the abolition of slavery. The subject's given name was Isabella Baumfree, but she later changed her name to Sojourner Truth.

Clinton, Catherine. ***When Harriet Met Sojourner.*** **New York: Katherine Tegen Books, 2007.**

A common goal, different strategies. Two women, one world. Traveling through the perils of time, two great freedom fighters worked hard to tell the truth and set people free. This is their story.

Colbert, David. ***Michelle Obama: An American Story.*** **Boston: Houghton Mifflin Harcourt, 2009.**

In this book, the author gives a descriptive account of the early life of First Lady Michelle Obama. From her background to her life at the White House, Obama's story is a most interesting one that is bound to motivate young girls to strive and settle for nothing but the best. A descendant of a former slave—her grandfather from South Carolina—she never settled for second best and always strived to become her best. One can't help but chuckle while reading this book because whatever her brother did, she wanted to do better. Although Michelle never wants folks to say that she's special, her brother thinks she is because of her determination, devotion, dedication, and love for all people.

Crews, Donald. ***Bigmama's.*** **New York: Scholastic, 1991.**

Young readers will be fascinated with the author's description of farm life. This delightful story is reminiscent of what it's like to spend the summer on the farm with Grandmama. There are many jobs and activities to do on the farm, and this book is a must-read for those studying or interested in farm life. The story has a surprising ending.

Edwards, Roberta. ***Michelle Obama: Mom-in-Chief.*** **New York: Grosset & Dunlap, 2009.**

Learn more about the first African American woman who became the First Lady of the United States. This talented woman is highly educated with a degree in law and a successful career behind her. This book tells about her role as First Lady, mother, and community leader.

Evans, Mari. ***I Am a Black Woman.*** **New York: Quill, 1970.**

This collection of poems focuses on African American women—their lives, hardships, battles, and triumphs.

Ferris, Jeri Chase. ***With Open Hands: A Story About Biddy Mason.*** **Minneapolis, MN: Carolrhoda Books, 1999.**

Biddy Mason never knew her parents and was raised by a caring slave couple in the slave quarters. By the time she reached her teens, her medical skills were exceptional. She knew how to look for the right roots to heal the sick as well as how to deliver babies.

Lasky, Kathryn. ***Vision of Beauty: The Story of Sarah Breedlove Walker.*** **Cambridge, MA: Candlewick Press, 2000.**

Beautiful illustrations support the text in this biography, which provides encouragement to readers by telling of one whose life was anything but good; yet she pursued her dream and became the first African American female millionaire by manufacturing cosmetics.

Lindbergh, Reeve. ***Nobody Owns the Sky: The Story of "Brave Bessie" Coleman.*** **Cambridge, MA: Candlewick Press, 1996.**

Bessie Coleman wanted the birds to know that one day she would join them in the sky. When her dreams were shattered at home, she decided to move to another country in pursuit of her dream. Faced with discrimination, called names, and often simply ignored, Bessie persevered. Readers will delight in knowing that she did join the birds in the sky—Bessie was determined, and she did soar.

McGovern, Ann. **"*Wanted Dead or Alive.*"** ***The True Story of Harriet Tubman.*** **New York: Scholastic, 1965.**

Harriet Tubman, called the "Black Moses" by her people, worked day and night to free enslaved men and women. Slave owners were determined to catch her, but she always managed to find safe havens along the way on the dangerous journey from the South to the North via the Underground Railroad.

McKissack, Lisa Beringer. ***Women of the Harlem Renaissance.*** **Minneapolis, MN: Compass Point Books, 2007.**

Black women in America have carved their way into history since they first arrived here. This book takes a look specifically at African American women in the 1920s and 1930s. Readers are introduced to heroines who were relentless in the pursuit of their dreams and aspirations. Some were even rejected by their own families or communities because of the color of their skin, so they traveled to Harlem in search of a better life. They often found inspiration and encouragement from such male figures as W. E. B. Du Bois, whose primary interest was in helping his race move forward. This was an important foundation to the Harlem Renaissance. Based on their persistence and perseverance, these women's stories serve as motivational tools for young adult readers.

McKissack, Patricia, and Fredrick McKissack. *Sojourner Truth: Ain't I a Woman?* New York: Scholastic, 1992.

The McKissacks have written yet another powerful book. Readers will marvel at the stamina and charisma of this former slave who worked hard to buy her freedom and that of her son. The title of this work is taken from the speech that she delivered in 1851 at a Women's Rights Convention in Akron, Ohio. Although many worked hard to prevent her from speaking, the impact of the speech is still felt today.

Pinkney, Andrea. *Sojourner Truth's Step-Stomp Stride.* New York: Jump at the Sun, 2009.

This is an easy read for young readers who are just beginning to understand the important contributions made to U.S. history by African American women. Readers will follow and understand Sojourner's "stomp" across the country, steppin' to eradicate slavery and racism.

Pinkney, Gloria Jean. *In the Forest of Your Remembrance.* New York: Phyllis Fogelman Books/An Imprint of Penguin Putnam, 2001.

The "greatest story ever told" is from the most highly read volume of literature—the Holy Bible. In this volume of inspirational stories, Gloria Pinkney has poured her heart and soul into the writing and telling of thirty-three stories confirming how powerful one's life can become if faith is practiced.

Chapter 16

SLAVES, SLAVERY, AND THE UNDERGROUND RAILROAD

Lesson Plan: Knowing How to Approach the Slavery Issue

Websites
http://www.mediainstitute.org/NFSW/2007/index.html
http://www.famousquotes.me.uk/speeches/Mary-Reynolds/
http://www.historyplace.com/speeches/douglass.htm
http://www.blackpast.org/?q=african-american-history-major-speeches

Brief Summary

This material is designed to provide ideas, suggestions, and resources for educators as they prepare to present this chapter to students. Although many of these stories are heartbreaking, it is valuable to have firsthand knowledge of how people worked together to encourage and empower each other in their quest for personal freedom. These books should be read, shared, and discussed with students.

Focus

- Be sensitive to students who may struggle with the subject or books in this chapter.
- Help students understand the power in being free.

Teacher Input

- Use this online resource to discuss Freedom of Speech: http://www.timcforkids.com/TFK/teachers/minilessons/wr/0,28171,1588219,00.html.
- Show the following online resource to the class for celebrating National Freedom of Speech Week: Free to Express Feelings Without Being Disrespectful: http://www.randomhouse.com/highschool/resources/guides3/censorship.html#2.

Guided Practice

- Create a Freedom Box and Freedom Strips. Ask students to write one statement about a destructive behavior or habit they may be facing on the Freedom Strips. Place the completed strips in the Freedom Box.
- Using the list of statements drawn from the Freedom Box, lead a discussion of what freedom means, and allow students time to brainstorm possible solutions to take in breaking free of destructive behaviors.

Independent Practice

- Divide the class into four groups. Ask each group to choose a major speech delivered by a slave. Instruct the groups to read and analyze their chosen speech and to then present their interpretations of the speech to the class.

Closure

- Invite students to express their gratitude for being free.
- Students discuss how understanding what slavery was like might enable them to help those who are in bondage today.
- Plan to celebrate National Freedom of Speech Week, or create your own classroom celebration around freedom.

Assessment

- Group discussions, analyzing and interpreting slave speeches, and Freedom Box contributions and discussion of resolves.

Feelings, Tom. *The Middle Passage*. New York: Dial Books, 1995.

About the Author

Tom Feelings. n.d. http://www.nathanielturner.com/tomfeelings.htm (accessed October 30, 2010).

Literary Elements	Lexile Range	Teacher Resources and Supplies
Art Coretta Scott King Book Award	—	Book Wordless picture books Index Cards Worksheet
Reading Level Grades 5 and up	**Accelerated Reader** —	

Additional Titles
Feelings, Tom. ***My Soul Looks Back in Wonder.***
Lester, Julius. ***To Be a Slave.***

Websites
http://k-8visual.info
http://www.fno.org/PL/vislit.htm
http://www.juneteenth.com/middlep.htm
http://www.edselect.com/visual.htm
http://www.nga.gov/kids/kids.htm
http://www.nhptv.org/kn/vs/artlab5.asp
http://www.ilike.com/artist/Stevie+Wonder+&+Melba+Moore/track/Lift+Every+Voice+And+Sing

Brief Summary

This is no "hearsay" book. Tom Feelings gives those who pick up this book the opportunity to see, interpret, feel, and understand the story. This soul-searching, heartfelt work reveals the passion of an artist and his ability to use the paintbrush to tell a story.

Focus

- Wordless Picture Books
- Freedom of Expression
- Types of Communication

Teacher Input

- Invite the students to comment on whether they ever felt they were misunderstood.
- Ask students if they know what "visual literacy" is. Explain the term if they do not.
- Check school or public libraries for wordless picture books for students to use to during Guided Practice.
- Introduce this book, discuss its title, and write on the board the following letters and what they represent:
    - Respect for self and classmates during discussions of this book.
    - Group participation and respect for individual opinions within the group.
    - Project completion.

Guided Practice

- Distribute wordless books to students for a story-writing activity. At least three books should rotate among students to determine whether their interpretations of these books are similar or varied. Students write stories to go with the illustrations.
- Instruct students to use the following site to explore and gain new knowledge about the visual arts: http://www.edselect.com/visual.htm.
- Allow students to use this interactive online site to express to others what they see in their hearts: http://www.nga.gov/kids/kids.htm.

Independent Practice

- To enhance visual literacy while making a statement at the same time, suggest that each student think of an event, place, or item to draw. Have them name their drawings, "The message I'm trying to convey."
- Instruct each student to create a ten-page wordless book. Review with each student his thoughts for the project prior to the design to make certain that his or her focus does not conflict with school or district policies.
- Ask students to brainstorm why they believe Feelings wrote, "My Soul Looks Back In Wonder."
- Assign students to develop a visual biographical report on Tom Feelings, the illustrator.

Closure

- Students analyze the significance of using wordless books with readers and nonreaders and explain what the lesson teaches about visual literacy.

Assessment

- Student feedback to teacher questions and classroom discussions, eagerness to interpret projects, and production of projects.

"I Get the Message" Worksheet

Draw a Picture Here and Write the Message of the Picture on the Back

Share your interpretation of ***The Middle Passage***.

____

____

____

____

Write about Tom Feelings and his works.

____

____

____

____

What poem did you read from ***My Soul Looks Back in Wonder***?

____

____

Levine, Ellen. *Henry's Freedom Box: A True Story from the Underground Railroad.* New York: Scholastic Press, 2007.

About the Author

Ellen Levine. Scholastic Inc. 1996–2010. http://www2.scholastic.com/browse/contributor.jsp?id=3318 (accessed December 24, 2010).

Literary Elements Coretta Scott King Book Award Imagery Historical Fiction Narrative	**Lexile Range** AD380L	**Teacher Resources and Supplies** Book Box Worksheet
Reading Level Grades 1 and up	**Accelerated Reader** Points: 0.5 Book Level: 3.0	
Additional Title Hamilton, Virginia. ***Many Thousand Gone: African Americans from Slavery to Freedom.*** **Websites** http://www.spartacus.schoolnet.co.uk/slavery.htm http://www.nmm.ac.uk/freedom/links.cfm		

Brief Summary

Boxed to go—please handle with care. This was no ordinary box. The contents could breathe, feel, and love and had a soul. And the soul, just like a little bird, wanted to be free. This is the story of a young man in search of a better life for himself and the people he loved. When opened in a state that allowed free blacks to know and celebrate their birthdays, the contents from the box stepped into a place that offered hope.

Focus

- Perseverance
- Slaves and Slavery
- Slave Trade

Teacher Input

- Show a box and brainstorm with students the many ways that people use boxes. List the reasons the students give on the board.
- Show the class a box before it is folded together and introduce the book as the box is set up (use this site to learn to build a box: http://illuminations.nctm.org/LessonDetail.aspx?id=L570).
- See this website for a digital copy of the 1816 book written by Henry Box Brown: http://docsouth.unc.edu/neh/brownbox/menu.html. This book can be used with all ages.
- Arrange with a merchant to collect different sizes of boxes for a classroom activity titled, "***It's in the Box!***"
- Ask students to share what they understand about slavery.

- Discuss the types of slavery that exist using the following resource: http://www.living-prosperity.com/modern-day-slavery.html.

Guided Practice

- Instruct first- and second-grade students to draw a picture of a box with a man inside and call it Henry's Picture, or decorate a small box and name it Henry's Box.
- Lead a discussion about slavery with the class. Allow students to comment on ways slaves tried to escape. Have students use one of several resources located online to support their comments (e.g., http://www.whispersofangels.com/secrets.html).
- Write down various secret codes and distribute quilt patterns (http://www.osblackhistory.com/quiltcodes.php). Organize the class into two teams. Distribute code patterns to Team One and code meanings to Team Two. Ask each student on Team One to locate the student on Team Two holding the match or meaning of the pattern code.
- Assign students an essay using the theme "***What I Like About Freedom.***"

Independent Practice

- Have students choose one slave from a list of well-known former slaves and develop a plan to help that person to freedom. Students must identify the slave and his or her location, plan a "Boxed for Freedom" escape, and tell what contribution(s) the slave makes after obtaining freedom.

Closure

- Students present group and individual project reports.

Assessment

- Respectful reaction to topic, respect for individual points of view, brainstorming, and project completion.

Set Me Free Worksheet

Locate and read these online resources to determine the commonalities between Henry "Box" Brown, Aunt Jemima, Uncle Ben, and Rastus. Share your point of view about the articles in the space provided.

Online Resource	Your Point of View
Henry Brown http://www.encyclopediavirginia.org/Brown_Henry_Box_ca_1815	
Aunt Jemima's Pancakes http://www.auntjemima.com/aj_history http://www.npr.org/templates/story/story.php?storyId=6709995	
Uncle Ben's Rice http://www.unclebens.ca/en-ca/About/BenStory.aspx	
Rastus—Cream of Wheat http://www.ferris.edu/jimcrow/tom/ http://www.petitiononline.com/cw3r6525/petition.htm	

Henry built a box. Identify an issue or problem, then describe what you will build to flee from it.

What do you like about freedom?

Nelson, Marilyn. *Fortune's Bones: The Manumission Requiem.* Asheville, NC: Front Street, 2004.

About the Author

Marilyn Nelson. Poet.org. Poetry, Poems, Bios & More. Academy of American Poets. 1997–2010. http://www.poets.org/poet.php/prmPID/97 (accessed October 30, 2010).

Literary Elements	Lexile Range	Teacher Resources and Supplies
Capitol Choices: Noteworthy Books for Children Coretta Scott King Book Awards History Music Notable Children Poetry Science	—	Book Worksheet
Reading Level Grades 6 and up	**Accelerated Reader** Points: 0.5 Book Level: 5.6	
Additional Title Rinaldi, Ann. ***Numbering All the Bones.*** **Websites** http://www.wtnh.com/generic/ct_style/waterbury_symphony_orchestra http://www.fortunestory.org/fortune/who.asp http://www.npr.org/templates/story/story.php?storyId=1433035		

Brief Summary

An award-winning and heartfelt book of poems that describe the historic reconstruction of the life of a slave named Fortune, who died in 1798. His owner preserved Fortune's skeleton to teach anatomy, and the bones were then donated to a museum many years later. Nelson uses poetry to help readers feel Fortune's pain and to express compassion for Dinah, his wife. Nelson describes how Dinah felt when directed to clean the room where the bones of her husband were stored. To help readers understand the full meaning of this powerful book, the author has provided resources for additional research.

Focus

- Poetry
- Servitude
- Requiem

Teacher Input

- Present this book to the class by playing an introduction by the author, Marilyn Nelson, from one of these sites:
  - http://www.wtnh.com/generic/ct_style/waterbury_symphony_orchestra
  - http://www.teachingbooks.net/book_reading.cgi?id=3662&a=1

- Find pictures of Nelson here: http://www.google.com/search?sourceid=navclient&ie=UTF-8&rlz=1T4TSNA_en___US387&q=marilyn+nelson+photo.
- If desired, show the trailer to the film *Amistad* and the interactive map of Waterbury, Connecticut. On the *Amistad* slave ship, the slaves revolted, and their bodies were never recovered. In the book *Fortune's Bones*, a faithful slave's body is lost until it is rediscovered and history is generated to keep his legacy alive. For more information, see http://www.fortunestory.org/waterburyinthe18thcentury/mapframes.htm.
- Explain to the students that not all African Americans were slaves.
- Introduce the singing group ***Sweet Honey and the Rock*** to students (http://www.sweethoney.com).

Guided Practice

- Instruct students to use this interactive map to navigate their way around Waterbury, Connecticut: Make certain the students understand what a requiem is. Allow students time to locate information on how to compose a requiem.
- Give students an assignment to compose a poem expressing what they think about slavery.
- Invite students to comment on what they know about the modern-day slave trade.
- Have students listen to Nelson's reading of "***Dinah's Lament***" at http://www.teachingbooks.net/book_reading.cgi?id=3662&a=1. Brainstorm how you would have reacted to Miss Lydia's request to clean around your dead husband's (or wife's) bones.
- Assign students to read the Author's Notes and name the groups to whom she dedicated her requiem.
- Read aloud the words expressed by the Vietnamese Buddhist monk Thich Nhat Hanh. See http://www.pbs.org/wnet/religionandethics/episodes/september-19-2003/thich-nhat-hanh/1843.
- Allow students to describe a time in their lives when they lost all hope.

Independent Practice

- Divide the class into groups of two or three and allow them to report on specific jobs held by free blacks during the slavery era.
- Guide the students in a discussion on why good or kind slave masters may have had more devoted and dedicated slaves than harsh, cruel slave masters.
- Have students locate and read online biographies on Marilyn Nelson and Dr. Ysaye M. Barnwell, a vocalist with the African American a cappella ensemble Sweet Honey in the Rock.

Closure

- Suggest that students start a fund-raising drive for world hunger.
- Students list the names of at least ten slaves who fought for freedom and made a major contribution toward abolishing slavery.

Assessment

- Student participation, reports, and project design.

Vocabulary Worksheet

Define these words:

Cantata ____

Requiem ____

Servitude ____

Bibliography

Author Dennis Fradin. n.d. http://www.scbwi-illinois.org/FradinD.html (accessed October 30, 2010).

Ellen Levine: Scholastic.com. 1996–2010. http://www2.scholastic.com/browse/contributor.jsp?id=3318 (accessed October 30, 2010).

Feelings, Tom. *The Middle Passage.* New York: Dial Books, 1995.

Fradin, Dennis Brindell. *Bound for the North Star: True Stories of Fugitive Slaves.* New York: Clarion Books, 2000.

Home-Julius Lester. n.d. http://juliuslester.net (accessed October 30, 2010).

Lester, Julius. *Day of Tears.* New York: Jump at the Sun/Hyperion Books for Children, 2005.

Levine, Ellen. *Henry's Freedom Box: A True Story About the Underground Railroad.* New York: Scholastic Press, 2007.

Marilyn Nelson. Poet.org-Poetry, Poems, Bios & More. Academy of American Poets. 1997–2010. http://www.poets .org/poet.php/prmPID/97 (accessed October 30, 2010).

Nelson, Marilyn. *Fortune's Bones: The Manumission Requiem.* Ashville, NC: Front Street, 2004.

Tom Feelings. n.d. http://www.nathanielturner.com/tomfeelings.htm (accessed October 30, 2010).

Webliography

Adam Lambert—The Tracks of My Tears (free MP3 download). Beemp3.com. n.d. http://beemp3.com/download.php?file=7357892&song=The+Tracks+of+My+Tears (accessed December 24, 2010).

African American History: Major Speeches. The Black Past: Remembered and Reclaimed. 2007–2009. http://www.blackpast.org/?q=african-american-history-major-speeches (accessed November 5, 2010).

Africans in America/Part 4/Narrative: Fugitive Slaves and Northern Racism. WGBH/PBS. n.d. http://www.pbs.org/wgbh/aia/part4/4narr3.html (accessed December 23, 2010).

Aunt Jemima—Our History. Quaker Oats Company. 2010. http://www.auntjemima.com/aj_history (accessed December 25, 2010).

Black Dancers. Son of South. 2003–2008. http://www.sonofthesouth.net/slavery/african-american-art/black-dancers.htm (accessed November 28, 2010).

The Demise and Removal of the Rastus/Cream of Wheat Icon Petition. Artifice. 1999–2005. http://www.petitiononline.com/cw3r6525/petition.html (accessed December 25, 2010).

Elliott, Pat. *Visual Arts.* October 31, 2010. http://www.edselect.com/visual.htm (accessed December 23, 2010).

Fanny Kemble and Pierce Butler. WGBH. n.d. http://www.pbs.org/wgbh/aia/part4/4p1569.html (accessed December 25, 2010).

Flight to Freedom: Slavery and the Underground Railroad in Maryland. Maryland State Archives. 2010. http://www.mdslavery.net/html/antebellum/ba.html (accessed December 24, 2010).

Fortune's Bones: The Manumission Requiem. TeachingBooks.net. 2001–2010. http://www.teachingbooks.net/book_reading cgi?id=3662&a=1 (accessed December 26, 2010).

Frederick Douglass Speech: The Hypocrisy of America. Great Speeches Collection. The History Place. n.d. http://www.historyplace.com/speeches/douglass.htm (accessed December 26, 2010).

Freedom: Slavery Links. UK Museums. n.d. http://www.nmm.ac.uk/freedom/links.cfm (accessed November 10, 2010).

The Freeman's Bureau. n.d. http://freedmensbureau.com (accessed December 23, 2010).

Henry Box Brown, b. 1816 Narrative of the Life of Henry Box Brown, Written by Himself. University Library. The University of North Carolina at Chapel Hill 2004. http://docsouth.unc.edu/neh/brownbox/menu.html (accessed December 25, 2010).

Her Day as a Slave: Famous Speech by Mary Reynolds. n.d. http://www.famousquotes.me.uk/speeches/Mary-Reynolds (accessed December 26, 2010).

Hidden Museum Treasures: Fortune's Bones: NPR. n.d. http://www.npr.org/templates/story/story.php?storyId=1433035 (accessed December 26, 2010).

Interactive Map of Fortune's Waterbury. n.d. http://www.fortunestory.org/waterburyinthe18thcentury/mapframes.htm (accessed December 26, 2010).

Jim Crow Museum of Racist Memorabilia at Ferris State University. n.d. http://www.ferris.edu/jimcrow/ (accessed November 4, 2010).

John Brown, fl. 1854, Slave Life in Georgia: A Narrative of the Life, Suffering, and Escape of. University Library. 2004. http://docsouth.unc.edu/neh/jbrown/jbrown.html (accessed December 23, 2010).

Johnson, Dr. Kenneth R. *A Slave's Family Struggle for Freedom.* 1978. http://www.rootsweb.ancestry.com/~alcolber/aa-struggle.htm (accessed December 24, 2010).

Libba Moore Gray (1937–1995). n.d. http://www.utc.edu/Academic/TennesseeWriters/authors/gray.libba.html (accessed October 26, 2010).

Mann, Dr. Bob. *Illuminations: Building a Box.* National Council of Teachers of Mathmatics. 2000–2010. http://illuminations.nctm.org/LessonDetail.aspx?id=L570 (accessed December 24, 2010).

Margaret Garner. AALBC.Com. 1997–2010. http://aalbc.com/authors/margaret.htm (accessed December 24, 2010).

Marilyn Nelson Photos. n.d. http://www.google.com/search?sourceid=navclient&ie=UTF-8&rlz=1T4TSNA_en_US387&q=marilyn+nelson+photo (accessed December 26, 2010).

McKenzie, Jamie. *Visual Literacy and the Net.* 1998. http://www.fno.org/PL/vislit.htm (accessed December 26, 2010).

The Middle Passage—Tom Feelings. Juneteenth.com. n.d. http://www.juneteenth.com/middlep.htm (accessed December 26, 2010).

Modern Day Slavery. Living-Prosperity.com. 2010. http://www.living-prosperity.com/modern-day-slavery.html (accessed December 25, 2010).

Moss Kendrix: The Advertiser's Holy Trinity: Aunt Jemima, Rastus, and Uncle Ben. The Museum of Public Relations. 2010. http://www.prmuseum.com/kendrix/trinity.html (accessed December 25, 2010).

Moyer, Judith. *Step-by-Step Guide to Oral History.* Oral History Association. 1999. http://dohistory.org/on_your_own/toolkit/oralHistory.html (accessed December 24, 2010).

National Freedom of Speech Week. CreationDepot. n.d. http://www.mediainstitute.org/NFSW/2007/index.html (accessed December 26, 2010).

National Gallery of Art NGAKids Art Zone. National Gallery of Art, Washington. 2010. http://www.nga.gov/kids/zone/zone.htm (accessed November 6, 2010).

New Georgia Encyclopedia: William and Ellen Craft (1824–1900; 1826–1891). Georgia Humanities Council. 2004–2010. http://www.georgiaencyclopedia.org/nge/Article.jsp?id=h-622 (accessed December 24, 2010).

NHPTV Knowledge Network—Visual Arts for Kids. New Hampshire Public Television. 2010. http://www.nhptv.org/kn/vs/artlab5.asp (accessed December 26, 2010).

Pathways to Freedom: About the Underground Railroad. Maryland Public Television. 2010. http://pathways.thinkport.org/about/about11.cfm (accessed December 24, 2010).

Quotes. ThinkExist.com. 1999–2010. http://thinkexist.com/quotation/tears_are_words_the_heart_can-t/339969.html (accessed December 24, 2010).

Revisting Aunt Jemima: "Slave in a Box." National Public Radio. 2010. http://www.npr.org/templates/story/story.php?storyId=6709995 (accessed December 25, 2010).

Runaway Slaves: Ohio History Central. Ohio Historical Society. 2010. http://www.ohiohistorycentral.org/entry.php?rec=626&nm=Runaway-Slaves (accessed November 10, 2010).

Scales, Pat. *Censorship. Random House for High School Teachers. Teacher's Guides.* 2005. http://www.randomhouse.com/highschool/resources/guides3/censorship.html#2 (accessed December 23, 2010).

Slave Narratives. The MoAD Salon—Museum of the African Diaspora. n.d. http://www.moadsf.org/salon/exhibits/slave_narratives/index.html (accessed December 24, 2010).

The Slave Trade. n.d. http://www.spartacus.schoolnet.co.uk/slavery.htm (accessed November 10, 2010).

Solomon Northup. Twelve Years a Slave: Narrative of Solomon Northup, a Citizen of New-York Kidnapped in Washington City in 1841 and Rescued in 1853. University Library. 2004. http://docsouth.unc.edu/fpn/northup/northup.html (accessed December 26, 2010).

Summary of the Story of the Life of John Anderson, the Fugitive Slave. The University Library. 2004. http://docsouth.unc.edu/neh/twelvetr/summary.html (accessed December 24, 2010).

A Teenager's Guide to Emancipation. Legal Assistance Resource Center. 2008. http://www.larcc.org/pamphlets/children_family/teen_emancipation.htm (accessed December 23, 2010).

Top Five Causes of the Civil War. About.com. 2010. http://americanhistory.about.com/od/civilwarmenu/a/cause_civil_war.htm (accessed December 23, 2010).

The Trail of Tears and the Forced Relocation of the Cherokee Nation. n.d. http://www.nps.gov/nr/twhp/wwwlps/lessons/118trail/118trail.htm (accessed November 10, 2010).

Turner, Patricia A. *The Rise and Fall of Eliza Harris.* National Endowment for the Humanities. 2007. http://utc.iath.virginia.edu/interpret/exhibits/turner/turner.html (accessed December 24, 2010).

Uncle Ben's Story. Mars Incorporated. 2008. http://www.unclebens.ca/en-ca/About/BenStory.aspx (accessed December 25, 2010).

Underground Railroad—Runaway Slaves Method of Escape. n.d. http://www.whispersofangels.com/secrets.html (accessed December 26, 2010).

Understanding the First Amendment. Time for Kids. Classroom: Mini-Lessons. Time Inc. 2010. http://www.timeforkids.com/TFK/teachers/minilessons/wr/0,28171,1588219,00.html (accessed December 22, 2010).

Visual Literacy K–8. Black Cuckatoo Publishing. 2010. http://k-8visual.info/ (accessed November 10, 2010).

Waterbury Symphony Orchestra. Connectcut Style, WTNH.com. 2000–2011. http://www.wtnh.com/generic/ct_style/waterbury_symphony_orchestra (accessed December 26, 2010).

Who Was Fortune? Mattatuck Historical Society. 2004. http://www.fortunestory.org/fortune/who.asp (accessed November 10, 2010).

The Weeping Time. PBS/WGBH. n.d. http://www.pbs.org/wgbh/aia/part4/4p2918.html (accessed November 10, 2010).

Additional Reading Materials

Allen, Thomas B. *Harriet Tubman, Secret Agent: How Daring Slaves and Free Blacks Spied for the Union During the Civil War.* Washington, DC: National Geographic, 2006.

Brave men and women like Harriet Tubman risked their lives to advance the cause of freedom during the Civil War. They secretly read documents, listened, and traveled for the Union Army during a very turbulent time in our nation's history.

Cooper, Michael L. *Slave Spirituals and the Jubilee Singers.* New York: Clarion Books, 2001.

Michael Cooper recounts the songs of slavery sung by the renowned Frisk Jubilee Singers in this book. These spirituals are beautiful to the ears of most any listener.

Fradin, Judith Bloom, and Dennis Brindell Fradin. *5,000 Miles to Freedom: Ellen and William Craft's Flight from Slavery.* Washington, DC: National Geographic, 2006.

This clever, real-life couple disguised themselves as master and servant traveling together to reach a state where they could live free. Readers will be fascinated by light-skinned Ellen Craft's role (she dressed as a rich white man) and that of her husband (who pretended to be her slave) as they navigate through danger.

Hamilton, Virginia. *Many Thousand Gone: African Americans from Slavery to Freedom.* New York: Alfred A. Knopf, 1993.

With Virginia Hamilton's descriptive writing and Leo and Diane Dillon's fine artwork, the stories of the fugitive slaves come to life for the reader. Living in harsh conditions, these men and women were willing to risk losing their lives to the Underground Railroad rather than continue living in captivity.

Hatt, Christine. *Slavery from Africa to the Americans.* London: Evans Brothers, 1997.

This informative book is a great resource for student research. It consists of documents that slave owners kept, as well as narratives from both slaves and free blacks. A glossary helps readers to fully understand the articles. Black-and-white and color photographs and maps complement the text.

Lester, Julius. ***From Slave Ship to Freedom Road.*** **New York: Dial Books, 1998.**

This is a riveting book about the lives, living conditions, and perseverance of a group of strong men and women who endured slavery and fought to abolish it. Lester's innovative way of crafting words inspires readers to see, feel, and relive the lives of those involved.

Lester, Julius. ***To Be a Slave.*** **New York: Dial Books , 1968.**

In this book, Lester uses texts derived from a variety of primary documents to tell the story of what it was like to live the life of a slave. The text and the illustrations portray the emotions the slaves must have felt during that tumultuous time.

Rinaldi, Ann. ***Numbering All the Bones.*** **New York: Scholastic, 2002.**

This is the painful story of a young girl who is a house slave on a Georgia plantation. She describes what her life is like, the fate of one of her brothers and the escape of another, and how she was befriended by Clara Barton.

Sherman, Pat. ***Ben and the Emancipation Proclamation.*** **Grand Rapids, MI: Eerdmans Books for Young Readers, 2010.**

A young slave boy secretly improves his life by learning to read. Although slaves were not allowed to read and would be punished if caught doing so, Ben acquires this skill by working as an apprentice. Determined to earn the gold dollar his mother promised him if he masters this skill, he uses his wits and creative talents to learn to read. He becomes a role model to other slaves as he understands and communicates what is happening outside the bounds of slavery.

Stroud, Bettye. ***The Patchwork Path: A Quilt Map.*** **Somerville, MA: Candlewick Press, 2007.**

This is an incredible book about a young slave girl and her father who bravely sought freedom by relying on the security of a quilt that her dead mother taught her how to make, stitched with encouragement, love, and endurance.

Chapter 17

SPECIAL CHALLENGES

Teach your students to develop empathy, tolerance, and respect for children and adults who have special challenges, including mental and physical disabilities and chronic and terminal illnesses.

Altman, Linda Jacobs. *Singing with Momma Lou.* New York: Lee & Low Books, 2002.

About the Author

Linda Jacobs Altman. Jacketflap.com. 2010. http://www.jacketflap.com/persondetail.asp?person=94984 (accessed October 30, 2010).

Literary Elements	Lexile Range	Teacher Resources and Supplies
Disability Best Children's Books of the Year—Banks Street College Music Myers Outstanding Book Awards Honorable Mention Neuroscience	—	Book Paper Pencils Crayons Binder combs Digital camera Flip camera Worksheet
Reading Level Grades: 1–4	**Accelerated Reader** Points: 0.5 Book Level: 3.8	
Additional Title Hamilton, Virginia. ***Sweet Whispers, Brother Rush.*** **Websites** http://www.mayoclinic.com/health/alzheimers/HQ00216 http://www.negrospirituals.com		

Brief Summary

Tamika's grandmother has Alzheimer's disease, and Tamika finds it difficult to be around her. Her father becomes upset when Tamika leaves the care center one day without saying goodbye to her grandmother. Tamika knows she must find a way to communicate with her grandmother. What she does will delight readers and help those who may also have relatives with this or a similar illness.

Focus

- Alzheimer's Disease
- Grandmothers

Teacher Input

- Introduce the book by using the following online resources:
  - http://www.alz.org/living_with_alzheimers_just_for_kids_and_teens.asp
  - http://www.youtube.com/watch?v=GVwJNg4Wgq4
- Lead students in a discussion about Alzheimer's disease. Invite them to tell what they know about the disease and whether they know anyone who has it.
- Use the following online resource to help students better understand Alzheimer's disease: http://www.mayoclinic.com/health/alzheimers/HQ00216.
- Ask students to list hymns or spirituals that Momma Lou may have sung while sitting in the community room: http://www.negrospirituals.com.
- Ask students what is means to give someone the "silent treatment."
- Invite students to comment on whether any one of them is the first grandchild.

Guided Practice

- Invite students to share a time when they made a visit to a nursing home and tell why they were there.
- Help students locate and listen to Civil Rights protest songs. Have them view photos from the Civil Rights movement.
- Assign students to research and write a brief report on understanding people who have mental illnesses. Use the following online resource:
  - http://www.mhasp.org/coping/guardians.html
  - http://www.aacap.org/cs/root/facts_for_families/talking_to_kids_about_mental_illnesses
- Invite students to predict how they believe Tamika will respond to her Momma Lou after looking through her scrapbook.
- Have students collaborate and produce a "Grandmothers' Video."

Independent Practice

- Suggest that students design a "My Granny" scrapbook that reflects how they describe their grandmothers.

Closure

- Invite grandmothers to class to watch the special project presentations.

Assessment

- Student brainstorming, discussions, project planning, development, and presentations.

My Granny Worksheet

Grandmother's Memory Comes Back

Create a storyboard for your book and video here. You can use additional paper if necessary.

My Fun Work Section.

Respond to the following questions and statements.

1. What is Alzheimer's Disease?

2. Have you ever given anyone the "silent treatment"?

3. Three things I like most about staying at my mother's Momma's house.

4. Here are three songs my grandmother may have sung just to remember "the good ole days."

5. What I love or remember about my father's mother.

6. What I love or remember about my mother's mother.

7. Do my grandmothers remember the Civil Rights movement?

8. Do you or a friend of yours have no memories of a grandparent?

Krull, Kathleen. *Wilma Unlimited: How Wilma Rudolph Became the World's Fastest Woman.* New York: Voyager Books, 1996.

About the Author

Kathleen Krull: Children's Author. n.d. http://www.kathleenkrull.com (accessed October 30, 2010).

Literary Element Biography	**Lexile Range** AD730L	**Teacher Resources and Supplies** Book Index cards Worksheet
Reading Level K–Grade 5	**Accelerated Reader** Points: 0.5 Book Level: 5.1	
Additional Title Barasch, Lynne. ***Knockin' on Wood.*** **Websites** http://www.wilmarudolph.net http://www.youtube.com/watch?v=igl8DmcKRhQ http://kidshealth.org/parent/system/ill/phys_therapy.html http://www.achievement.org/autodoc/page/sal0bio-1		

Brief Summary

Determined to use her mind to heal her body, a young girl whose physical condition almost shattered her life is featured in this book. Through hard work, a determined mind, and strong faith, she beat the odds, using her talent and triumphs to bridge the racial gap in her hometown and across the country.

Focus

- Perseverance
- Achievement
- Racial Dignity

Teacher Input

- Introduce the book by using this online resource: http://www.wilmarudolph.net.
- Discuss health issues and how vaccines are available today to prevent children and adults from contracting certain diseases or illnesses.
- Ask students to share a monologue of Wilma's thoughts as she sat in her wheelchair watching the children play outside.
- Present the "Let's Track Our Concentration" Card Activity to the class. Each card has a question about a well-known African American female athlete with a web resource to find the answer (see the reproducible for the cards later in this section). You may choose to develop a PowerPoint presentation of this game or simply show the cards. Reward students who score a perfect ten.
- Invite students to comment on what they think is the meaning of faith and whether they live by faith.

Guided Practice

- Invite students to participate in the "Let's Track Our Concentration" activity. This activity is relevant to the challenges Wilma knew she would have to face while learning to walk again.
- Have students create a collage or draw pictures of their favorite female athletes.
- Have students view "Let's Run Through Wilma's Life" at http://www.youtube.com/watch?v=igl8DmcKRhQ.
- Lead the students in a discussion of how Wilma used her successful experiences to help others. Point out that she refused to visit certain places or participate in certain events because of racism.

Independent Practice

- Suggest that students create a PowerPoint track of women athletes using names from the card activity.

Closure

- Present class projects.
- Invite a female athlete from a nearby college or professional team to speak at your school.
- Poll students to determine who is involved in school and community athletics.

Assessment

- Student interest, participation, and project design.

Let's Run with Wilma!

What is polio? See http://www.cyh.com/HealthTopics/HealthTopicDetailsKids.aspx?p=335&np=285&id=2876. ____

Name the doctor who developed the polio vaccine. ____

How did Wilma Rudolph fight bullying? ____

Locate Clarksville, Tennessee, on a map. Describe its current population and special tourist attractions. ____

Let's Track Our Concentration Game Cards

Teacher prints the information for this activity on index cards.

Game Card 1: http://www.infoplease.com/spot/marionjones1.html

In the Olympics, Jones won ________________ medals.

Game Card 2: http://womenshistory.about.com/od/gibsonalthea/a/althea_gibson.htm

Gibson was the first African American woman to compete in ________________________.

Game Card 3: http://www.venuswilliams.com

Her sister's name was ________________. They are both ______________ players.

Game Card 4: http://womenshistory.about.com/od/jackiejoynerkersee/p/joyner_kersee.htm

Many consider this woman the ______________________ in the world.

Game Card 5: http://www.florencegriffithjoyner.com/

She was known to the sports world as ____________________________________.

Game Card 6: http://www.alicecoachman.org

In what year did she win the Olympic Medal?__________________.

Game Card 7: http://www.thehistorymakers.com/biography/biography.asp?bioindex=190

Willye became the first American woman to win in which competition?________________.

Game Card 8: http://hoopedia.nba.com/index.php?title=Cheryl_Miller

Cheryl Miller is known for her skills in which sports?______________________________

Game Card 9: http://www.wnba.com/playerfile/cynthia_cooper/index.html

________________ is the name of the team for which Cynthia played basketball.

Game Card 10:

http://womenshistory.about.com/od/gibsonalthea/a/althea_gibson.htm

After she retired from track, what did Wilma Rudolph become? ______________________

Answers: 1. 5; 2. Tennis; 3. Serena, tennis; 4. "best-all around;" 5. "Flo-Jo;" 6. 1948; 7. Long jump; 8. Basketball; 9. Comets; 10. A teacher and coach.

Bibliography

Altman, Linda Jacobs. *Singing with Momma Lou.* New York: Lee & Low Books, 2002.

Hamilton, Virginia. *Bluish.* New York: The Blue Sky Press/Scholastic, 1999.

Jeanne Whitehouse Peterson (1939–). Biography, Personal, Career, Writings, Sidelights. Net Industries. 2010. http://biography.jrank.org/pages/1552/Peterson-Jeanne-Whitehouse-1939.html (accessed October 30, 2010).

Kathleen Krull: Children's Author. n.d. http://www.kathleenkrull.com (accessed October 30, 2010).

Krull, Kathleen. *Wilma Unlimited: How Wilma Rudolph Became the World's Fastest Woman.* New York: Voyager Books, 1996.

Linda Jacobs Altman. Jacketflap.com. 2010. http://www.jacketflap.com/persondetail.asp?person=94984 (accessed October 30, 2010).

Mathis, Sharon Bell. *Ray Charles.* New York: Lee & Low Books, 2001.

Peterson, Jeanne Whitehouse. *I Have a Sister, My Sister Is Deaf.* New York: HarperCollins, 1977.

Sharon Bell Mathis. The Brown Book Shelf. February 13, 2010. http://thebrownbookshelf.com/2010/02/13/sharon-bell-mathis (accessed October 26, 2010).

Virginia Hamilton—America's Most Honored Writer of Children's Literature. Hamilton Arts. 2009. http://www.virginiahamilton.com/biography (accessed October 20, 2010).

Webliography

50 Interesting Facts About the Great Depression. Random History.com. 2007–2010. http://facts.randomhistory.com/2009/04/12_great-depression.html (accessed December 27, 2010).

Alice Coachman. Track and Field Foundation. January 9, 2008. http://www.alicecoachman.org (accessed December 27, 2010).

Althea Gibson. About.com. 2010. http://womenshistory.about.com/od/gibsonalthea/a/althea_gibson.htm (accessed December 27, 2010).

Alzheimer's: Helping Children Understand the Disease. Mayo Foundation for Medical Education and Research. 1998–2010. http://www.mayoclinic.com/health/alzheimers/HQ00216 (accessed November 10, 2010).

America the Beautiful: Ray Charles '91. n.d. http://www.youtube.com/watch?v=ghz4_kikLkE&feature=related (accessed December 26, 2010).

Barasch, Lynne. *Knockin' on Wood.* New York: Lee & Low Books, 2004.

CancerCare for Kids. CancerCare. 2010. http://www.cancercare.org/get_help/special_progs/cc_for_kids.php (accessed November 10, 2010).

Charles, Ray (1930–2004). The Free Online Encyclopedia of Washington State History. n.d. http://www.historylink.org/index.cfm?DisplayPage=output.cfm&file_id=5707 (accessed December 27, 2010).

Cheryl Miller. Hoopedia. n.d. http://hoopedia.nba.com/index.php?title=Cheryl_Miller (accessed December 27, 2010).

Childhood Cancer. The Nemours Foundation. 1995–2010. http://kidshealth.org/parent/medical/cancer/cancer.html (accessed November 10, 2010).

Composers Official Site of Negro Spirituals, Antique Gospel Music. n.d. http://www.negrospirituals.com/composers.htm (accessed October 24, 2010).

Florence Griffith Joyner: Official Website. CMG Worldwide represents many famous legends of the 20th Century. Estate of Florence Griffith Joyner. n.d. http://www.florencegriffithjoyner.com (accessed December 27, 2010).

Helping Children Understand Mental Illness: A Resource for Parents and Guardians. November 7, 2001. http://www.mhasp.org/coping/guardians.html (accessed December 27, 2010).

The HistoryMakers. 2008. http://www.thehistorymakers.com/biography/biography.asp?bioindex=190 (accessed December 27, 2010).

Jackie Joyner-Kersee. About.com. 2010. http://womenshistory.about.com/od/jackiejoynerkersee/p/joyner_kersee.htm (accessed December 27, 2020).

Jonas Salk Biography. American Academy of Achievement. 1996–2010. http://www.achievement.org/autodoc/page/sal0bio-1 (accessed December 26, 2010).

Learning American Sign Language. Yahoo. 2010. http://www.associatedcontent.com/article/327682/learning_american_sign_language.html?cat=25 (accessed December 27, 2010).

"Lift Every Voice and Sing" and Stevie Wonder Medley. n.d. http://www.youtube.com/watch?v=bQcc5eoU0CU (accessed December 27, 2010).

Living with Alzheimer's: Just for Kids & Teens. Alzheimer's Association National Office. 2010. http://www.alz.org/living_with_alzheimers_just_for_kids_and_teens.asp (accessed December 26, 2010).

Marion Jones: Fastest Woman on Earth. Infoplease.com. Pearson Education. 2000–2010. http://www.infoplease.com/spot/marionjones1.html (accessed December 27, 2010).

Memory by Barbara Streisand. n.d. http://www.youtube.com/watch?v=GVwJNg4Wgq4 (accessed December 26, 2010).

National Grandparents Day—Preserving Precious Memories Introduction. National Grandparents Day Council. 2010. http://www.grandparents-day.com/ (accessed October 26, 2010).

Nolen, Jerdine. *Hewitt Anderson's Great Big Life.* New York: Simon & Schuster Books, 2005.

Play the Piano Online! A Virtual Piano Online—Java Piano. n.d. http://www.pianoworld.com/fun/javapiano/javapiano.htm (accessed December 26, 2010).

Polio. Kid's Health—Topics. May 24, 2010. http://www.cyh.com/HealthTopics/HealthTopicDetailsKids.aspx?p=335&np=285&id=2876 (accessed December 26, 2010).

Ray Charles—Free Listening, Videos, Concerts, Stats, & Pictures. Last.fm. February 11, 2009. http://www.last.fm/music/Ray+Charles (accessed December 27, 2010).

Ray Charles—I Can't Stop Loving You (free MP3 download). Beemp3.com. n.d. http://beemp3.com/download.php?file=3377979&song=I+Can%26%23039%3Bt+Stop+Loving+You (accessed December 27, 2010).

Ray Charles—Pre-order Rare Genius. n.d. http://raycharles.com/splash (accessed December 27, 2010).

Ray Charles. Lift Every Voice and Sing Lyrics. ListenMusic. 2010. http://listenmusic.fm/track/Lift-Every-Voice-and-Sing-by-Ray-Charles-with-lyrics-2184711 (accessed December 27, 2010).

Ray Charles Timeline. The Rock and Roll Hall of Fame and Museum. 2010. http://rockhall.com/story-of-rock/timelines/raycharles/basic/ (accessed December 27, 2010).

Sign Language for Children. Activities: PBS Kids Sprout. Children's Network. 2005–2010. http://www.sproutonline.com/sprout/activities/listing.aspx?preset=signlanguage&ppreset=cgoodnightshow (accessed December 27, 2010).

St. Jude Children's Research Hospital—Partners in Hope—Video Tour. St. Jude's Research Hospital. 2010. http://www.partnersinhope.org/video_tour.html (accessed December 26, 2010).

Stevie Wonder. November 16, 2010. http://www.steviewonder.org.uk/index.htm (accessed December 27, 2010).

Stevie Wonder: I Just Called to Say I Love You (free MP3 download). Beemp3.com. n.d. http://beemp3.com/download.php?file=2428107&song=I+Just+Called+To+Say+I+Love+You (accessed December 27, 2010).

Stevie Wonder and Ray Charles: Living for the City Video. Remixation, Inc. 2010. http://vodpod.com/watch/347504-stevie-wonder-and-ray-charles-living-for-the-city (accessed December 27, 2010).

Talking Hands Video. Videolinks4u.net. n.d. http://www.videolinks4u.net/v/lFbxhH0VyHw/talking-hands (accessed December 27, 2010).

Talking to Kids About Mental Illness. American Academy of Child & Adolescent Psychiatry. 2010. http://www.aacap.org/cs/root/facts_for_families/talking_to_kids_about_mental_illnesses (accessed December 27, 2010).

Teachers Network: Lesson Plans: ABC's in ASL. Teachers Network. 2010. http://library.thinkquest.org/5875/ (accessed December 26, 2010).

Teens Living with Cancer. 2009. http://www.teenslivingwithcancer.org/ (accessed November 3, 2010).

Troupe, Quincy. *Little Stevie Wonder.* New York: Houghton Mifflin, 2005.

Venus Williams. Alexander, James III. n.d. http://www.venuswilliams.com (accessed December 27, 2010).

Wilma Rudolph—An Uphill Battle. n.d. http://www.youtube.com/watch?v=igl8DmcKRhQ (accessed December 26, 2010).

Wilma Rudolph.net. Biography, Picture, Videos, & Quotes. Mosaic. n.d. http://www.wilmarudolph.net/ (accessed December 26, 2010).

WNBA.com: Cynthia Cooper Player Info. WNBA Enterprises. 2010. http://www.wnba.com/playerfile/cynthia_cooper/index.html (accessed December 27, 2010).

Additional Related Reading

Barasch, Lynne. *Knockin' on Wood.* New York: Lee & Low Books, 2004.

This is a highly motivational true story about a young boy who refused to allow his disability to stand in the way of his dream to dance. After a severe accident at an early age that left him with only one leg, Clayton "Peg Leg" Bates became a famous dancer recognized around the world. Barasch has provided encouragement to children with disabilities by penning this story of a young boy in pursuit of developing a career in dance.

Hamilton, Virginia. *Sweet Whispers, Brother Rush.* New York: Philomel Books, 1982.

Walking into a room and seeing a person in the middle of a table will quickly get your attention. That is exactly what happened to Teresa, nicknamed Tree, when she walked into the little sunny room where she often drew or had quiet time to herself. The mystery behind the ghost in the center of the table will change her life forever. Readers will be enthralled by this amazing Newbery Honor Award book.

Negron, Ray. *The Greatest Story Never Told.* New York: HarperCollins, 2008.

It begins with what we say to our children. It depends on how we say it to our children. It ends when we model for our children what we want them to know about cultural diversity. This is a great book for all ages revealing racial discrimination of two terminally ill children and how they dealt with racism during their trials.

Nolen, Jerdine. *Hewitt Anderson's Great Big Life.* New York: Simon & Schuster Books, 2005.

Determined not to allow size to interfere with his ability to think and perform, a small boy encourages those who may feel limited due to their size.

Troupe, Quincy. *Little Stevie Wonder.* New York: Houghton Mifflin, 2005.

This is a delightful little book that shares tidbits of biographical information about the early life of Grammy Award Winner Stevie Wonder. The author creates the story by providing a timeline of Wonder's accomplishments from the onset of his blindness to the tribute he received from fellow musicians for his musical genius.

Chapter 18

VALUES THAT SHAPE CHARACTER

Teach your students character-building values such as courage, determination, teamwork, persistence, integrity, and commitment through the books and activities featured in this chapter. Share with your students the examples of others who used these values in their lives to build self-esteem and pursue their dreams.

Edelman, Marian Wright. *I Can Make a Difference: A Treasury to Inspire Our Children.* New York: HarperCollins, 2005.

About the Author

Marian Wright Edelman Institute—Homepage. n.d. http://edelman.sfsu.edu (accessed October 31, 2010).

Literary Elements	Lexile Range	Teacher Resources and Supplies
Biography Language Arts Music Poetry	—	Book Worksheet Photo Photo of Bell Photo of Hammer
Reading Level Grades 2–5	**Accelerated Reader** —	
Additional Title Dungy, Tony. ***You Can Do It!*** **Websites** http://video.nationalgeographic.com/video/player/movies/god-grew-tired/cultural-differences-ggtu.html http://www.cdc.gov/HealthyYouth/keystrategies/pdf/make-a-difference.pdf		

Brief Summary

In this powerful collection of stories, poems, and excerpts from prominent world leaders and literary figures, well-known child advocate Marian Wright Edelman once again inspires all children to never lose hope in their quest to make a difference in the world.

Focus

- Self-esteem, Confidence
- Making a Difference
- Character and Values

Teacher Input

- Show the class a picture of yourself as a child, a picture of a bell, and a picture of a hammer. Explain how each of these resources can be used to accomplish something worthwhile in life.
- Using the following online resources, show Haley Farm and introduce students to Marian Wright Edelman, its founder: http://www.childrensdefense.org/who-is-cdf/cdf-contacts-state-offices/cdf-haley-farm.

Guided Practice

- Have students watch the online resource listed below, discuss the cultural differences observed, and share their perspectives on how people of various cultures are treated: http://video.nationalgeographic.com/video/player/movies/god-grew-tired/cultural-differences-ggtu.html.
- Invite students to comment on ways they can take on the responsibility for making a difference in school when another student is harassed by bullying.
- Have students devise a plan showing what they can do to make a difference when they observe bullying in the school, at home, or in the community.
- Assign students to work in groups to write a poem on the topic "I Can Make a Difference—Yes, We Can!" Students will write four verses (see template following this lesson plan). Verses one and three must be the individual student's thoughts and contributions. Verses two and four must be developed by the group. The poem should flow and have one main theme throughout.
- Have students listen to John Legend's song "If You're Out There" and write their interpretation of the lyrics: http://www.last.fm/music/John+Legend/_/If+You're+Out+There.
- Instruct students to use the Healthy Youth online resource (http://www.cdc.gov/HealthyYouth/obesity) to gather information for a school television production, "Youth and Good Health." Have students use the template provided at the end of this lesson plan.

Independent Practice

- Suggest that students choose one individual from the book and draw a poster or develop another type of project showing that individual's contribution to mankind.

Closure

- Students present their projects.

Assessment

- Student project designs, poems, and personal plans to combat bullying.

Poem Template Worksheet

"I Can Make a Difference—Yes, We Can!"

Develop an individual verse first, then work with a group to develop a second verse. Note how by working together, a group can make a difference.

(Individual)

Line 1: ______________________________

Line 2: ______________________________

Line 3: ______________________________

Line 4: ______________________________

(Group Input)

Line 5: ______________________________

Line 6: ______________________________

Line 7: ______________________________

Line 8: ______________________________

(Individual)

Line 9: ______________________________

Line 10: ______________________________

Line 11: ______________________________

Line 12: ______________________________

(Group Input)

Line 13: We Can ______________________________

Line 14: We Can ______________________________

Line 15: ______________________________

Line 16: ______________________________

Template for Creating School News Show on Youth and Good Health

Work with health and physical education teacher in your school to develop this product

Define and discuss obesity.

Define and discuss body mass index (BMI).

Demonstrate how students may use the BMI Percentile Calculator found at http://www.cdc.gov/HealthyYouth/obesity.

Ask students to keep a log of what they eat and drink, what activities they participate in (e.g., watching television, using the Internet, studying), and how much they exercise for one week. Logs will be turned in to health or physical education teacher.

"Good Body Students" will be recognized over school television.

Holman, Sandy Lynne. *Grandpa, Is Everything Black Bad?* Davis, CA: Culture CO-OP, 1999.

About the Author

Sandy Lynne Holman. n.d. http://dcn.davis.ca.us/~gizmo/1998/holman.html (accessed October 31, 2010).

Literary Elements Tolerance Social Studies	**Lexile Range** —	**Teacher Resources and Supplies** Book Map or globe
Reading Level Grades 1–4	**Accelerated Reader** Points: 0.5 Book Level: 3.6	
Additional Title Barnwell, Ysaye M. ***No Mirrors in My Nana's House.*** **Websites** http://www.youtube.com/watch?v=Bm5cNeH6KPw&feature=related http://www.infoplease.com/spot/colors1.html http://www.calacademy.org/exhibits/africa/kids.htm http://www.ibike.org/library/africakids.htm		

Brief Summary

In this insightful story, a young boy wonders if black is bad and carries his concerns to his grandpa, who reassures him that any color can be bad—if used the wrong way. To build his grandson's self-esteem and pride in his heritage, Grandpa takes him on a visual journey back to their native homeland to show him how powerful and gifted the people of his race are. Grandpa tells him of the knowledge and skills of his people and how they used drums as a communication tool.

Focus

- Four-Leaf Clover or Shamrock (Some children grow up believing that shamrocks bring good luck. In the book reviewed, the author's goal is to help young people realize that color has nothing to do with false ideologies or superstitions.)
- Self-esteem
- Pride

Teacher Input

- Introduce this book to the class by playing James Brown's song, "***Say It Loud, I'm Black and I'm Proud.***"
- Read the poem by Dr. Margaret Burroughs, "What Do We Tell Our Children Who Are Black?" to the class and lead a discussion about the poem.
- Allow students the opportunity to explore Africa through this online resource: http://pbskids.org/africa/myworld/index.html.

Guided Practice

- Allow students to take a virtual field trip to Africa by using this online resource: http://www.ibike.org/library/africakids.htm.
- Have students view the following website to learn about many of the great things that Grandpa tells Montsho about the beauty of Africa: http://www.yourchildlearns.com/africa_map.htm.
- Invite students to share their personal feelings about the word "black" and the impact it has on their own lives. See http://www.youtube.com/watch?v=Bm5cNeH6KPw&feature=related.
- Encourage the students to participatc in an "I've Got That Feeling" Game. Have them write the first thing that comes to their minds as you hold up a color flash card.
- Instruct students to write a classroom play using the meanings and power of colors. The title of the play will be "That's Good, That's Bad."
- Suggest that students plan a Mood Week at school. Each day they will wear a specific color to school. They will keep a log to discuss how wearing a certain color may have affected mood swings, changes, or performance.

Independent Practice

- Instruct students to draw a map of Africa and list all the "good" things they learned about this great continent inside of the outline.
- Have students respond to Dr. Burroughs' poem with one of their own, "***We're Making Strides and That's a Fact!***"
- Suggest that students design their own ***Black Pride Magazine*** that shows the things they like that are black.

Closure

- Report results from the card game, production of *Black Pride Magazine,* and presentation of the classroom play.

Assessment

- Student excitement, involvement, and project presentations.

Myers, Walter Dean. *Looking Like Me*. New York: Egmont, 2009.

About the Author

Walter Dean Myers Author. n.d. http://www.walterdeanmyers.net (accessed October 10, 2010).

Literary Elements Character Education	**Lexile Range** —	**Teacher Resources and Supplies** Book Mirror Worksheet
Reading Level Grades 4 and up	**Accelerated Reader** Points: 0.5 Book Level: 2.6	
Additional Title Barnwell, Ysaye M. ***No Mirrors in My Nana's House.*** **Websites** http://www.youtube.com/watch?v=GD57KULeIgg http://www.dollslikeme.com/html/esteem.html http://www.more-selfesteem.com/self_esteem.htm		

Brief Summary

Filled with encouraging words to boost self-esteem, this book is rejuvenating to young people with a variety of diverse learning styles. Myers makes it very clear that who you are, what you are, how you look, or where you live has nothing to do with your ability to dream or believe.

Focus

- Self-esteem
- Family
- School
- Community

Teacher Input

- Bring a mirror to class and use it with the video listed below to introduce Myers's book: http://www.youtube.com/watch?v=GD57KULeIgg.
- Instruct students to use Walter Dean Myers's website to learn more about his writings and his son, Christopher Myers.

Guided Practice

- Have students use small mirrors to look at themselves. Ask them to write descriptions of their own images, which will be used later in a group activity.
- Assign numbers to students for this activity. When the teacher calls their assigned number, students take turns posing as models to give their classmates the opportunity to study and write about their appearance. The topic

of their essays should be, "What I See in the Person Standing Before Me." Instruct students that their comments abut the models must be positive, uplifting, and encouraging.

- Have students create a collage of their lives using newspaper headings, magazine photographs, and online images. The collage title will be, "Bam! Here I Am!"
- Using online resources from the self-esteem website, have students create a flip chart, photo story, or PowerPoint "bamming" self-esteem into themselves or to a friend or relative.
- Invite students to compare the similarities and differences between how they described themselves and what their classmates saw in them.
- Read Ecclesiastes 9:11 to the class. Lead the class in a discussion on what they think the passage means: "I returned, and saw under the sun, that the race is not to the swift, nor the battle to the strong, neither yet bread to the wise, nor yet riches to men of understanding, nor yet favour to men of skill; but time and chance happeneth to them all."

Independent Practice

- Suggest that students choose one confidence builder described by the author, such as a dreaming, writing, dancing, or the like, and bring that talent to life through drama, dance, writing, or storytelling.

Closure

- Invite an older adult to participate in a "***How to Build Character Chat***" with the students.

Assessment

- Student interest, group discussions and project development.

Here's Looking at You Worksheet

This Is How I See Myself (Self-Image):
This Is How I'm Perceived by Others:
My Explanation of "***Ecclesiastes 9:11***":

Robinson, Sharon. *Jackie's Nine: Jackie Robinson's Values to Live By.* New York: Scholastic, 2001.

About the Author

Sharon Robinson. Scholastic. 1996–2010. http://www2.scholastic.com/browse/contributor.jsp?id=2004 (Sharon Robinson) (accessed October 10, 2010).

Literary Elements Character Nonfiction	Lexile Range 1040L	Teacher Resources and Supplies Book Nine baseballs, with each ball labeled with one of the value traits Worksheet
Reading Level Grades 6 and Up	**Accelerated Reader** Points: 4.0 Book Level: 7.3	

Additional Titles
Robinson, Jackie. ***I Never Had It Made*** (Coretta Scott King Book Award).
Robinson, Jackie. ***Promises to Keep.***
Uhlberg, Myron. ***Dad, Jackie and Me.***

Websites
http://www.jackierobinson.com
http://www.bluekids.org/teensandkids/ga_choices.asp
http://www.sharonrobinsonink.com

Brief Summary

The daughter of the sport's figure who broke the color barrier in baseball tells how her father used the character menu to order up the necessary values needed to obtain his personal goals in life, while clearing the path of opportunity for others at the same time.

Focus

- Courage, Determination
- Teamwork, Persistence
- Integrity, Citizenship
- Justice, Commitment, Excellence

Teacher Input

- Introduce this book to the class using baseball props and playing the song "Take Me Out to the Ball Game: http://beemp3.com/download.php?file=4250695&song=Take+me+out+to+the+ball+game.
- Ask the students to define what credibility means and lead them in a discussion by providing examples.
- Introduce students to Sharon Robinson, the daughter of Jackie Robinson, through her website: http://www.sharonrobinsonink.com.

Guided Practice

- Assign students to write a song to the tune of "***Take Me Out to the Ball Game,***" using the nine values described in Robinson's book: http://beemp3.com/download.php?file=4250695&song=Take+me+out+to+the+ball+game.
- Have students describe ways to apply the values listed in "Jackie's Nine." On a scale from one to nine, with nine being the most important, have students list their nine values.
- Divide the class into two groups. Group One will develop a survey listing all nine values listed in the book. Group Two will conduct the survey to show which values in the book are most often practiced in the classroom.
- Assign an essay titled "Break the Barriers, Let's Build a Bridge!"
- Instruct students to design a "Beginner's Guide for Understanding Baseball for Amateurs." Have students examine the following online database for an explanation of terms: http://mlb.mlb.com/mlb/official_info/baseball_basics/lingo.jsp.
- Have students identify people referenced in Jackie's Nine and search online for additional information regarding the values described in Robinson's book.
- Invite students to bring in old baseball cards for "Show and Discuss."

Independent Practice

- Instruct students to complete the "My Nine Values" Worksheet while viewing the online video of Jackie Robinson: http://video.tvguide.com/The+Jackie+Robinson+Story/4048188.
- Have each group design a "Top Values" PowerPoint presentation using teamwork. The presentation must consist of nine slides illustrating each value. Information obtained may come from online research.

Closure

- "Let's Play Ball!": students present their papers and projects.

Assessment

- Student interest, brainstorming, working together, and presentations.

My Nine Values Worksheet: The Things I Value in Life

Bibliography

Edelman, Marian Wright. *I Can Make a Difference; A Treasury to Inspire Our Children.* New York: HarperCollins, 2005.

Holman, Sandy Lynne. *Grandpa, Is Everything Black Bad?* Davis, CA: Culture CO-OP, 1999.

Hudson, Wade. *Powerful Words: More than 200 Years of Extraordinary Writings by African Americans.* New York: Scholastic, 2004.

Just Us Books. AALBC.com, LLC. 1997–2010. http://aalbc.com/writers/justusbooks.htm (accessed October 31, 2010).

Marian Wright Edelman Institute—Homepage. n.d. http://edelman.sfsu.edu/ (accessed October 31, 2010).

Myers, Walter Dean. *Looking Like Me.* New York: Egmont, 2009.

Robinson, Sharon. *Jackie's Nine: Jackie Robinson's Values to Live By.* New York: Scholastic, 2001.

Sandy Lynne Holman. n.d. http://dcn.davis.ca.us/~gizmo/1998/holman.html (accessed October 31, 2010).

Sharon Robinson. Scholastic. 1996–2010. http://www2.scholastic.com/browse/contributor.jsp?id=2004 (accessed October 10, 2010).

Walter Dean Myers Author. n.d. http://www.walterdeanmyers.net (accessed October 10, 2010).

Webliography

Africa for Kids—My World. PBS. n.d. http://pbskids.org/africa/myworld/index.html (accessed December 28, 2010).

Africa Map: Interactive Map of Africa With Countries and Capitals. CIA World Fact Book. 2000–2009. http://www.yourchildlearns.com/africa_map.htm (accessed December 28, 2010).

Barnwell, Ysaye M. *No Mirrors in My Nana's House.* New York: Harcourt Children's Books, 1998.

Color Psychology—Infoplease.com. Pearson Education. 2000–2010. http://www.infoplease.com/spot/colors1.html (accessed November 7, 2010).

Cultural Differences. National Geographic Society. 1998–2010. http://video.nationalgeographic.com/video/player/movies/godgrew-tired/cultural-differences-ggtu.html (accessed December 28, 2010).

Dr. Henry Clarke Tell Our Children Our History, Part 3. n.d. http://www.youtube.com/watch?v=Bm5cNeH6KPw&feature=related (accessed December 28, 2010).

Dred Scott Case. WGBH. n.d. http://www.pbs.org/wgbh/aia/part4/4h2933.html (accessed December 27, 2010).

Games and Activities: Making Choices. Children's Health Education Center. n.d. http://www.bluekids.org/teensandkids/ga_choices.asp (accessed December 27, 2010).

Healthy Youth: Make a Difference at Your School. http://www.cdc.gov/HealthyYouth/keystrategies/pdf/make-a-difference.pdf. January 2008. http://www.cdc.gov/HealthyYouth/keystrategies/pdf/make-a-difference.pdf (accessed November 6, 2010).

John Legend "If You're Out There." n.d. http://www.last.fm/music/John+Legend/_/If+You're+Out+There (accessed December 28, 2010).

Just for Kids. California Academy of Sciences. n.d. http://www.calacademy.org/exhibits/africa/kids.htm (accessed December 28, 2010).

Just Us Books. http://aalbc.com. 1997–2010. http://aalbc.com/writers/justusbooks.htm (accessed December 27, 2010).

Mozer, David. *Africa Kids Page: Games, Books, Knowledge, Fun.* International Bicycle Fund. 1995–2010. http://www.ibike.org/library/africakids.htm (accessed December 28, 2010).

Negro Leagues = MLB.com: History. MLB Advanced Media, L.P. 2001–2010. http://mlb.mlb.com/mlb/history/mlb_negro_leagues.jsp (accessed October 10, 2010).

No Mirrors in My Nana's House. n.d. http://www.youtube.com/watch?v=GD57KULeIgg (accessed December 27, 2010).

The Official Site of Jackie Robinson. n.d. http://www.jackierobinson.com (accessed October 13, 2010).

Perera, Karl. *Build Self Esteem and Confidence.* 2003. http://www.more-selfesteem.com/self_esteem.htm (accessed November 6, 2010).

Self Esteem Activities. Self-Esteem-Experts.com. 2009–2010. http://www.self-esteem-experts.com/self-esteem-activities.html (accessed December 28, 2010).

Self-Esteem in Children of Color. DollLikeMe.com. 2009. http://www.dollslikeme.com/html/esteem.html (accessed November 5, 2010).

Sharon Robinson. 2006. http://www.sharonrobinsonink.com (accessed December 27, 2010).

Take Me Out to the Ball Game. (free MP3 download). Beemp3.com. n.d. http://beemp3.com/download.php?file=4250695&song =Take+me+out+to+the+ball+game (accessed December 27, 2010).

Watch the Jackie Robinson Story. (free full episode, online video guide). n.d. http://video.tvguide.com/The+Jackie+Robinson+ Story/4048188 (accessed December 27, 2010).

Welcome to African American Quotes.com. 2007. http://africanamericanquotes.org (accessed November 6, 2010).

Whitney Houston "Greatest Love of All" (music video). Dailymotion. 2005–2010. http://www.dailymotion.com/video/x2aqg4_ whitney-houston-greatest-love-of-al_music (accessed December 28, 2010).

Additional Reading Materials

Barnwell, Ysaye M. *No Mirrors in My Nana's House.* New York: Harcourt Children's Books, 1998.

A young girl knows that she is loved every time she looks into her nana's eyes. Her living conditions or surroundings don't matter, she knows that she is deeply loved.

Belton, Sandra. *Pictures for Miss Josie.* New York: Greenwillow Books/An Imprint of HarperCollins, 2003.

A young boy's father takes him to meet his mentor. The boy finds this proud black woman intimidating because of her size. When this woman discovers the boy's interest in drawing, she allows him to use his creativity freely to discover a whole new world. He takes her advice to use his gift, which becomes a lifetime career.

Dungy, Tony. *You Can Do It!* New York: Little Simon Inspirations, 2008.

Tony Dungy tells a delightful story of a family and how they allowed their faith to guide them in developing their professions. Readers will learn from the example of the older brother who, despite his younger brother's doubt, continues to encourage him to be patient in seeking a career.

Evans, Kristina. *Cherish Today; A Celebration of Life's Moments.* New York: Jump at the Sun, 2007.

This is a refreshing, poetic book for young readers that will inspire them to pursue their dreams and never give up, even when they experience turbulent times, because through faith, prayer, and hard work, one can persevere.

Morrison, Toni, and Slade Morrison. *The Big Box.* New York: Jump at the Sun, 1999.

Various sectors of the community feel that three children should be confined to a box because of their behavior. Although these children are provided with many luxuries in life, such as toys, gimmicks, and other items of interest to children, the fact that they no longer have their freedom diminishes their character.

Tarpley, Natasha Anastasia. *I Love My Hair!* New York: Little, Brown and Company, 1998.

The author takes a girl's hair and creates a work of art. Using powerful objects and places a child can identify with, her hair builds self-esteem and removes the negative thoughts that have often been associated with African American hair.

Wyeth, Sharon Dennis. *Something Beautiful.* New York: Bantam Doubleday, 1998.

Students will develop a better appreciation for their surroundings after reading or listening to this story. A young girl refuses to accept the harsh conditions that she sees in her neighborhood. So after searching for "something beautiful" from family, friends, the neighbor, and the community, she discovers that beauty comes from what she does and how she contributes to her neighbors.

Chapter 19

YOUTH ISSUES

Introduce your students to books and activities about the issues some young people face and actions they take to improve or resolve them. Physical appearance, self-esteem, cultural diversity, bullying, homelessness, and drug addiction are some of the topics explored in this chapter.

Flake, Sharon. *The Skin I'm In.* New York: Hyperion, 1998.

About the Author

Sharon G. Flake. 2008. http://www.sharongflake.com/ (accessed October 26, 2010).

<table>
<tr><td>Literary Elements
Coretta Scott King Book Award
Reading
Self-Esteem
Realistic Fiction
Writing</td><td>Lexile Range
670L</td><td rowspan="2">Teacher Resources and Supplies
Book
Worksheet</td></tr>
<tr><td>Reading Level
Grades 9–12</td><td>Accelerated Reader
Points: 4.0
Book Level: 4.1</td></tr>
<tr><td colspan="3">Additional Title
Mendez, Phil. The Black Snowman.

Websites
http://www.soundvision.com/Info/teens/pbs.asp</td></tr>
</table>

Brief Summary

What do you do when you don't like the way you look and you can't change your physical appearance? Do you hang with the first gang that accepts you for who you are, even though you know that you're being used? Or do you allow a strange teacher with a visible defect—that you think is even worse than yours—to enter your space and bring out the best in you? Maleeka Madison can no longer hide behind a wall of insecurity. There's a new teacher in town, and she plans to bring out the gifts that she sees hiding inside of Maleeka. But doing so is a slow process. Maleeka makes great strides but then disappoints when she tries to offend the one person who believes in her.

Focus

- Skin Tone
- Self-Esteem

- Bullies
- Academic Achievement

Teacher Input

- Invite students to share personal thoughts about being African American or another race/ethnicity.
- Play James Brown's record "Say It Loud, I'm Black and I'm Proud."
- Read aloud *The Black Snowman* and divide the students into three groups to read and discuss.
- Ask students to comment on the meaning of the question, "How can you expect others to love you if you don't love yourself?" See http://www.soundvision.com/Info/teens/pbs.asp.
- Discuss with the class how physical appearance might dominate a student's striving for academic excellence. Provide examples.

Guided Practice

- Assign student groups to act out a simulated skit of Jacob and the Black Snowman.
- "***Beauty Is in the Eyes of the Beholder.***" Divide the class into three groups. The groups then brainstorm as a team about what makes a person "beautiful." Distribute tear sheets for students to use for this activity. Have students list things they like about Charlese and things they did not. Ask them to share their thoughts about Corey.
- After reading their assigned chapters, instruct student groups to compare and contrast ***The Black Snowman*** and ***The Skin I'm In***.

Independent Practice

- Divide the class into two groups. Give one group the Temptations' song "***Beauty Is Only Skin Deep***" and the other group "***God Bless the Child.***" Ask each group to listen to, interpret, and make an oral report on what each song means to them.
- Suggest that students write a positive essay titled "***What My Face Says to the World.***"
- Introduce students to Open Diary Online: http://www.opendiary.com.

Closure

- Students share group project activities.

Assessment

- Student reports, teamwork, discussions, worksheets, and project designs.

My Self-Esteem Worksheet

1. List five things that determine how people see and the labels they place on others.

1.
2.
3.
4.
5.

2. List "favorable or "unfavorable" behaviors in the classroom that turn others on or off.

Favorable Behaviors—Turn On	Unfavorable Behaviors—Turn Off

3. Write an essay titled "What My Face Says to the World" on the back of this sheet.

4. Compare and contrast the two songs. Based on personal experiences and knowledge of the African American race, describe which song title has more meaning in your life.

God Bless the Child	Beauty Is Only Skin Deep

Lester, Julius. *Let's Talk About Race.* New York: HarperCollins, 2005.

About the Author

Home-Julius Lester. n.d. http://juliuslester.net (accessed October 30, 2010).

Literary Elements	Lexile Range	Teacher Resources and Supplies
Social Justice	—	Book Worksheet
Reading Level Grades 1–5	**Accelerated Reader** Points: 0.5 Book Level: 3.0	

Additional Titles
Adoff, Arnold. ***All the Colors of the Race.***
Cole, Heidi. ***Am I a Color Too?***

Websites
http://abcnews.go.com/video/playerIndex?id=8179413
http://www.freemaninstitute.com/cultures.htm

Brief Summary

Julius Lester has written a wonderful book to discuss race with young people. He reveals the many positive aspects of himself rather than what some people may have said about him without really knowing him. Lester is an example to everyone who wants to bring understanding, peace, and harmony to diverse groups.

Focus

- Race, Cultural Diversity, Respect

Teacher Input

- Play the song by Lee Greenwood, "***I'm Proud to Be an American***" in preparation for a later activity and to fill out the worksheet.
- Ask students to describe why people are sensitive about discussing race. See http://abcnews.go.com/video/playerIndex?id=8179413.
- Create a book display for the class featuring peoples and cultures around the world.
- Discuss special days and celebrations that recognize different cultures and peoples.
- Invite students to comment on which special days are celebrated or recognized by students' families.

Guided Practice

- Lead students in a brainstorming session about ways that people from diverse cultures can work together to bring about racial harmony and maintain peace during these turbulent times. See http://www.stlyrics.com/songs/l/leegreenwood2271/proudtobeanamerican279965.html

- Assign students to write an essay titled "I'm Proud to Be [race/ethnicity].
- Have students list rules, habits, and actions that some cultures have that may offend or otherwise negatively affect people of other cultures.

Independent Practice

- Suggest that students create a picture story of their lives in the form of a poster, collage, flip chart, or PowerPoint presentation.
- Sponsor a "Get-to-Know-Me Day." Each student will use Lester's suggestions from the book to present his or her life and learn more about the lives of others.

Closure

- Students share their projects.

Assessment

- Student discussions, writings, and project creativity and presentations.

Let's Race to These Special Days to Celebrate Worksheet

Do you have a favorite time of day? If so, write about it in the space below.

Explain songwriter Lee Greenwood's lyrics, "I'm Proud to Be an American."

List five reasons why you're proud of your race and nationality.

1.____

2.____

3.____

4.____

5.____

Here's My Story What's Yours?

Get

to

Know

Me

Day

Lyon, George Ella. *You and Me and Home Sweet Home.* New York: Atheneum Books for Young Readers, 2009.

About the Author

Official Site of George Ella Lyon, writer and teacher. Ella Lyon George. 2010–2014. http://www.georgeellalyon.com/ (accessed October 31, 2010).

Literary Elements Bank Street Best Books of the Year CCBC Choices (Cooperative Children's Book Council) Notable Social Studies Trade Book	**Lexile Range** AD530L	**Teacher Resources and Supplies** Book
Reading Level Preschool–Grades 2	**Accelerated Reader** Points: 0.5 Book Level: 2.8	
Additional Title Gunnings, Monica. ***A Shelter in Our Car.*** **Websites** http://www.habitat.org http://www.habitat.org/youthprograms/parent_teacher_leader/kidsonly.aspx		

Brief Summary

A young girl watches day by day as her new home is built. She's fascinated by the many hands that put her house together and she keeps the reader informed by naming the procedures involved each day. Her excitement earns her the right to "tell and explain" to her classmates the house that the community, love, and colorless hands built.

Focus

- Poverty
- Home Building
- Habitat for Humanity
- Homeowners
- Community Involvement

Teacher Input

- Ask students to explain the meaning of the phrase "***between a rock and a hard place.***"
- Write the word "faith" on the board and lead a discussion with students about what faith means.
- Introduce students to the Habitat for Humanity website to participate in online activities: http://www.habitat.org/youthprograms/parent_teacher_leader/kidsonly.aspx.
- Read aloud the book *A Shelter in Our Car* to the class and lead a discussion on the similarities and differences between that book and *You and Me and Home Sweet Home*.

Guided Practice

- Have students search for the meaning of the word "***humanity.***"
- Have students express the importance and power of "faith" in action. Give them an assignment to write their own "A Better World Prayer."
- Have students design and construct a house using craft sticks.
- Instruct students to list the day-by-day procedures involved in building a house. There should be at least fourteen procedures listed.
- Divide students into two groups. Each group will compose a "Build My House" song using such words as measuring, sawing, drilling, or hammering.

Independent Practice

- Suggest that students compose a poem titled "***Jack Didn't Build This House, I Did!***"

Closure

- Invite a contractor who builds houses to speak to the class about careers and opportunities in this field.

Assessment

- Student work, projects, and interests.

Myers, Walter Dean. *Amiri & Odette: A Love Story.* New York: Scholastic, 2009.

About the Author

Walter Dean Myers Author. n.d. http://www.walterdeanmyers.net (accessed October 10, 2010).

Literary Elements Ballet Dance	**Lexile Range** —	**Teacher Resources and Supplies** Book Worksheet
Reading Level Grades 7 and up	**Accelerated Reader** Points: 0.5 Book Level: 4.6	
Additional Title Price, Leontyne. ***Aida.*** **Websites** http://www.ilike.com/artist/Tchaikovsky/track/Swan+Lake+Ballet http://www.fancast.com/tv/Ghetto-Ballet/106015/1383895452/-Ghetto-Ballet—Preview-%28HBO%29/videos http://www.ballethnic.org/company		

Brief Summary

This story is about a ballet depicting the lives of two young people who fall in love at first sight. Promising to love Odette to the end yet knowing her fate, young Amiri fights for his true love. He is determined to release her from Big Red's captivity and break the spell at any cost—even if that means losing his own life. This is a retelling of Tchaikovsky's *Swan Lake* for the hip-hop generation. The reader will see the love and admiration that draws the two characters together forever.

Focus

- Ballet
- Black Dancers

Teacher Input

- Ask students to define the term "biography." Display a photo of Tchaikovsky on the board and lead the class in a discussion about this great composer.
- Discuss Amiri's basketball skills and how he used the ball as a means to release stress or anxiety.
- Divide the class into two groups. Group one will consist of the boys and group two will consist of the girls in the class. Ask students to read and discuss item three on the worksheet.
- Read aloud to the class Joyce Hansen's book, *The Heart Calls Home*.

Guided Practice

- Have students research and list additional ballets written by Tchaikovsky.
- Instruct students to view "The Ghetto Ballet" at this website: http://www.tubehome.com/watch/ghetto-ballet. Students will observe how ballets are choreographed and filmed by referring to the online resource. After viewing, have students work in three groups to plan, choreograph, and record ballets for project sharing.

- Have students conduct research online to conclude whether it is difficult for black dancers to pursue a career in ballet: http://www.columbia.edu/itc/journalism/gissler/anthology/webrhone.html.
- Assign student groups to create a "Trying to Connect" rap.
- Have students cite the similarities and differences between Joyce Hansen's love story *The Heart Calls Home* and Myers's *Amiri & Odette: A Love Story*.

Independent Practice

- Suggest that students search online resources and read background information about *Swan Lake* to determine how they would rewrite and produce it. Students may use online resources in search of additional African American ballets.

Closure

- Students present their own production of ***Swan Lake.***

Assessment

- Group work and participation, class discussions and production of ***Swan Lake.***

Amiri & Odette: Discussion and Worksheet

1. Define the word "ballet."

2. List other well-known ballets written by Tchaikovsky.

3. Create a "*Trying to Connect*" rap with your group.

4. Cite the similarities and differences between Leontyne Price's ***Aida*** and Myers's ***Amiri & Odette: A Love Story.***

Similarities	Differences

5. Explain "The Ghetto Ballet."

Bibliography

Adoff, Arnold. *All the Colors of the Race.* New York: Lothrop, Lee & Shepard Books, 1982.

Flake, Sharon. *The Skin I'm In.* New York: Hyperion, 1998.

Home-Julius Lester. n.d. http://juliuslester.net (accessed October 30, 2010).

Janet Cheatham Bell. n.d. http://janetcheathambell.com/ (accessed October 31, 2010).

Lester, Julius. *Let's Talk About Race.* New York: HarperCollins, 2005.

Lyon, George Ella. *You and Me and Home Sweet Home.* New York: Atheneum Books for Young Readers, 2009.

Myers, Walter Dean. *Amiri & Odette: A Love Story.* New York: Scholastic , 2009.

Official Site of George Ella Lyon, writer and teacher. 2010–2014. http://www.georgeellalyon.com/ (accessed October 31, 2010).

Sharon G. Flake. 2008. http://www.sharongflake.com (accessed October 26, 2010).

Stretch Your Wings: Famous Black Quotations for Teens. Selected and edited by Janet Cheatham Bell and Lucille Usher Freeman. New York: Little, Brown and Company, 1999.

Walter Dean Myers, Author. n.d. http://www.walterdeanmyers.net (accessed October 10, 2010).

Webliography

AR BookFinder US: Quick Search. Renaissance Learning. 2010. http://www.arbookfind.com/Default.aspx (accessed December 7, 2010).

Ballethnic Dance Company. 2008–2009. http://www.ballethnic.org/company (accessed November 7, 2010).

Celebrating Cultural Diversity! The Freeman Institute. n.d. http://www.freemaninstitute.com/cultures.htm (accessed November 6, 2010).

Dr. Carter Woodson Quotes and Quotations. Inspiring Quotes and Stories. 2006. http://www.inspiring-quotes-and-stories.com/carter-woodson-quotes.html (accessed December 29, 2010).

Ghetto Ballet. TubeHome.com. 2010. http://www.tubehome.com/watch/ghetto-ballet (accessed December 29, 2010).

Habitat for Humanity Int'l. 2010. http://www.habitat.org/default.aspx (accessed November 6, 2010).

Habitat for Humanity Int'l. "Kids Only" pages. Habitat for Humanity International. 2010. http://www.habitat.org/youthprograms/parent_teacher_leader/kidsonly.aspx (accessed December 29, 2010).

Lee Greenwood: Proud to Be an American Lyrics. StLyrics.com. 2002–2010. http://www.stlyrics.com/songs/l/leegreenwood2271/proudtobeanamerican279965.html (accessed December 29, 2010).

The Lexile Framework for Reading. Lexile.com. MetaMetrics. 2010. http://lexile.com (accessed November 2, 2010).

Open Diary. womenforum.com. 1998–2010. http://www.opendiary.com (accessed December 29, 2010).

Rhone, Nedra. *Swan Lake Dreams.* n.d. http://www.columbia.edu/itc/journalism/gissler/anthology/webrhone.html (accessed December 29, 2010).

Swan Lake Ballet by Tchaikovsky. iLike. 2010. http://www.ilike.com/artist/Tchaikovsky/track/Swan+Lake+Ballet (accessed December 29, 2010).

The Truth Behind Teen Culture. Sound Vision Foundation. 2010. http://www.soundvision.com/Info/teens/pbs.asp (accessed December 29, 2010).

Watch "Ghetto Ballet" Preview (HBO): Ghetto Ballet Previews Online. http://www.liveleak.com/view?i=1ef_1282147302

Welcome to African American Quotes.com. 2007. http://africanamericanquotes.org/ (accessed December 27, 2010).

Will Obama's Beer Help Race Relations? ABC News. n.d. http://abcnews.go.com/video/playerIndex?id=8179413 (accessed December 29, 2010).

Additional Reading Resources

Adoff, Arnold. ***All the Colors of the Race.*** **New York: Lothrop, Lee & Shepard Books, 1982.**

"In your face." Yes, that's an expression. However, this is the way a young child describes the color of the people going to and fro in this book. What a great read for young people who can relate to people of every color who are involved in every aspect of life today.

Childress, Alice. ***A Hero Ain't Nothin' but a Sandwich.*** **New York: Penguin Putnam Books for Young Readers, 1973.**

Everyone but Benji knows that he is in trouble. He has already devalued his life at the age of thirteen by hanging out with the wrong group and getting hooked on drugs. Benji is living in denial and ignoring the advice of his loved ones until the day that Butler, a father figure, finally tells him that no advice can help him until he is ready to stop his drug and alcohol use.

Grimes, Nikki. ***Bronx Masquerade.*** **New York: Dial Books, 2002.**

In this book, there are no top students in the class. Why? Because nobody else can see what each of the students described sees from his or her own heart. They write what they see, feel, and hope for from their perspective, and then share it with a group of "hopers" in a classroom that is no longer boring.

Gunning, Monica. ***A Shelter in Our Car.*** **Children's Book Press, 2004.**

A young Jamaican girl's dreams of having a home in the United States seem dismal as she climbs into the backseat of her mother's car to sleep for the evening. Still, she learns how to handle difficult times, such as having little to eat and enduring bullying, as she befriends other homeless children.

Holt, Kimberly Willis. ***Mister and Me.*** **New York: G. P. Putnam's Sons, 1998.**

After her father dies, a young girl resents the man who has entered her mother's life. After creating several opportunities to express her displeasure of him, she finally succumbs when his actions reflect a loving and caring individual whose purpose is not to replace her real father.

Hoose, Phillip. ***Claudette Colvin: Twice Toward Justice.*** **New York: Melanie Kroupa Books/Farrar, Straus & Giroux, 2009.**

This award-winning book tells the story of someone who initiated the bus-ride debate and motivated Civil Rights leaders to consider legal actions against the courts long before Rosa Parks appeared on the scene. In this book, the reader can see evidence of racism within racism due to the difference in treatment of the individuals involved in the bus rides. Prejudice can even occur within one's own race, as seen in this book. Young Claudette Colvin wasn't treated the same as Rosa Parks and her resistance did not spark the same type of community reaction as Rosa Parks's did because of Claudette's socioeconomic status.

Mendez, Phil. ***The Black Snowman.*** **New York: Scholastic Paperbacks, 1991.**

The magic of kente cloth on a snowman takes Jacob Miller, a young boy who doesn't like being black, to the Mother Country of Africa, revealing the proud historic accomplishments and achievements of his ancestry.

Myers, Walter Dean. ***The Young Landlords.*** **New York: Puffin/Penguin, 1979.**

Sometimes you get more than you bargained for. This happened to a group of teens who complained to their landlord about their shabby living conditions. Their complaints gained them ownership of the building. Now these young people must figure out a way to improve the property, eliminate the fights, get the community involved in renovation, and generate additional income for maintenance. This is an outstanding read for young adults to learn that behind every complaint there must be a bank of possible solutions.

Myers, Walter Dean. ***Monster.*** **New York: Amistad, 2000.**

How do you turn a tragedy into a movie script? Steve Harmon knew that he had to remove the stigma attached to his life if he was ever to have a life again. On trial for murder, he knew that a change in his behavior together with his ability to write would both be therapeutic and provide a tool for recovery.

The Voice of the Children. **Collected by June Jordan and Terri Bush. New York: Henry Holt, 1999.**

Little voices can make remarks that lead to big changes. Here are the voices of children speaking the truth that comes from the heart.

Chapter 20

THE CORETTA SCOTT KING BOOK AWARDS

About Mrs. Coretta Scott King

The King Center. The King Center. 2010. http://www.thekingcenter.org/MrsCSKing (accessed October 31, 2010).

Brief Summary

The Coretta Scott King Book Awards for books that are written and/or illustrated by black Americans and address the black experience. Each book has its own special purpose and will motivate some readers, encourage others, and stimulate still others to understand why the book was honored with the award.

Focus

- Coretta Scott King
- History of Book Awards
- The Book Awards

Teacher Input

- Distribute the Coretta Scott King Book Awards Prereading Survey to the students.
- Ask students the following focus questions: "What award or awards have you received? What was the honor for?" "What makes a book good to you?"
- Share with students the many ways an author, an illustrator, or a new writer may receive one of the three awards: Author Award, Illustrator Award, and the John Steptoe Award for New Talent in writing and illustration.

Guided Practice

- Suggest that students create their own new book award.
- Discuss with students the criteria they'll use to select a winner. Have students write down their answers.
- Invite students to share the results of their Coretta Scott King Book Awards surveys.

Independent Practice

- Suggest that students examine genres of the Coretta Scott King Book Awards and select one to read. Students who select the same book to read will compare and contrast ideas for project design.
- Require students to locate and read an online resource about Mrs. Coretta Scott King and then summarize what they read in their own words.

Closure

- Collect the Coretta Scott King Book Awards survey sheets from the students.
- Have students announce the title of the book they selected for individual reading.

Assessment

- Student excitement, participation, and eagerness to share what they learned about Mrs. King and the Coretta Scott King Book Awards.
- Creativity and Innovative Project Ideas.

Online Resources

- http://www.teachingbooks.net/crc.cgi?id=1

Coretta Scott King Book Awards Prereading Survey

Please respond to this reading survey honestly. You do not have to put your name on this survey.

Name:____Grade:__________

Gender:____Age:__________

<u>How Much Do You Read?</u>

__________Very Little __________ Only Assigned Readings __________ Often

What activities would you like to participate in to increase your interest in reading?

______ Oral Book Reports

______ Books on a specific subject (name subject)______________________________

______ Books that will give me the opportunity to develop a project.

Are you familiar with the Coretta Scott King Book Awards?

_____Yes _____ No _____ Somewhat

Describe what you know about the Coretta Scott King Book Awards.

Would you be interested in organizing and presenting a class project after reading one or more of these books?
_____Yes _____ No

After reading one of these books and hearing your classmates give various reports about them, would you like to have one of these award-winning books added to your classroom library in your honor?

If so, why?

If not, tell why.

Coretta Scott King Book Awards Project Planning Form

Project Based Curriculum

Name:____Group Name:______________________

1. Describe your project. What do you envision it will look like when finished?

2. How will you begin to put your project together? What are some procedures you will use to complete it?

3. What materials will you need for your project?

4. Is there a certain topic you are already interested in? Is there any book you know you want to use?

Coretta's Books Activity

The teacher leads this Coretta Scott King Book Awards fingerplay and response activity, and students will respond.

Leader: Coretta's Books will help children know.

Coretta's Books will give some children pride.

Coretta's Books will help children grow.

That's the literacy fertilizer the brain needs inside.

So,

If you read Coretta's Books, clap your hands!

If you read Coretta's Books, clap your hands!

If you read Coretta's Books, and like what you read

If you read Coretta's Books, clap your hands.

Leader: Would you please share these books with your class?

Audience Responds: Yes, I will! Oh, yes, I will.

Leader: Would you please share these books with your class?

Audience Responds: Yes, I will! Oh, yes, I will.

Leader: If you will share just one that you've read,

A reading need will be fed.

Leader: Would you please share these books with your class?

Audience Responds: Yes, I will! Oh, yes, I will.

Leader: There's humor in Coretta's Book, let us laugh!

Audience Responds: Ha, Ha, Ha!

Ha, Ha, Ha, Ha!

Leader: There's sorrow in Coretta's Book, let us sob.

Audience Responds: Sob, Sob, Sob!

Sob, Sob, Sob, Sob!

Leader: There's drama, let's take a stand

Join hand-in-hand!

And, there's love to share across the land.

Coretta Scott King Book Awards Project Planning Form

Project Based Curriculum (Middle and High School)

Name:____Group Name:_________________

1. Describe your project. What do you envision it will look like?

2. How will you begin to put your project together? What are some procedures you will use to complete it?

3. What are the materials that you need or plan to use in your project? List them below.

4. Is there a certain topic you are already interested in? Any book you know you want to use?

Teachers may use this as a cover page to develop a Coretta Scott King reading list of the award-winning books to use in a CSK Book Week theme for observation leading up to the celebration of the National Dr. Martin Luther King, Jr. Day.

"***Ready to Dream***"

Book Club

Hughes, Langston. *The Negro Speaks of Rivers.* New York: Disney/Jump at the Sun, 2009.

About the Author

Langston Hughes. Academy of American Poets. 1997–2010. http://www.poets.org/poet.php/prmPID/83 (accessed October 10, 2010).

Literary Elements	Lexile Range	Teacher Resources and Supplies
Poem and Rhyme Coretta Scott King Illustrator Honor Award Culture Personal Narratives Speech Social Studies	—	Book Worksheet Rhyming Dictionary Online
Reading Level Grades 4 and up	**Accelerated Reading** —	

Brief Summary

Langston Hughes's poem is an interpretation of the boldness and strength flowing through the minds of a people in control of their own destiny. Despite their muddy past, they live on to a lead more responsible and adaptive lives.

Focus

- Goal Setting
- Poets, Poetry, Poet Laureate
- Mothers and Sons

Teacher Input

- Introduce the book by leading a discussion about the things that students remember, both good and bad, about a classroom activity, an event, or a place.
- Have students discuss the importance of water. Poll students to find out who lives near the water, and ask them to share their experiences on or near the water.
- Introduce students to other works by Langston Hughes by using this online site: http://www.poemhunter.com/poem/mother-to-son. Read the poem "Mother to Son." Ask students to interpret the poem.
- Show students how to create their own rhymes by demonstrating how to use the online resource at http://www.rhymezone.com.
- Distribute the "**Sink or Swim**" Worksheet for students to complete.

Guided Practice

- Ask students to reflect on their lives, choose a particular situation, person, or thing that is important to them, and write a speech about it. The speech should begin with "I've known . . ."
- Ask this focus question: "In what way did you use water before you left home today?"

- Write the following on the board: "Now That I Think About It, That Was Wasting Water." Ask each student to list ways they see people wasting water.
- Instruct students to describe how they are affected by the sound of water.
- Allow students to explore the early writing and contributions by Langston Hughes using this website: http://kirjasto.sci.fi/lhughes.htm.
- Explore and learn more about rivers across the United States by having the students play the game at http://www.sheppardsoftware.com/web_games.htm.

Independent Practice

- Instruct students to use "Mother to Son" as an example to construct a poem or create a PowerPoint slide show speaking to their mother from their perspectives on and about life.
- If students live near the ocean or a river, have them develop a flip chart to show the flow of water and how it's used for entertainment.

Closure

- Play water theme music to the class (e.g., http://www.youtube.com/watch?v=4JjjzlrdtgA; http://www.youtube.com/watch?v=k0gsduLrfSU).
- Have students locate and read other works by Langston Hughes.

Assessment

- Student involvement and teamwork, project sharing.

"Sink or Swim" Worksheet

The Impact of Rivers on Slavery and the Quest for Freedom

1. Discuss the Ohio River and the role it played in the history of slavery. Use this resource to learn more: http://www.slaveryinamerica.org/scripts/sia/gallery.cgi?term=&collection=ugrr&index=6.

2. Read and analyze the lyrics to "Jordan River—One More River to Cross."

3. Research the rivers listed below and their impact on slavery. Provide one important fact about each one.

1. Missouri River	Fact:
2. Ohio River	Fact:
3. Mississippi River	Fact:

4. Is there a river in your hometown? What do you know about it?

Nelson, Vaunda. *Bad News for Outlaws: The Remarkable Life of Bass Reeves, Deputy U.S. Marshal.* Mankato, MN: Carolrhoda Books, 2009.

About the Author

Vaunda Micheaux Nelson. n.d. http://thebrownbookshelf.com/2009/02/16/vaunda-micheaux-nelson (accessed October 30, 2010).

Literary Element(s)	Lexile Range	Teacher Resources and Supplies
Biography History, Social Studies Oklahoma U.S. Government	860L	Book Law enforcement badge Map of Oklahoma Fact sheet with stats on youth and guns (Distribute sheet while introducing this book.)
Reading Level Grades 5 and up	**Accelerated Reader** Points: 0.5 Book Level: 5.2	
Websites http://www.ojjdp.gov/pubs/reform/ch2_h.html http://life.familyeducation.com/safety/school/34435.html http://life.familyeducation.com/school-safety-month/violence/29712.html http://www.saf.org/default.asp?p=rkba_protections http://www.policyalmanac.org/crime/guns.shtml http://www.ncjrs.gov/pdffiles/redyouth.pdf		

Brief Summary

This book describes the remarkable life of Bass Reeves, a black deputy U.S. marshal. Born a slave, Reeves never learned to read, yet he refused to let this determine his destiny. This lawman was smart, honest, and skillful in developing the necessary strategies for capturing outlaws, keeping the law, and making friends in the territory.

Focus

- Black Lawmen
- Character
- Education
- The Right to Bear Arms and Gun Control

Teacher Input

- Ask students if they know what the term "squatter" means.
- Lead the class in a discussion about what it means to have good character.
- Bring several masks to class and lead a discussion on disguises. Ask students to name celebrations during the year when people wear disguises for fun.

- Lead the class in a discussion about what "The Right to Bear Arms" means.

Guided Practice

- Explore the thought "nothing but right in his heart." Invite the students to comment on what they think the author meant by this statement.
- Ask students what the significance was of Bass Reeves using good character in his decision making.
- Instruct students to identify and list reasons they believe the Native Americans accepted Reeves into their tribe.
- Ask students to discuss ways they have observed law enforcement officers providing positive services in their community.
- Invite students to comment on whether they think the right to bear arms is important.
- Allow students to find information online about whether there is a difference in the way law enforcement personnel handle various issues based on race, gender, social status, and location.
- Instruct students to research online to find out where high-ranking African American law enforcement officers are serving today.
- Have students discuss what they think the author means by the statement, "***How can you be respected and hated at the same time?***"

Independent Practice

- Instruct students to read Paul Laurence Dunbar's poem "We Wear the Mask" (see http://www.potw.org/archive/potw8.html). Have them share their thinking about what the poem means and discuss why Reeves disguised himself. Have them discuss whether Dunbar's poem is relevant to Reeves's disguises. Students may then design their own masks and write a poem explaining why such a mask would be worn.
- Have students design a poster, create a PowerPoint presentation, or develop a chart describing at least two ways to reduce youth gun violence. Use this website as a resource: http://www.ncjrs.gov/pdffiles/redyouth.pdf.

Closure

- Invite a representative from local law enforcement to discuss service projects in the neighborhood or local community with the class.

Assessment

- Students' questions for law enforcement representative, their feelings expressed about law enforcement, and reports on African American law enforcement across the country.

Rapport, Doreen. *Martin's Big Words.* New York: Jump at the Sun, 2001.

About the Author

Doreen Rapport. HarperCollins. 2010. http://www.harpercollins.com/authors/12630/Doreen_Rappaport/index.aspx (accessed October 31, 2010).

Literary Element(s)	Lexile Range	Teacher Resource and Supplies
Biography Civil Rights Coretta Scott King Book Award Family	AD410L	A photo of Dr. King Basket of words Dictionary Small white balls Box of Cheerios Worksheet
Reading Level Grades 2 and up	**Accelerated Reader** Points: 0.5 Book Level: 3.4	
Additional Title(s) Farris, Christine King. ***My Brother Martin.*** King, Martin Luther. ***Why We Can't Wait.*** Watkins, Angela Farris. ***My Uncle Martin's Big Heart.*** **Websites** http://www.thekingcenter.org http://www.cnn.com/SPECIALS/2007/king.papers http://www.fun-with-words.com/word_longest.html http://www.salemcountyava.org/Martin_Luther_King.htm http://www.webenglishteacher.com/king.html http://www.lebanon.k12.mo.us/profdev/picturethis_20070418.pdf		

Brief Summary

This is a book of big words to encourage little people. Big words can come from little people when they learn how to listen and interpret their meaning. Here is a book that is definitely appropriate for groups of various ages to learn valuable life skills lessons.

Focus

- Civil Rights
- Biography
- Reading
- Dictionary and Thesaurus

Teacher Input

- Introduce the concepts of increasing one's vocabulary and learning new long words by using this online site: http://www.fun-with-words.com/word_longest.html.
- Ask students to explain how words are used.
- Middle and high school teachers should introduce Dr. King's works by using excerpts from his speech "The Drum Major Instinct," located at this site: http://www.thekingcenter.org.

Guided Practice

- Select words that students are not familiar with and use them in sentences. Determine how students react when new words are presented.
- Introduce the dictionary and thesaurus to younger students and explain the activity to those who are familiar with both resources. Give each student a small ball. Ask them to use the dictionary to locate and learn definitions for as many new words and their meanings that can be written on the ball.
- Using the same activity above, review parts of speech with students. Teacher will ask students to share words listed on their balls, which will then be recorded on the board. Each word will then be reviewed to identify parts of speech.
- Instruct students to keep a list of five new words they have learned in addition to weekly spelling words. Students in upper grades record five new words, define them, and say what part of speech they are.
- Develop a "**You May Have to Eat Those Words**" **Activity.** Each student will receive a sandwich bag of Cheerios and a dictionary. The Cheerios are to be used to "spell out" the words. Have students use the dictionary to look up new words. As students discover new words, they will list words on their worksheet. When the activity is completed, allow students to "eat their words."

Independent Practice

- Suggest that students share their new words by writing stories titled "I Can Use These Words Because I Know What They Mean!"
- Plan a Word Ball: Throwing Your Words Around. Students will bring balls from home labeled with new words discovered from the "You May Have to Eat Those Words" activity. This is a follow-up activity designed for family involvement. Collect all the balls and record the number of new words each student discovered before the Word Ball activity begins. Announce the number of new words discovered. To compare and contrast how students are similar and differ, and that no two students have the same thoughts, this activity motivates students never to be afraid of failure.

Closure

- Write new words on a Word Wall or in a class "Writing Manual."

Assessment

- Student involvement in the "Eat My Words" activity.

I've Got Your Word—Worksheet

	http://www.fun-with-words.com/word_longest.html Use this online site to locate the five longest words in the world.
Five Long Words	What are the longest Welsh Words?
Find three new words from a dictionary to add to the classroom Word Basket and provide their meanings.	Word 1: Definition: Your Name:
	Word 2: Definition: Your Name:
	Word 3: Definition: Your Name:
I Had to Eat My Words: list the new words you discovered and ate!	

Bibliography

Chocolate, Debbi. *The Piano Man.* New York: Walker & Company, 1998.

Hughes, Langston. *The Negro Speaks of Rivers.* New York: Disney/Jump at the Sun, 2009.

Nelson, Vaunda. *Bad News for Outlaws: The Remarkable Life of Bass Reeves, Deputy U. S. Marshal.* Mankato, MN: Carolrhoda Books, 2009.

Rapport, Doreen. *Martin's Big Words.* New York: Jump at the Sun, 2001.

Walter, Mildred Pitts. *Justin and the Best Biscuits in the World.* New York: Lothrop, Lee & Shepard Books, 1986.

Webliography

123 Free Watch Online Movie Bass Reeves Video. ponderousproductions. n.d. http://123nonstop.com/watch_online_movie_video/Bass_Reeves (accessed December 5, 2010).

Broadway. The American Musical. Stars over Broadway. Bert Williams. PBS. Educational Broadcasting Corporation. 2004. http://www.pbs.org/wnet/broadway/stars/williams_b.html (accessed December 4, 2010).

Coretta Scott King Book Award Curriculum Resource Center. TeachingBooks.net. February 10, 2010. http://www.teachingbooks.net/crc.cgi?id=1 (accessed December 7, 2010).

Duke Ellington Was Not a Street. n.d. http://www.youtube.com/watch?v=7qq5xKPtsqM (accessed December 5, 2010).

Escape From Slavery: Underground Railroad Student Activity. Scholastic. 2010–1996. http://teacher.scholastic.com/activities/bhistory/underground_railroad/escape.htm (accessed December 5, 2010).

The Facts About Kids and Guns. Pearson Education Inc. 2000–2010. http://life.familyeducation.com/school-safety-month/violence/29712.html (accessed December 6, 2010).

Free Silent Movies to Download or Watch. pdcomedy.com. n.d. http://www.pdcomedy.com/AllTheSilents.html (accessed December 4, 2010).

The King Center. n.d. http://www.thekingcenter.org/ (accessed December 7, 2010).

"*Mother to Son" by Langston Hughes.* n.d. http://www.poemhunter.com/poem/mother-to-son/ (accessed December 4, 2010).

Reducing Youth Gun Violence: An Overview of Programs and Initiatives. Office of Juvenile Justice and Delinquency Prevention. n.d. http://www.ncjrs.gov/pdffiles/redyouth.pdf (accessed December 5, 2010).

RhymeZone: Rhyming Dictionary and Thesaurus. Datamuse. 2010. http://www.rhymezone.com (accessed December 6, 2010).

Second Amendment Foundation Online. 2000–2010. http://www.saf.org/default.asp?p=rkba_protections (accessed December 5, 2010).

See the Show. University of Georgia. 2004. http://virtualvaudeville.com/shows.htm (accessed November 4, 2010).

U.S.A. Rivers: Learning Level Online Learning. Sheppard Software. n.d. http://www.sheppardsoftware.com/web_games.htm (accessed December 4, 2010).

Word Records: Longest Words. Fun-with-words.com. 1999–2010. http://www.fun-with-words.com/word_longest.html (accessed December 6, 2010).

Please refer to the complete list of Coretta Scott King Book Awards Titles at the link below:

http://www.ala.org/ala/mgrps/rts/emiert/cskbookawards/recipients.cfm

Index

About the Author

DOROTHY LITTLEJOHN GUTHRIE is a retired School Library Director with Gaston County Schools in Gastonia, North Carolina. After retirement from North Carolina, she was employed by the Clover School District where she currently serves as school librarian at Crowders Creek Elementary School. She has written several articles for Cable In The Classroom, a magazine produced by Time Warner Cable. As a school librarian, Guthrie was named School Librarian of the Year for three consecutive years in Gaston County. She received the Gertrude Coward Award from Charlotte Mecklenburg Schools, North Carolina Media and Technology Specialist of the Year Award, and The National Teacher Award from Time Warner Cable. She is the recipient of the Ben Craig Outstanding Educators' Award, Paul Harris Fellows Award and Founder of Foothills Yarnspinners Storytelling League.

She serves on the Executive Board of The Black Caucus of The American Library Association, is a member of the Coretta Scott King Book Awards Committee, a former Coretta Scott King Book Awards Breakfast Chair and Jury.

Dorothy coordinated the first Gaston County Diversity Book Fair. She has conducted workshops at the University of Wisconsin at Madison and throughout North and South Carolina.